THE FOURTH
OLD HOUSE CATALOGUE

Cover illustration: "Pinegrove," Pittstown, New Jersey. Photographed by Frank Mahood.

Stair hall, Charles Bissell House, Rochester, New York. Photographed by Hans Podelt, Historic American Buildings Survey.

THE FOURTH
OLD HOUSE CATALOGUE

Compiled by Lawrence Grow

Jan S. Cohen, General Editor

THE MAIN STREET PRESS • PITTSTOWN, NEW JERSEY

General Editor:	Jan Cohen
Staff Writers:	Vicki Brooks
	Jan Cohen
	Martin Greif
	Salena Kern
Research Assistant:	Terese Parisi
Art:	Frank Mahood
	M. Henri Katz
	Donald Rolfe

No part of this book may be utilized or reproduced in any form or by any means, electronic or mechanical, including photocopying, recording, or by any information storage and retrieval system, without permission in writing from the publisher.

Published by
The Main Street Press, Inc.
William Case House
Pittstown, New Jersey 08867

Distributed in the United States by
Kampmann & Company, Inc.
9 East 40th Street
New York, New York 10016

Published simultaneously in Canada by
Methuen Publications
2330 Midland Avenue
Agincourt, Ontario M1S 1P7

Cover design by Frank Mahood

Printed in the United States of America

Library of Congress Cataloging in Publication Data

Grow, Lawrence
  The fourth old house catalogue.

  Includes index.
  1. Historic buildings—United States—Conservation
and restoration—Catalogs. 2. Buildings—United States—
Conservation and restoration—Catalogs. I. Title.
TH3411.G75 1984   728.3′7′0288029473   84-15488
ISBN 0-915590-52-2 (pbk.)

Contents

Introduction

Since the publication of the first *Old House Catalogue* in 1976, the reproduction and renovation supplies market has greatly expanded. This increase is largely due to the growth in public appreciation of period architecture and design. More and more people simply do not choose to live in square, unadorned boxes—whether houses or apartments—and seek ways to make better use of older buildings. In doing so, they search for quality materials which are appropriate for a particular style—whether it be Victorian, Colonial, Art Deco, or Art Nouveau—and craftsmen who can execute various types of decorative work.

When *The Third Old House Catalogue* was issued two years ago, new building construction was in the doldrums because of the recession. Since that time, the pace has increased dramatically. The new house market, however, is somewhat different than it used to be. The public vogue for traditional building styles is being catered to by many architects and construction firms. New "Victorian" houses replete with verandas and turrets are taking a place alongside the more common suburban split-levels; timbered English Tudor mansions, the likes of which have not been seen since the 1920s, are rising in the fields of exurbia. In the city, developers are putting up condominium units which look very much like the neighboring Georgian Colonial Revival town houses of the early 1900s.

Where is all the decorative millwork, the reproduction hardware, the ornamental ironwork coming from for these new "old" buildings? From the same suppliers who serve the old-house market. As one New York dealer in architectural antiques (fomerly known as salvage) reported recently, "It is getting awfully crowded down here in Soho on weekends."

The increase in demand for traditional building and decorative materials has had mixed results. On the one hand, more and more young people are learning traditional crafts such as blacksmithing, woodworking, plastering, and decorative painting. Old techniques like graining, wax casting, stone cutting, and hand-turning of wood, for example, are being resurrected in schools and workshops. All of this has resulted in improved craftsmanship among small suppliers of specialty items. On the other hand, more commercial purveyors of home products have all too quickly stamped out so-called "Colonial" and "Victorian" items which have neither the texture nor the substance of the originals.

The buyer of any type of old-house service or product,

therefore, must proceed with caution. It is still unlikely that what one needs—whether it be a simple doorknob or a complicated cornice molding—can be found on impulse in a nearby hardware store or home center. More often, one must locate a quality supplier through the mail or make a trip to a specialty outlet. *The Fourth Old House Catalogue* is the only restoration/renovation resource book which offers more than listings of names and addresses. The detailed information which accompanies each of the hundreds of write-ups in eleven different chapters concerns specific products or services. Restoration experts throughout North America with practical experience in solving building and design problems have helped to pinpoint the most imaginative and useful craftsmen and manufacturers.

Advertising plays no part in *The Fourth Old House Catalogue.* No one can buy his way onto these pages. As in the past, only a small portion of the large number of suppliers contacted have been selected for inclusion. Yet, what they have to offer is so diverse and intriguing that every reader who appreciates authentic styling will profit from reading through these pages.

Once again we must express our thanks to the many persons and organizations who have assisted in the compiling of this biennial publication. Jan Cohen, who has developed her own "hands-on" skills as a home restorer, has guided the Main Street staff in locating new sources of supply and in evaluating and organizing material. In the important job of record-keeping, she was assisted by Terese Parisi. Together, they have written thousands of letters and made countless calls to produce an avalanche of information that is thoroughly up-to-date. As in the past, staff members of the National Trust for Historic Preservation have provided useful leads to suppliers as well as information on local and regional preservation organizations. We are also indebted to the American Institute of Architects and to members of the National Park Service's regional offices for their assistance in tracking down one-of-a-kind services and suppliers.

Lawrence Grow
Pittstown, New Jersey
August 1984

THE FOURTH
OLD HOUSE CATALOGUE

Defining the Architectural Styles

Whether decorating, renovating, or restoring an older home, each home owner wants to know something about its style. North American houses are popularly thought to fall into one of three simple categories: Colonial, Victorian, or Modern. When a friend asked an architectural historian what style her house was, he studied the façade and answered, "bracketed Italianate." The building is a square brick one with a relatively flat overhanging roof and bracketed eaves, and round-headed windows and entrance-way. It probably dates from the mid-1800s. My friend responded that she had thought it was "Victorian." She was right, and so was the historian. Such terms as "Colonial" and "Victorian" are all-inclusive and therefore limited when it comes to describing a particular building.

The following pages on domestic building styles common in North America from the 17th century through the early 1900s suggest, but by no means exhaust, the variety displayed in most geographic areas. The categories—eighteen in all—are broadly sketched so as to allow for stylistic variations. Not all Second Empire homes, for example, have mansard roofs; neither does every Greek Revival residence sport a columned portico. Every house tells its own story, and the joy of living in an old house lies in the discovery of its own special style.

Early Colonial,
1600s-1750s

Georgian Colonial, 1730s-early 1800s

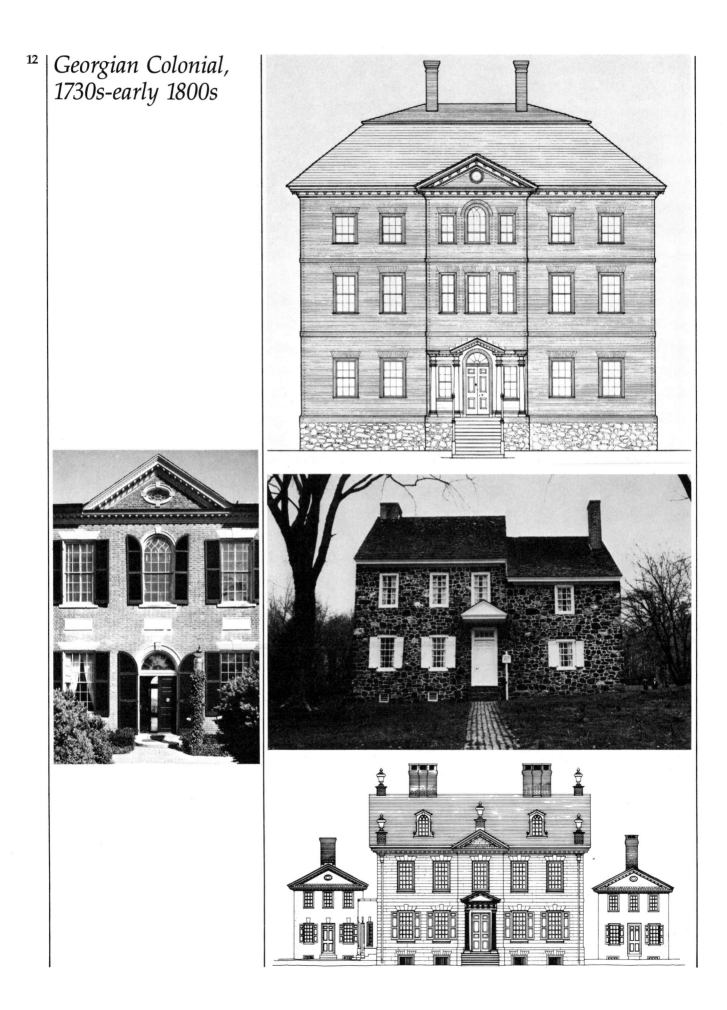

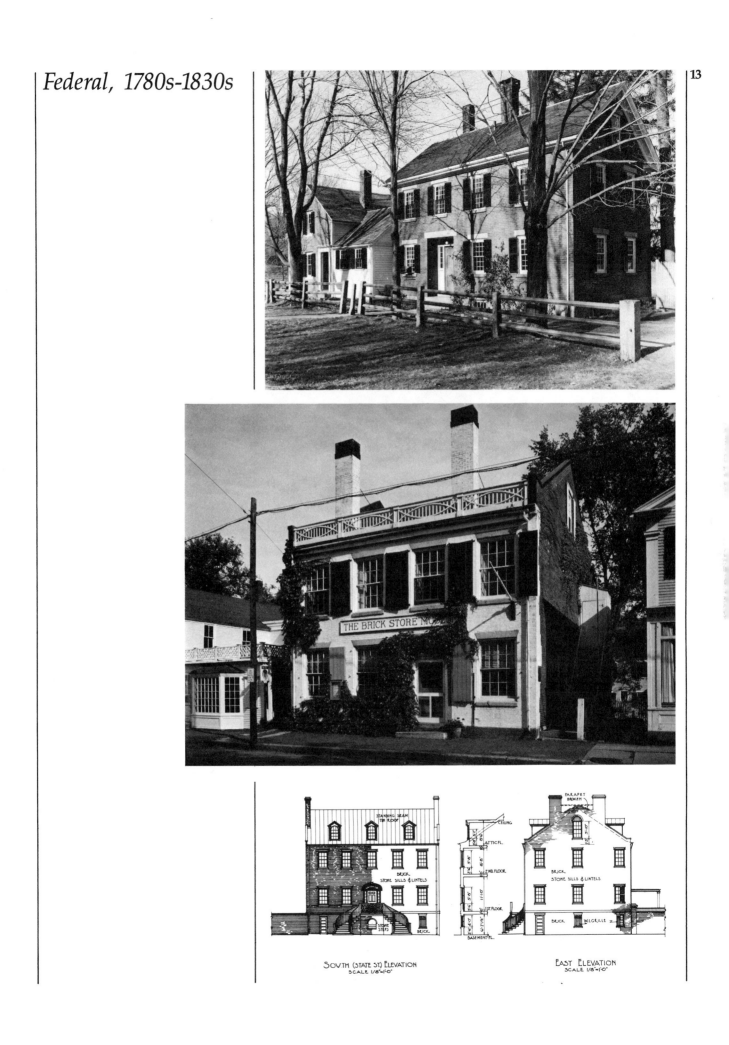

SOUTH (STATE ST) ELEVATION
SCALE 1/8"=1'-0"

EAST ELEVATION
SCALE 1/8"=1'-0"

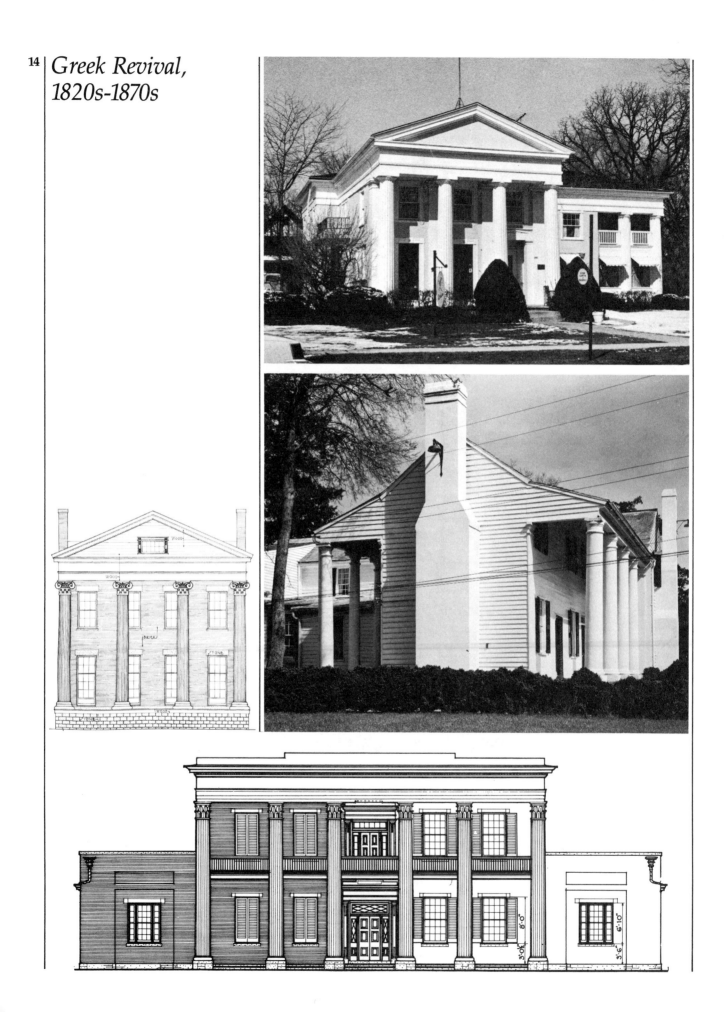

Gothic Revival,
1820s-1860s

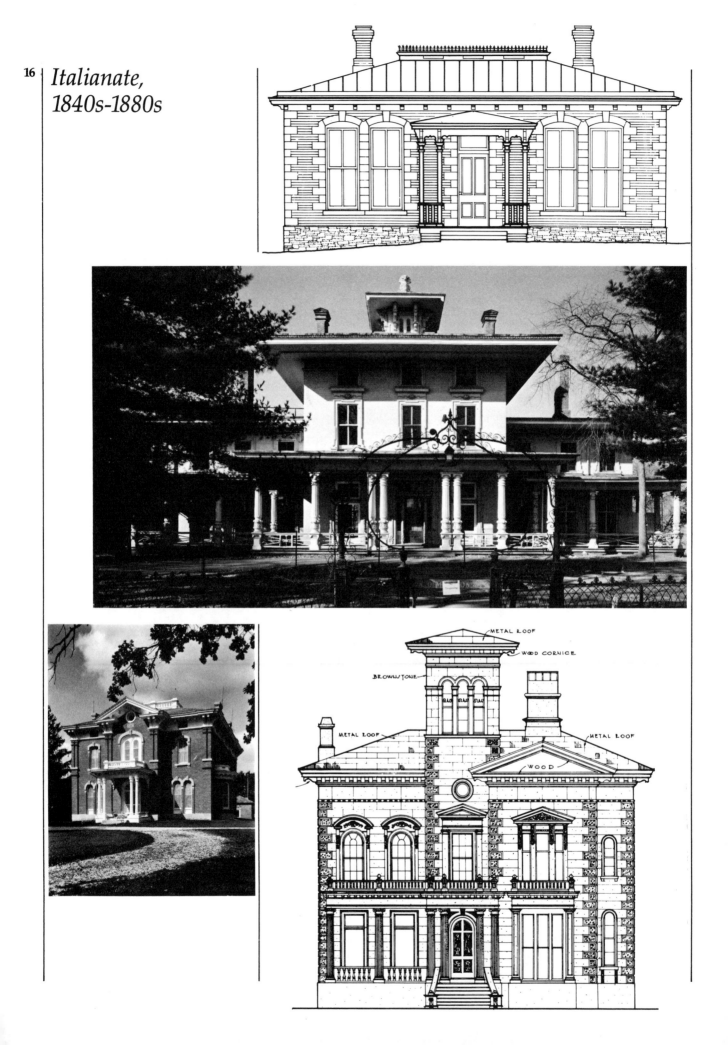

Renaissance Revival, 1850s-1890s

The Second Empire Style, 1860s-1890s

The Shingle Style, 1870s-early 1900s

The Stick Style, 1870s-early 1900s

The Queen Anne Style, 1880s-early 1900s

Romanesque Revival, 1880s-early 1900s

English Tudor, 1880s-1920s

Georgian Colonial Revival, 1890s-1940s

The Bungalow Style, 1890s-1930s

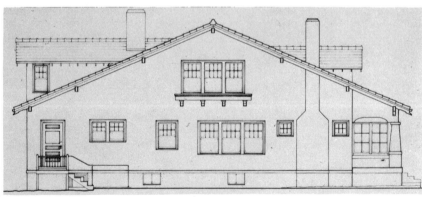

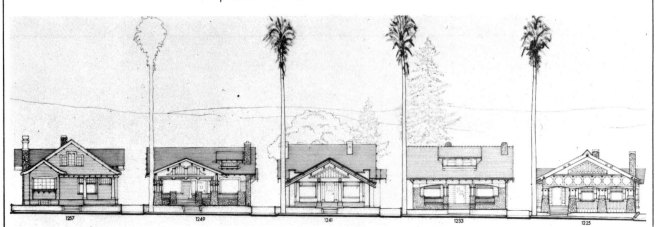

1257   1249   1241   1233   1225

Spanish Colonial Revival, early 1900s-1930s

The Prairie Style, early 1900s-1940s

The Modern Style,
1930s-1950s

1.

Structural Products and Services

Buying an old house is rather like a marriage—you take it with all its faults, pleasures, and hidden surprises. In an old house, the area most likely to surprise and challenge is the structural condition of the building. Before the curtains are hung and the floors are refinished, the sheltering frame of the house must be solid, tight, and harmonious. This may be a matter of replacing beams, repairing window sash, redesigning a front porch, and generally curing all the ills the house's flesh is heir to.

In this chapter, our bias is decidely towards resources that provide authentic materials and towards professionals and artisans who understand the special nature of old buildings. It is always better to try to replicate what can't be repaired and to add only what will be in keeping with elements already there, although any such attempts at architectural purism should not be done at the expense of living comfortably.

It is heartening to know that, over the last several years, a wide range of material sources and services has become available to the old-house owner. Almost every area of the country has a source of architectural salvage for windows, mantels, stair parts, and the like. There are many fine craftsmen and businesses that are prepared to produce and repair slate roofs, stone chimneys, metal ceilings, and other structural elements. There is also a growing availability of instruction and schools for the do-it-youselfer.

While some of these essential elements may sound intimidating or less interesting than the decorative aspects of remodeling or restoring, good materials and quality workmanship have a special beauty of their own that can only enhance the overall look and feel of your old house.

Architectural antiques, Architectural Antiques Exchange, Philadelphia, Pennsylvania.

Architectural Salvage

The pace at which old architectural America is being ripped down has increased recently as the recession of 1981-83 has come to an end. New building often means the loss of the old, even if it is only a barn or a decayed tenement. Wreckers, unlike those of the recent past, however, no longer scatter everything to the wind. More and more individuals are rushing in to save building materials and ornamentation before they are reduced to dust. It is not only valiant to do so; it is economically advantageous. The number of architectural antiques emporiums across North America is increasing—and they are having no problem in disposing of such items as old bricks, mantels, hardware, flooring, windows, and doors. These outlets are valuable sources of supply when the need arises. Remember, however, that stock constantly changes. The objects inventoried in such stores and warehouses are largely one-of-a-kind.

Architectural Antiques

This Little Rock store is filled with over 36,000 square feet of architectural artifacts. The firm stocks a fine collection of antique pieces ranging from a 26-foot mahogany bar and a twin-staircase English pulpit to a restored brass and copper bank clock and a terrific assortment of original mantels and stained glass. One of owner Darlene Bell's recent coups was the rescue of much of the interior fittings of the Kellogg mansion in Chicago. When the structure was scheduled for demolition, Ms. Bell and her crew salvaged entire rooms, including paneling, silver fixture hardware, staircases, plaster moldings, and brass and copper French doors. This is an inventory we wish every reader could see!

For further information, contact:

*Architectural Antiques
1321 E. 2nd
Little Rock, AR 72202
(501) 372-1744*

Architectural Antiques Exchange

Whatever the period, Architectural Antiques Exchange can probably provide unusual and appropriate artifacts to suit a client's needs. Aside from the expected inventory of trim, glass, woodwork, etc., this company also carries one-of-a-kind pieces such as ticket booths, gingerbread entryways, apothecary fixtures, restaurant booths, and backbars. The Exchange is well known for its restaurant projects around the country, but caters to the individual client as well. Some of the available items are shown in the frontispiece to this chapter.

Brochure available.

*Architectural Antiques Exchange
709-15 N. 2nd St.
Philadelphia, PA 19123
(215) 922-3669*

Architectural Antique Warehouse

With a large and continuously changing supply of old-house artifacts, one could start with a shell of a house and end up with a Victorian mansion—all from the Architectural Antique Warehouse. The firm's stock includes complete verandas, window frames, mantels, letterslots, fretwork, and marble sink tops, just to list a small part of the inventory. Also available now are metal ceiling panels and cast-iron spiral staircases in kit form.

The retail store is located at 1583 Bank Street, in Ottawa. Mail inquiries should be directed to the address below:

*Architectural Antique Warehouse
Box 3065, Station D
Ottawa, Ontario, Canada K1P 6H6
(613) 526-1818*

Architectural Emporium

Betty Rimert, owner of this Indiana company, carries a changing inventory of antique building materials, including mantels, doors, plumbing fixtures, brackets, columns, and other commercial and residential salvaged items. She also provides a "finding" service for clients searching for a specific article. The Architectural Emporium offers, in addition, a wide selection of new reproductions. The warehouse is open by appointment only, and an initial phone call to Ms. Rimert's office is suggested.

For further information, contact:

*Architectural Emporium (office)
1011 S. 9th St.
Lafayette, IN 47905
(317) 423-1500*

*Architectural Emporium (warehouse)
315 Sheridan Rd.
Lafayette, IN 47905*

Artifacts

A well-known Virginia source of old house materials, Artifacts carries a full range of salvaged items, including plumbing fixtures, stair parts, doors, columns, and 18th- and 19th-century mantels. Fans take note—proprietor Elsa Rosenthal has moved her business to Middleburg from Alexandria and should, by now, be comfortably ensconced at the new address.

For further information, contact:

*Artifacts, Inc.
Box 1787, Federal St.
Middleburg, VA 22117
(703) 687-5957*

The Bank

Buyers for The Bank tap the rich architectural resources of New Orleans and the Mississippi River Valley region to provide an extensive selection of architectural antiques. And now owner Mike Wilkerson and his staff have expanded The Bank's horizons by acquiring select items from Mexico, Central America, Portugal, and Spain. Their inventory features authentic wooden architectural elements, from cypress plantation doors to handcrafted moldings, as well as stained glass and antique fixtures.

Brochure available.

The Bank
1824 Felicity St.
New Orleans, LA 70113
(504) 523-2702

E. Cohen's Architectural Heritage

Five years ago, Eric Cohen gathered his extensive collection of antique house materials under one roof, an old army barracks building, and now carries what may be the largest stock of architectural antiques in Ontario. He can provide authentic pieces from the Victorian, Art Nouveau, and Art Deco periods, including hand-painted stained-glass windows, Victorian gingerbread, ornate metal grillwork, plaster ceiling rosettes, and much more. There is a fully-equipped shop on the premises to repair glass, metalwork, and woodwork, and items can be purchased "as is" or repaired and restored.

For further information, contact:

E. Cohen's Architectural Heritage
1804 Merivale Rd.
Nepean, Ontario, Canada K2G 1E6
(613) 226-2979

The Conservatory

Situated in the restored community of Marshall, Michigan, this shop carries antique and reproduction products for the home. Among the architectural artifacts offered are restored Victorian lighting fixtures, bronze hardware, and marble sink tops, to name a few. In addition, books of interest to house restorers are available, as is professional design consultation.

For further information, contact:

The Conservatory
209 W. Michigan Ave.
Marshall, MI 49068
(616) 781-4790

1874 House

For over twenty years, 1874 House has been providing the Portland area with quality architectural antiques. The firm carries stained glass, doors, mantels, moldings, columns, and hardware for buildings and furniture, among other items. Since the stock is constantly renewed, frequent visits to this architectural emporium are recommended.

For further information, contact:

1874 House
8070 S.E. 13th
Portland, OR 97202
(503) 233-1874

Florida Victoriani

Concerned with the frequent demolition of architecturally significant properties in central Florida, Mark Shuttleworth formed this company in 1981 to preserve artifacts and details from these buildings. In addition, the company offers refinishing services, short-term rentals of articles, and appraisals. Some of the inventory is shown here. Shuttleworth tells us that, while all of his items are antique, the mask of Comedy, bottom left, is reproduced from a casting rescued from a theater facade by two retired miners who happened to be walking by the building during demolition. They climbed a stepladder and chiseled around the surrounding block of the ornament for two hours to save it from destruction. Lovers of the old and irreplaceable are apparently to be found everywhere.

Brochure available. (SASE requested.)

Florida Victoriani Architectural
*   Antiques*
901 W. First St. (Hwy 46)
Sanford, FL 32771
(305) 321-5767

Hanks Architectural Antiques

Unlike many restoration sources, this Texas firm specializes in materials from Europe, although it does carry some American items. In general, Hanks's inventory includes antique stained glass, cut glass, paneling, bars, flooring, and ironwork. Shown here is one of the firm's more flamboyant items, an enormous clock, which, while not for just any old house, would be marvelous somewhere. Hanks does not publish a catalogue, but announcements of new shipments are sent to people on its mailing list. Specific inquiries are also encouraged.

For further information, contact:

Hanks Architectural Antiques
311 Colorado
Austin, TX 78701
(512) 478-2101

Irreplaceable Artifacts

This ever-expanding company might well be renamed "irresistable artifacts," for only a lack of space keeps us from walking off with all of its marvelous salvaged treasures. Who could pass up a neo-Gothic carved oak staircase or a Victorian cast-iron balcony from New Orleans or, for that matter, a pair of marble and sandstone Byzantine style columns from a Harlem apartment house? A visit to the new showroom as well as to the warehouse outlet is a must.

Mail inquiries should be directed to the office address below:

Irreplaceable Artifacts (office)
526 E. 80th St.
New York, NY 10021
(212) 288-7397

Irreplaceable Artifacts (showroom)
14 Second Ave.
New York, NY 10003
(212) 982-5000

Irreplaceable Artifacts (warehouse
*   outlet)*
259 Bowery
New York, NY 10002
(212) 982-5000

Jerard Paul Jordan Gallery

Jordan has a large inventory of 18th- and early 19th-century building materials, including doors, raised panel walls, room ends, wainscoting and sheathing, shutters, mantels, and other architectural components essential for many Colonial and Federal homes. He can also supply old bricks, hearthstones, and flooring for old or reproduction homes. If it is an entire old house or barn that you are seeking, especially one of early New England ancestry, look no further—Jordan may have just the right one for you. He will also consult on the proper use of everything from a hand-wrought nail to a complete 18th-century home.

Catalogue, $4.

Jerard Paul Jordan Gallery
Slade Acres, Box 71
Ashford, CT 06278
(203) 429-7954

Old Mansions

Old Mansions continues to provide a large and eclectic selection of antique architectural material. The firm's fine inventory features mantels, paneling, cabinetry, Victorian bars, mirrors, slate and granite, plaster ornaments, and many more quality items. Because of the enormous warehouse space to be covered, admission is limited to adults—particularly those with definite wants—and browsing is not encouraged. Don't let this deter you from a visit. If there is an architectural artifact you need, Old Mansions probably has it. An appointment is required.

For further information, contact:

Old Mansions
1305 Blue Hill Ave.
Mattapan, MA 02126
(617) 296-0737 or 296-0445

Restoration Treasures

This company was formed in 1981 by a group of professionals already involved in the preservation and museum worlds. Their constantly-changing inventory is salvaged only from buildings in danger of imminent demolition and is offered in unrestored condition, which makes their prices pleasantly reasonable in a field where the sky is all too often the limit. Among the current items for sale are 1,600 square feet of 19th-century oak wainscoting, but like all of their one-of-a-kind items, the wainscoting is subject to prior sale. The firm will be glad to provide photos and full descriptions of specific items of interest, which should reassure the long-distance shopper. Restoration Treasures will also keep a "want list" of particular pieces a client may be searching for.

Illustrated listing, $1.

Restoration Treasures
Box 724
Cooperstown, NY 13326
(315) 858-0315

Structural Antiques, Inc.

Old house lovers in the South Central states will be happy to know there is a good source of American architectural antiques in Oklahoma City. Structural Antiques has a large selection of wood trim, mantels, columns, and marble and wood flooring, among other items. The firm also offers restoration services for the materials it sells. Structural Antiques offers no brochure, but mail and phone inquiries will be answered.

For further information, contact:

Structural Antiques, Inc.
1406 NW 30th St.
Oklahoma City, OK 73118
(405) 528-7734

Urban Archeology

Located in Manhattan's Soho district, Urban Archeology has helped in recent years to raise the layman's consciousness of the value of architectural antiques. One of the earliest and trendiest in the "salvage as antiques" genre, this large store houses a marvelous collection of turn-of-the-century New York interiors, furnishings, and fixtures. No one visiting the Big Apple should fail to make an appointment to see it.

For further information, contact:

Urban Archeology
137 Spring St.
New York, NY 10012
(212) 431-6969

Reproduction Building Materials

It is amazing just how sophisticated the market for reproduction building materials has become. For years there has been a plentiful supply of period fabrics, papers, and lighting fixtures. Now, one can also purchase new old-style brick, whole tin ceilings, doors and windows, lumber for flooring or wainscoting, roofing materials, and stair systems suitable for various types of old houses. This happy circumstance is due largely to a renaissance in traditional craftsmanship. More and more people have learned how to use old methods to produce materials such as mortise-and-tenon paneled white pine doors and 12-over-12 windows. Of course, the demand for old style products has grown proportionally. Sometimes you have to wait in line to get what you want from a particular craftsman, but your investment of time and money will be amply rewarded.

Since the quantity and quality of reproduction building materials have grown almost geometrically in the past few years, the listings that follow are organized by subject, viz., Brick and Stone, Ceilings, Doors and Windows, Lumber, Roofing Materials, and Stairs.

Brick and Stone

Locating supplies of the type of masonry material originally used in an older building is a task requiring considerable patience. Whether your aim is to patch up a small area, restore a whole expanse of wall, or add a complementary addition, you will have to seek out the specialty dealer or producer. Architectural antiques suppliers sometimes carry an inventory of old brick; salvage yards are another good source. Manufacturers of old-style brick may be able to help you if you forward a sample to them. Stone is somewhat easier to come by, as most varieties popular in the past, such as brownstone, slate, fieldstone, marble, and granite, are still quarried today.

Gladding, McBean

Terra cotta offers many advantages as a facing material. It can be sculptured into a design with permanent, non-fading glazes adding an extra dimension in color and texture. Gladding, McBean has been producing terra cotta for almost 100 years. The company has supplied materials for many historic structures and is expert at matching existing ornamental facades. It also carries a large selection of stock shapes for cornices, allowing the client to create or replicate almost any cornice profile.

For further information, contact:

Gladding, McBean & Co.
Box 97
Lincoln, CA 95648
(916) 645-3341

Glen-Gery Brick

Nothing looks more jarring than an old brick structure patched with brand-new, machine-made, bright-orange brick. Fortunately, Glen Gery offers a handmade brick which can match most existing brickwork. Its Colonial-style product is hand-formed in wooden molds to produce bricks with individual surface textures and colors. They are available in an extensive range of colors, from shades of white to buffs, browns, and reds. In addition, custom brick shapes can be manufactured to specification.

For further information, contact:

Glen-Gery Corp.
Drawer S, Rte. 61
Shoemakersville, PA 19555
(215) 562-3076

Rising & Nelson

Rising & Nelson is best known as the principal North American supplier of green slate, a gray-green shade often termed Sea Green that weathers beautifully with age when used for exterior purposes. There are other shades, as well, that come from the Vermont quarries—a dark, reddish purple; variegated purple; mottled green and purple; and red. For roofing or other purposes, a mixture of colors can be very pleasing. The company also stocks random irregular or rectangular slate flagstone for flooring, stair treads and risers, fireplace facing and mantels, window sills, and walkways. The flags are from ¾" to 1" or ½" to ⅝" in thickness. Best of all for home restorers, Rising & Nelson can match slate from samples supplied them for whatever purpose.

Brochure available.

Rising & Nelson Slate Co., Inc.
West Pawlet, VT 05775
(802) 645-0150

Structural Slate

Since 1918, this company has been marketing the production of five major quarries located in the heart of northeast Pennsylvania's famed slate region. The interior/exterior architectural slate is available in several finishes ranging from rough with textural variations to an even, stippled finish to semipolished and smooth. Being true Pennsylvania slate, whatever its finish, it comes only in various shades of gray. This beautiful natural material can be put to use quite imaginatively for stairs, floors, shower stalls and baths., exterior facing, and hearths and mantels. Structural is, of course, a primary supplier of roofing slate. For information on this type of material, consult the listing under roofing materials in this chapter.

Free brochure available.

The Structural Slate Co.
222 E. Main St., Box 187
Pen Argyl, PA 18072
(215) 863-4141

Ceilings

Modern ceiling treatments are often so hideous that few old-house enthusiasts make use of them. An acoustical drop ceiling never makes any sense in a period room, and the swirled plaster ceilings which first became popular in the 1950s are equally inappropriate. Decorative plasterowrk ceilings can be very expensive, and are discussed in the following chapter; there are, however, other alternatives such as the use of metal ceilings and panels of synthetic materials which effectively simulate fancy plasterwork.

Entol Industries

As an alternative to plaster or metal ceilings, Entol fabricates decorative ceiling panels, moldings, and medallions in a standard polyurethane material or in a non-combustible version in gypsum cement. In spite of the use of modern, high-tech materials, each panel is handmade with meticulous design detail. The photograph shows Entol's Baroque ceiling panel which is designed to drop into a standard grid system. It measures 2' by 2' and is just one of over 100 designs available

For further information, contact:

Entol Industries, Inc.
8180 NW 36th Ave.
Miami, FL 33147
(305) 696-0900

W. F. Norman

The W. F. Norman Corporation has occupied the same building since the turn of the century and still uses the original dies to stamp metal plates for decorative ceilings, sidewalls, and wainscoting. Being an original early 20th-century product line, the plates are authentic and architecturally correct for restoration or renovation work. Illustrated are two of some sixty plate designs to choose from, as well as examples of the sidewall and cornice designs. In style, the designs are representative of late-Victorian and early 20th-century decorative taste. The material, however, can be finished to complement various decorating styles: it can be painted any color, brass plated, or copper plated. In addition to the ceiling and wall plates and cornice moldings, Norman also offers ceiling centers, friezes, and borders.

The large ceiling panels in the photograph are models #406 (left) and #2670 (right), each 2' by 2' plates, the standard size for such elements.

Catalogue, $3.

W. F. Norman Corp.
Box 323, 214-32 N. Cedar St.
Nevada, MO 64772
(800) 641-4038
(417) 667-5552 (in MO)

Shanker Steel

The metal ceiling was introduced in the 1860s and increased in popularity until the early years of the 1900s as an inexpensive substitute for ornamental plasterwork. Shanker has led the resurgence in interest in this decorative material and is a leading manufacturer. Its panels are stamped from original 19th-century dies and range from mid-Victorian to Art Deco in design. They are sold in 2' by 8' sheets and have matching or complementary cornices and nosing elements as well as filler pieces. With over twenty designs to choose from, it is easy to find a sytle that would work well in the kitchen, bath, or even in a parlor.

Shanker sells directly to the

public as well as through regional distributors, two of which are given following Shanker's address. If none of these sources are convenient for you, contact Shanker for additional names and addresses of suppliers.

Brochure available.

Shanker Steel Corp.
70-32 83rd St.
Glendale, NY 11385
(212) 326-1100
(800) 221-6130 (NJ and New
England)

Another Eastern source for Shanker ceiling material is:

AA-Abbingdon
2149 Utica Ave.
Brooklyn, NY 11234
(212) 236-3251

Westerners can find Shanker metal ceilings at the following location:

Chelsea Decorative Metal Co.
6115 Cheena
Houston, TX 77096
(713) 721-9200

Cascade Mill & Glass Works

Cascade, in Colorado, offers a colletion of high-quality handcrafted screen, entry, and interior doors. The screen doors, in particular, couldn't be more fanciful or interesting. 1⅜" thick, generally constructed of pine and double-dowel jointing, these doors are suitable for late-Victorian homes. Handsome exterior doors, in a selection of woods ranging from red oak and Honduras mahogany to custom-ordered walnut, rosewood, teak, cherry, and pine, feature a variety of ornate glass patterns made from beveled or stained glass. Interior doors are just as gracious.

Brochure available.

Cascade Mill & Glass Works
Box 316
Ouray, CO 81427
(303) 325-4780

Customwood

Customwood, a New Mexico manufacturer of interior and exterior doors, offers a series of

Doors and Windows

As the openings to a house, doors and windows are those elements which are most directly affected by the weather. Old rattling or warped doors and windows often require replacment or reworking from time to time, depending on the age and situation of the house. It is always a shame, however, to see an old entryway replaced by one entirely inappropriate in scale, design, and materials. And it is disheartening to watch the replacement of multipane sash by modern one-piece sash. Such thoughtless substitutions need not be made. There are many excellent carpenters and cabinetmakers who will reproduce 18th- and 19th-century sash and doors that will last for many years.

Architectural Components

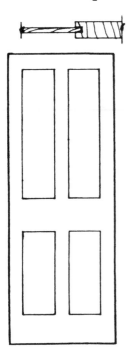

Architectural Components specializes in the reproduction of 18th- and 19th-century architectural millwork. Working from measured drawings and actual examples, the firm produces a line of authentic interior and exterior doors. Shown here is an example of an interior door: Shaker-style, it has four flat panels and is constructed of 1⅛" clear, kiln-dried Eastern white pine. The through-type mortise and tenon joint, held secure with square pegs, is used in the frame construction. The standard height for this door is 6'6" with widths ranging from 2' to 2' 8". Custom sizes for all doors can be arranged. Double-thickness exterior doors are available with additional insulation.

Brochure available.

Architectural Components
Box 246
Leverett, MA 01054
(413) 549-6230

hardwood doors inset with hand-crafted stained glass in unusual designs. 1¾″-thick doors are produced in 36″ by 80″ or 36″ by 84″ sizes. Shown here is a red oak door, part of Customwoods Vintage series, which is readily adaptable to many situations.

Catalogue available.

*Customwood
Box 26208
Albuquerque, NM 87125
(800) 545-6414*

French and Ball Woodworking

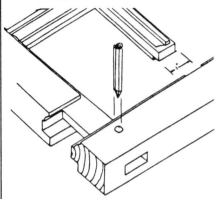

The window sashes made by this group of Massachusetts woodworkers are designed to duplicate or reproduce those of the 18th century. The traditional mortise and tenon method of construction is used. Sashes are made slightly oversized, unglazed, and with a sanded finish only. Plank frame windows that are fitted with French and Ball sash are also available. These must be custom ordered and come in eight sizes.

The double thickness clinch-nailed exterior doors made by French and Ball are accurate reproductions of 18th-century counterparts. Made of kiln-dried Eastern white pine, the exterior consists of four raised panels and the interior of vertical beaded sheathing. The two thicknesses are clinch-nailed together. Dimensions are 1¾″ thick, 6′ 6″ or 6′ 8″ high, and 32″ or 36″ wide. Also available are four-panel interior doors that are hand-planed on both sides and made of white pine.

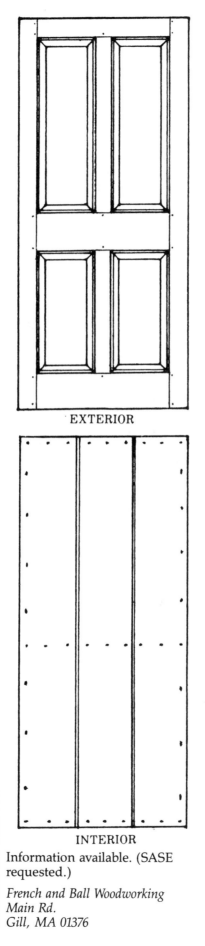

EXTERIOR

INTERIOR

Information available. (SASE requested.)

*French and Ball Woodworking
Main Rd.
Gill, MA 01376*

Gibbons Sash and Door

John Gibbons is a cabinetmaker who specializes in producing custom sash and doors. Among the variety of forms that he will undertake are French, frame, and panel doors of solid hardwood or pine; arch-top doors such as the example illustrated here; curved sash; curved and arch-top jambs and casing moldings; barred window sash; traditional counterweight double-hung windows; casement windows; and awning windows. Such is Gibbons' expertise that he was chosen to reproduce the doors of the Frank Lloyd Wright-designed Unitarian Meeting House in Madison, Wisconsin.

In addition to such custom work, Gibbons also offers designs of his own. His Windowworks Series is a handsome selection of door and sash designs appropriate for early 20th-century buildings. The four door models, including the arch-top example illustrated, are made of 1¾″ red oak glazed with laminated or tempered safety

glass. Four different styles of sash are made of pine, cherry, or Honduras mahogany and are 29½" wide by 29½" high by 1" thick. Three types of traditional transom windows are made of pine, measure 36" wide by 20" high by 1⅛" thick, and are sized to fit above a 36" entry door. All sash are glazed with single-strength window glass.

Gibbons wil also supply unfinished pine jamb and storm sash for his windows.

Brochure available.

Gibbons Sash and Door
Rte. 1
Hurley, WI 54534
(715) 561-3904

Kenmore Industries

Kenmore Industries has just introduced reproduction Georgian Colonial entryways, and we are pleased to be able to present one of the working drawings. It is of model #520, a hand-carved doorway 14' 5¾" high and 8' 9" wide; the pediment is 17" deep. This is one of three grand designs due from Kenmore this year. Details on materials, finishes, and requirements for installation of such a complex construction are not yet available, but can be secured by writing Kenmore.

The firm has made its reputation on delicately carved, lacelike fanlights and other over-door sash and decorative pieces. Kenmore carves all of these from high-quality mahogany. Illustrated is one of the four fanlight sash designs—number 101, which is fitted into frame number 107. The same sash design is available with a rectangular frame or can be supplied without any frame at all.

Catalogue, $3.

Kenmore Industries
44 Kilby St.
Boston, MA 02109
(617) 523-4008

John Lavoie

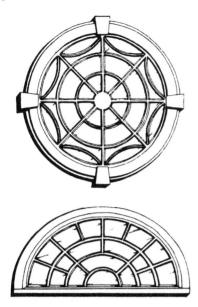

John Lavoie fashions imaginative fanlights; round, quarter-round, and oval windows; and transoms, all of whcih are guaranteed to delight any traditionalist. All of these are made up only by special order and are constructed of clear Eastern pine. Glass is double-strength with both sides of the window being back-glazed. Illustrated are examples of a round window (model 101) and a fanlight (model 629). It is always a pity to see lovely details like this lost in an old house. There is no reason for not replacing them when there are craftsmen such as Lavoie available today. His work should also draw the attention of post-modern architectural designers who are forever seeking new (read *old*) decorative forms with which to embellish their eclectic designs.

Brochure available.

John F. Lavoie
Box 15
Springfield, VT 05156
(802) 886-8253

Maurer & Shepherd

This Connecticut Valley firm recreates 17th- and 18th-century Colonial doors and entryways of the type found throughout New England. The work, all made to order, looks and feels authentic to the period. Carved pediments, rosettes, and swan necks adorn the Georgian Colonial entryway designs. Exterior doors, 1¾" thick, may feature raised panel fronts, either clinch-nailed to beaded batten boards or raised panel backs. Interior doors are ¹⁵⁄₁₆" thick and a far cry from the flimsy hollow-core Colonial-style pieces which pass as doors at the local building center. Maurer & Shepherd's interior doors are hand-planed and can be made up with any panel combination or other configuration. All of the work is done by hand, and mortise and tenon joinery is used throughout.

Brochure available.

Maurer & Shepherd Joyners, Inc.
122 Naubuc Ave.
Glastonbury, CT 06033
(203) 633-2383

Michael's Fine Colonial Products

Window sash is often the first element in an old house to self-destruct. If you have reached the point where you simply cannot reconstruct crumbling sash yet another time, Michael Bronfman can help you make up new ones just like the old. Send him a sketch, size required, and your preference of wood, and he will turn out a product that will be good for another several generations.

His standard work is double-hung sash of Eastern white pine in 1⅛", 1⅜", or 1¾" thicknesses. All come with real muntin bars. Bronfman can also supply wood storm sash and barn and cellear sash. A special item that he enjoys making is an octagonal window of Western pine with ¾" insulated glass and a removable grille. It measures 1' 10" in diameter. Windows of this type are often used for ventilation in the gable end of a residence or barn.

Brochure available. (SASE requested.)

Michael's Fine Colonial Products
Rte. 44, RD 1, Box 179A
Salt Point, NY 12578
(914) 677-3960

Nostalgia

Reproductions of elegant early- and mid-Victorian single and double exterior doors are made by this Savannah-based firm. The deep moldings and elaborate panel designs of the original doors found in the city's historic district have been expertly copied. Most of the available models feature stained, etched, beveled, or plain glass panels. Single doors measure 36" wide by 80" high, but these dimensions can be altered to suit other needs. Seasoned oak or mahogany are the woods used; others are available upon request. Double doors are a special-order item and can be made to suit almost any need.

Nostalgia also stocks antique doors that have been refurbished.

Catalogue, $2.50 (refundable with any purchase).

Nostalgia, Inc.
307 Stiles Ave.
Savannah, GA 31401
(912) 232-2324

Oak Leaves Wood Carving Studio

Few craftsmen with traditional skills can boast of working on the site of a covered bridge. Bill and Ronda Schnute built their own home and studio over a stream a few miles north of Iowa City, and this rustic setting helps to explain their unique work. Bill is a carver and his wife combines both this talent and that of design. Together they have created an unusual series of fine hardwood exterior doors that include extraordinary carved wildlife scenes. This type of work is not likely to interest the traditionalist, but the Schnutes's skills can be employed in other directions as well. If intricately sculpted custom work in wood is called for, here's a place to turn to.

Brochure, $1.

Oak Leaves Wood Carving Studio
RR 6, The Woods #12
Iowa City, IA 52240
(319) 351-0014

Walter E. Phelps

Craftsman and scholar Phelps has supplied 18th- and early 19th-century double-hung sash for some of the best residential restoration projects in the country. His custom work is of two types: sash with wide ovolo muntin bars of the type popular before the end of the Revolution, and the narrower ovolo muntin sash used through 1830 and later in remote areas of the country. Both types are available in 12 over 12, 12 over 8, 9 over 6, and 6 over 6 window sash combinations.

Recently Phelps has introduced a window unit that will interest anyone who lives in a cold climate—a window that is thermal efficient as well as historically accurate. The unit is made up of a removable double glazing panel which is attached to the outside of each sash. The panel creates a barrier that will reduce heat loss tremendously. Yet it does not alter the appearance of the window. The frame holding the sash is weatherstripped to further cut down on air infiltration. Window units of as many as 12 over 12 to 6 over 6 lights can be made up this way. Phelps has also developed a similar system for exterior doors.

For further information, have a contractor or architect contact the firm, as it does not deal directly with home owners.

Walter E. Phelps Co.
Box 76
Williamsville, VT 05362
(802) 348-6346

Renovation Concepts

This Minnesota door manufacturer offers a variety of woods—red oak, alder, cherry, and walnut—and quality workmanship at reasonable prices. Doors are of traditional Victorian designs. A variety of widths—30″, 32″, and 36″—and heights—80″, 84″, and 96″—are standard, but others are available on request. Shown here are two from the firm's Main Street Collection—the "Dakotah" (1¾″ thick, 3′ wide and 6′ 8″ or 7′ high) and the "Rochester" (1⅜″

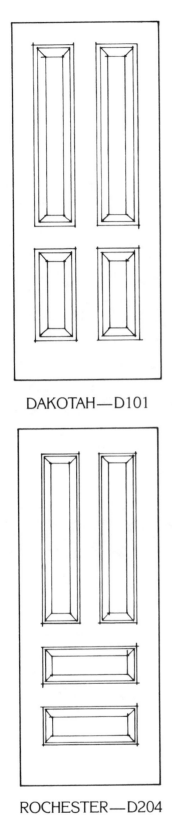

DAKOTAH—D101

ROCHESTER—D204

thick, 2' 6"; 2' 8", or 3' wide, and 6' 8" or 7' high).

Literature available.

Renovation Concepts, Inc.
213 Washington Ave., N.
Minneapolis, MN 55401
(612) 333-5766

Strobel Millwork

Strobel can make fine doors and windows for traditional or contemporary homes. The standard for both is the same—high. Most of the work is custom ordered, but the firm does maintain a small stock of standard door and window models. Mortise and tenon construction is used for all work, and all work is done by hand. The doors are simple panel and beaded board-and-batten designs common in North America from the 18th through the 19th centuries. Strobel can also supply the screen door of white pine illustrated here. The door has a recessed flush molding and is fitted with aluminum mesh wire screen. Preservative-treated, it is 1⅛" thick and comes in the following sizes—2' 6" wide by 6' 7" or 6' 9" high, 2' 8" wide by 6' 7" or 6' 9" high, and 3' wide by 6' 9" high.

One of Strobel's stock window designs is a radius-top fixed sash window. It can be framed in two

different ways, as illustrated. The center decorative pane of colored glass is sand-etched; the window can also be supplied with a clear pane. The same unit is available as a 2′ 8″ by 4′ 6″ double-hung window.

Information available.

Strobel Millwork
Rte. 7, Box 84
Cornwall Bridge, CT 06754
(203) 672-6727

Wallis's

Jack Wallis has been making Victorian-style doors accented with beveled, etched, and stained glass for fifteen years. Constructed of local oak and poplar, the doors can have glass panels that occupy one-half, three-quarters, or nearly the full frame. All components are made by hand—every joint, every bevel of glass. Yet Wallis manages to keep his prices moderate. Pictured here, behind the craftsman, are two limited-edition doors, which are only available in oak. In addition, Wallis will custom design

any door that combines glass and wood, from the very simple to the most intricately detailed.

Catalogue, $3.

Wallis's Stained Glass & Jack Wallis
*   Doors*
Rte. 1, Box 22A
Murray, KY 42071
(502) 489-2613

Woodstone

Woodstone interior and exterior doors are constructed using the traditional frame and panel system with pegged mortise and tenon joinery. Pine, oak, mahogany, cherry, or walnut—but no plywood or particle board—is used to make Woodstone doors, which may be special-ordered in any size. Of particular interest to those living in cooler climes is a specially insulated exterior door that has a foilated foam core sheathing sandwiched between the wood panels. Woodstone claims the door provides up to ten times the insulating value of an ordinary wood door. The insulated door is regularly stocked in pine or mahogany in two-, four-, and six-panel models. Of 1¾″ thickness, it is available in 2′ 6″ by 6′ 8″, 2′ 8″ by 6′ 8″, or 3′ by 6′ 8″ sizes.

Fanlights from Woodstone include wooden sash and trim that are

constructed using traditional pegged mortise and tenon joinery. This method allows for many varieties of shapes, sizes, and patterns. The windows come completely assembled with jamb and include all necessary curved trim and sash stops. Shown here is the use of a Gothic arch with round arc segments. A myriad of such designs is available, including Roman (round), elliptical, and Tudor arches.

Brochure, $1.

The Woodstone Company
Dept. OHC, Box 223
Patch Rd.
Westminster, VT 05158
(802) 722-4784 or 722-3544

Accurate Metal Weatherstrip Co.

Why ruin a beautiful exterior wood door with cheap weatherstripping? All too often the cheap, easy stuff sticks too well to paint, plaster, and your hands and not well enough to cut down on cold or heat. Accurate has been in business since 1898, producing metal weatherstripping of the highest quality. Zinc and bronze are the metals most frequently specified, but brass, aluminum, and stainless steel can also be supplied. Accurate also provides advice on proper nails or screws for attaching the material.

For information regarding Accurate products, contact:

Accurate Metal Weatherstrip Co., Inc.
725 S. Fulton Ave.
Mount Vernon, NY 10550
(914) 668-6042

Amherst Woodworking

With an extensive inventory of lumber, Amherst is a boon to the do-it-yourselfer. The stock usually includes cherry, aromatic cedar, South American mahogany, oak, pine, and maple (including curly and bird's-eye). The hardwoods are generally available in three thicknesses—1″, 1½″, and 2″—and are rough sawn to random widths and lengths. The lumber is kiln-dried and of select and better grades or first and second grades.

For those who are not eager to prove their own milling skills, Amherst will make up random-width board counters; stair treads, risers, and handrails; and tongue-and-groove paneling.

For further information, contact:

Amherst Woodworking & Supply,
 Inc.
Box 575, Hubbard Ave.
Northampton, MA 01061
(413) 584-3003

Lumber

If you are searching for boards or beams or even a small heavy strip of wood to replace a lintel or door saddle, you probably won't find what you want at the local lumberyard or home center. The usual response to a question concerning the availability of something other than the softest pine is that the better grade woods are simply not available any longer. That is not true. The truth is that the average bulding materials supplier makes his money from plywood, various types of composition board, sheetrock, and pine durable enough to

frame a house. Consequently, other specialty lumber dealers have established themselves throughout North America. All stock quantities of newly cut domestic and foreign timber such as quality white pine and oak, and many also keep a supply of recycled Southern heart pine. These dealers usually maintain an inventory of the more elegant woods used for interior work. If you need to have boards milled and finished in a particular manner, the specialty supplier probably can help.

A & M Wood Specialty

Canadian old-house owners will be glad to learn that A & M stocks many items of special interest to restorers and renovators. Available is a large selection of planks up to 40″ wide in cherry, oak, walnut, and ash, all suitable for flooring and paneling. A & M also carries half logs for wood turning in cherry, butternut, pear, ebony, and many other species. Veneers are available in over fifty species,

many of them exotics such as teak, rosewood, padauk, and olive wood. A & M will ship to the U.S. and the outer reaches of Canada.

Free price list available.

A & M Wood Specialty, Inc.
358 Eagle St. N., Box 3204
Cambridge, Ontario, Canada
 N3H 4S6
(519) 653-9322

Craftsman Lumber

This New England company specializes in supplying new pine boards in hard-to-find widths and in providing custom millwork for restoration projects. The wide pine boards are available in widths up to 24″ and in 1″ thickness. Craftsman also makes to order old-style wainscoting with beaded edge and center bead and a vee groove on the opposite side. Sometimes called "porch ceiling," this style was popular from about 1850 to 1930. It can be ordered in clear pine or clear oak. Another company specialty is clear or knotty white pine clapboard in any width and with any edging.

Brochure available.

Craftsman Lumber
Box 222
Groton, MA 01450
(617) 448-6336

Diamond K.

With its own sawmill, Canadian pine stand, and a wealth of salvaged materials, there is little that Diamond K. can't supply builders and restorers. The main products include rustic weathered barn wood, handhewn beams, rough-cut weathered beams, wide-plank pine, and old clapboard. All of these materials are available in a good selection of colors, widths, and lengths. We especially like Diamond K's handhewn chestnut beams which, unlike oak, keep their light golden color for generations without darkening perceptibly. Diamond K. will ship anywhere in the U.S.

Literature available.

Diamond K. Company, Inc.
130 Buckland Rd.
South Windsor, CT 06074
(203) 644-8486

Mad River Woodworks

The Victorian millwork executed by Mad River is described in chapter 2, but we think some of the firm's other products are also worth noting. Of special interest are ornamental redwood shingles, available in ten patterns, which would suitably adorn many Victorian homes. Mad River offers decorative redwood siding in five different profiles. All patterns are 7½" wide and may be painted, stained, or left in their natural finish. To complement the siding and shingles, Mad River makes redwood gutters, veranda posts, and fence pickets.

Catalogue available.

Mad River Woodworks
Box 163
Arcata, CA 95521
(707) 826-0629

Mountain Lumber

Along with a few other Southern lumber companies, Mountain lumber specializes in Southern longleaf heart pine. This handsome wood was originally used as construction lumber, but its scarcity now makes it economical only for decorative purposes, although—if your budget allows—it is hard to beat for structural needs. Heart pine, carefully remilled by Mountain, has several

advantages: it is practically bug-proof and won't rot; it is aesthetically pleasing; and it is amazingly strong. Mountain Lumber provides heart pine for use in paneling, flooring, and cabinetry, and will supply prices on such construction uses as floor joists, exposed beams, and porch framing. The wood is available in several grades and widths. The illustration is of heart pine flooring.

Free brochure and price list available.

Mountain Lumber
1327 Carlton Ave.
Charlottesville, VA 22901
(804) 295-1922 or 295-1757

Reisen Lumber

Besides a standard inventory of lumber and building materials, this New Jersey millwork company carries some items of particular interest to those restoring or renovating old buildings. Reisen stocks cedar shingles and shakes; cedar, cypress, and redwood siding; beaded wainscoting; beveled clapboard; and clear fir ceiling (which also works very well as wainscoting). In addition, the firm's mill can replicate custom patterns for molding, flooring, and paneling in any species. There is a minimum charge for most special orders.

For further information, contact:

Reisen Lumber & Millwork
1070 Morris Ave.
Union, NJ 07083
(201) 354-1500
(212) 267-8933 (NY)

Willis Lumber

Serving Ohio, Kentucky, Indiana, and West Virginia, this family business supplies top-quality furniture-grade domestic and imported hardwoods. Willis carries a good selection of tropical hardwoods, including teak, rosewood, and zebra wood. For small orders, customers are encouraged to hand select from the company's hardwood bins. Delivery is free within Ohio.

Catalogue available.

The Willis Lumber Co.
545 Millikan Ave.
Washington Court House, OH 43160
(614) 335-2601 (OH only)
(800) 346-3527

Roofing Materials

A roof is a necessary nuisance. It is hard to get to, and once you're on top of it, nearly impossible to stand on. If you have to replace or repair a roof, make sure that your contractor knows what he is doing and uses the best materials. With luck, you won't have to make another inspection trip up to this aery expanse for twenty or more years unless you particularly enjoy heights. Of the quality roofing materials, slate has always been considered number one. It is expensive, but will last for many years, as will also clay tile (not cement). But even a roof constituted of less durable materials such as wood shingling or mineral fibers will last a sufficient time if properly laid.

Jeff Alte

For something as important, structurally and aesthetically, as a roof, the home owner is wise to hire a specialist sensitive to the problems of period structures. In the New York metropolitan area, we have found Jeff Alte. He has rebuilt slate and cedar shingle roofs and created new ones with the look of the old. His crew is also equipped to handle copper gutters and leaders as well as built-in gutters, and his shop can fabricate custom gutters, ridge caps, and other elements that help to keep a house moisture free.

For further information, contact:

Jeff Alte Roofing
Box 639
Somerville, NJ 08876
(201) 526-2111

C & H Roofing

There is nothing in modern architecture that can match the gently rolling contours of an old-fashioned thatch roof. This style finds its origins in 16th-century rural England where the thatch for cottage roofs was made of water reeds. The style was transplanted to America, the thatch being made of wood shingles that were steamed and bent to fit the roof contours. Today, C & H Roofing, located in Sioux Falls, South Dakota, continues this splendid architectural tradition using Wetern red cedar shingles and its own steam-bending process. Luckily for those of us in the rest of the country, the C & H crew is prepared to travel extensively to restore thatch roofs or add them to new buildings. The photograph illustrates one of the firm's recent residential projects.

Free brochure available.

C & H Roofing
1713 S. Cliff Ave.
Sioux Falls, SD 57105
(605) 332-5060

Celestial Roofing

Roofing jobs are so easy to botch. There are valleys and peaks to contend with, and if the material is not carefully laid down with some thought given to the effect of heat, moisture, and cold, the whole house will suffer immeasurably. With a name like Celestial, you can be fairly certain that you are in heavenly hands when it comes to restoring or replacing a wood shingle, tile, or slate roof. Actually, the contractor's name is Ezra Wynn, a bit more down to earth. He and his assistants take great pride in the workmanship they achieve high above the ground—in the Berkeley, San Francisco, Oakland, and Piedmont, California area.

For further information, contact:

Celestial Roofing Co.
1710 Thousand Oaks Blvd.
Berkeley, CA 94707
(415) 549-3421

Evergreen Slate

Evergreen offers Vermont slate for roofing in five thicknesses and several textures. The slate comes in an unusual variety of colors, including semi-weathering gray-green, royal purple, blue-black, mottled green and purple, and our favorite, Rustic/Freaks, which has a variety of background colors and faces splotched with gold, bronze, and browns. Evergreen will ship throughout the country.

Literaure available.

Evergreen Slate Co., Inc.
Box 248
Granville, NY 12832
(518) 642-2530

A similar selection of Vermont roofing slate is available from Rising & Nelson. See previous listing for this firm under brick and stone building materials.

Follansbee Steel

Terne metal is a time-tested roofing material that has been in use in America since the early 18th century when it was imported from Wales. Several important historic buildings are still Terne roofed, including Monticello and the administration building of the Smithsonian Institution in Washington. Follansbee fabricates this material from prime copper-bearing steel coated with a tin/lead alloy. It is offered in seamless rolls of various sizes for use on most roof types.

For further information, contact:

Follansbee Steel Corp.
Follansbee, WV 26037
(800) 624-6906
(304) 527-1260 (WV)

Gladding, McBean

Aside from its terra-cotta products, described under brick and stone building materials, Gladding, McBean produces real clay roofing tile—not cement—in many styles suitable for period structures. Of particular interest is the firm's Cordova tile, the style of which derives from barrel mission tile made by the early Franciscan padres. The rounded shape and subtle color variations provide intricate and unusual textures. Cordova is offered in shades of red or in a combination of reds, browns, and buffs.

For further information, contact:

Gladding, McBean & Co.
Box 97
Lincoln, CA 95648
(916) 645-3341

Hilltop Slate

For over forty years, Hilltop has been manufacturing roofing slate, flooring, and flagstone from its own quarries. The roofing slate is predrilled and ready for installation. As is slate from other quarries, it is fire-proof, acid-resistant, and virtually unaffected by rain and snow. Slate from Hilltop is available in all colors, including several shades of green, purple, red, black, and gray.

For further information, contact:

Hilltop Slate Co.
Middle Granville, NY 12849
(518) 642-2770 or 642-1453

W. F. Norman

Long known for its metal ceilings, this firm also manufactures a line of metal roofing shingles. First introduced in 1908, they are available in several styles and are fabricated from galvanized steel or solid copper. Shown here is a Texas residence roofed in the Spanish Tile design. The company also has an interesting choice of Victorian-style tiles

which have decorative rounded or beveled edges.

For further information, contact:

San Valle Tile

For Spanish Colonial and Mission-style buildings, San Valle carries eight types of clay tile, from barrel mission to flat shingles. The curved tiles come in sizes from 17″ to 20″ long and chord widths of 7″ to 12″. Each is more than ½″ thick. Colors available range from natural red to brown and gold to a dark red-black.

The flat clay shake field tile, which is approximately 18″ long, comes in widths of 12″, 8″, 6″, and 4″, and is ⅝″ thick. It has a weathered rough finish, is predrilled for nailing, and is available in red or in a blend of reds and browns.

For further information, contact:

San Valle Tile Kilns
1717 N. Highland Ave.
Los Angeles, CA 90028
(213) 464-7289

Structural Slate

As a roofing material, slate has few equals. On the practical side, it is fireproof and non-absorbent and requires almost no upkeep.

W. F. Norman Corp.
Box 323, 214-32 N. Cedar St.
Nevada, MO 64772
(800) 641-4038
(417) 667-5552 (MO)

And it has an unusual and lasting beauty not found in many of today's synthetic roofing materials. Structural Slate offers handmade shingles of Pennsylvania blue-gray slate. While these high-quality materials can be expensive, longevity makes their use worthwhile. There are Structural Slate representatives throughout the country; contact the company for local distributors.

Brochure available.

The Structural Slate Co.
222 E. Main St., Box 187
Pen Argyl, PA 18072
(215) 863-4141

Supradur

Supradur continues to manufacture weatherproof and fireproof mineral fiber roofing shingles that are appropriate for many late-Victorian and early 20th-century houses and useful as a less expensive alternative to slate. The Supra-Slate line successfully imitates the look and texture of slate in Rutland Red, Vermont Green, Bangor Black, and Pennsylvania Gray colors. The standard size is a 9.35″ by 16″ rectangle; hexagonal shapes can also be supplied. With six-sided shingles, it is possible to duplicate a multicolor Victorian mansard roof.

Brochure available.

Supradur Manufacturing Co.
Box 908
Rye, NY 10580
(800) 223-1948
(914) 967-8230 (NY)

Stairs

A stairway can be among the most interesting and attractive features of an old house. It can also be among the shakiest and least secure. A stairway, however, is usually not a do-it-yourself weekend project. Professionals who can repair or rebuild any one of the many traditional types of stairways will save you money, considerable time, and free you from the threat of a lawsuit. These same stairbuilders and suppliers of stair systems are experienced in creating entirely new sturdy and elegant models that can be usd in spatially limited or lavish settings.

American General Products

Stairbuilding is a complex art, often beyond the skills of the do-it-yourselfer. American General manufacturers a curved wood staircase, Studio Stair S-90, designed to fit a standard eight-foot ceiling height; custom sizes are also available. It is constructed with hidden steel stringers which are permanenly screwed to the treads and risers. The treads are oak and the risers and stringers are birch or oak with matching cove molding. Balustrades and matching upper-story wood handrails are also available. Once in place, the Studio Stair S-90 has much of the grace of the elegant curving staircases found in many stately homes.

American General also carries an extensive line of steel and oak spiral stairs which, while not always appropriate to older houses, are well-constructed and

handsome and may be quite useful in certain cases.

Free brochures available.

American General Products, Inc.
1735 Holmes Rd.
Ypsilanti, MI 48197
(800) 732-0609
(313) 483-1833 (MI)

L. J. Bernard & Son

The Bernards have been in the woodworking business for four generations and produce high-quality custom woodwork. They specialize in Colonial and Victorian pieces, including paneling, molding, and mantels. Of particular interest are their custom stairways. They can build straight or curved staircases and will also supply the components for the home owner to assemble a stairway himself.

For further information, contact:

L. J. Bernard & Son Woodshop, Inc.
Rt. 3, Box 92A
Nixa, MO 65714
(417) 725-1449

James R. Dean

James Dean continues his exceptional work as a custom stairbuilder. He can fabricate any type of interior stair as well as match existing work. All parts are made to order in his shop and can be shipped—disassembled—anywhere. Installation is also available by special arrangement. Shown here is a cherry balustrade made by Dean to match an existing stair. The second photo illustrates a stair and balustrade reproduced from the Silas Dean House in Wethersfield, Connecticut.

For further information, contact:

James R. Dean
15 Delaware St.
Cooperstown, NY 13326
(607) 547-2262 or 547-2675

Every time we describe the products of this Canadian company, yet another imaginative design has been added to an already impressive collection of Victorian cast-iron stair units. The new spiral stair model, the Barclay, is shown here. It is 60" in diameter and uses twenty-five square feet of space. The bolt-together system provides convenient packing, shipping, and on-site assembly. The front rise and side panel have an intricate floral pattern with a closed tread surface. The Barclay is offered with an optional polished-brass side rail. Information is available on this and other spiral and straight staircase designs.

Literature available.

Steptoe & Wife Antiques Ltd.
3626 Victoria Park Ave.
Willowdale, Ontario, Canada
 M2H 3B2

Consultants and Architects

Almost everyone needs advice in putting an old house back together or in renovating some part of it. Consultants and architects can help tremendously with such preliminary steps as inspecting a building before it is purchased, digging out the building's history, and drawing up a recommended list of restoration or renovation steps to be taken. Once the direction is clear and the plans have been drawn up, a contractor is usually called in to perform most of the work. The architect or consultant need not step out of the picture entirely at this point; he is usually willing to supervise the contractual work.

Arch Associates

Arch Associates is an experienced Chicago-area architectural firm that offers various types of consulting services of interest to lovers of old houses. Even if you are only interested in finding the right house, Arch may be able to help you. And once the building is located, the firm will undertake its professional inspection.

Arch also provides complete restoration, rehabilitation, or remodeling plans and drawings—depending on your needs. Once the project is under way, the firm will supervise the work of a contractor.

For further information, contact:

Arch Associates
824 Prospect Ave.
Winnetka, IL 60093
(312) 446-7810

Architectural Resources Group

An architectural firm, ARG has extensive experience in restoration work throughout California, Nevada and Arizona. A job can be followed from the early planning stage through the supervision of construction details. It would be hard to disagree with the firm's stated philosophy: "Our interest in working with existing structures stems from the belief that the conservation and intelligent use of all of our resources are among the most critical challenges of our time. . . ." Judging from these photographs of a recently-completed residential restoration in San Francisco, this group is more than capable of fulfilling its goals.

For further information, contact:

Architectural Resources Group
Pier 9, The Embarcadero
San Francisco, CA 94111
(415) 421-1680

Bucher & Cope

This prestigious Washington, D.C., architectural firm specializes in fairly large-scale restoration and historic preservation projects. The firm offers complete architectural services, including engineering design, landscape and site planning, and interior restoration planning. Bucher & Cope has had extensive experience working with developers on rehabilitation projects, and much of the firm's expertise is focused on such major activities as campus planning and design and planning for commercial areas and historic districts.

For further information, contact:

Bucher & Cope
The Washington Design Center,
  Suite 300
1536 16th St., NW
Washington, DC 20036
(202) 387-0061

Carson, Dunlop & Associates

Toronto and its surrounding area has emerged in recent years as "old house territory." Much that has been valuable architecturally has been saved to be enjoyed again by a new generation of home owners. Anyone in the Toronto area stepping out into the world of old buildings for the first time would be wise to consult a professional home inspection team. Carson, Dunlop & Associates will make sure that the old house of your dreams does not become a nightmare when you take possession. Messrs. Dunlop and Carson are experienced engineers who work quickly and efficiently to provide you with a sound analysis of a structure's worth and potentiality.

Brochure available.

Carson, Dunlop & Associates, Ltd.
Home Inspection & Evaluation
597 Parliament St., Suite B5
Toronto, Ontario M4X 1W3
(416) 964-9415

Clio Group, Inc.

This Philadelphia firm has participated in numerous significant building restoration projects, among them Philadelphia's Academy of Fine Arts, 30th Street Station, and the Bellevue-Stratford Hotel. The group is known for its exhaustive research on the original condition of a building, after which it suggests appropriate alterations or additions

completely in keeping with the original. It will assist with historical register applications and with zoning surveys, and offers seriated paint and mortar analyses as well. Shown here is the stately three-story Victorian Charles Krauth Mansion in West Philadelphia which the Clio Group recently restored and rehabilitated.

Brochure available.

Clio Group, Inc.
3961 Baltimore Ave.
Philadelphia, PA 19104
(205) 386-6276

Allen Charles Hill, AIA

This historic preservation and architectural firm provides comprehensive professional assistance to property owners, architects, and historical commissions and societies—anyone, in short, interested in the care and maintenance of old buildings. At least half of its current projects involve private residences, with services ranging from historical research and technical consulting to full architectural services for restoration, rehabilitation, and adaptation. Although it generally works within a 150-mile radius of Boston, the firm is willing to travel even further. It will assist a client prior to the purchase of an old house and provide an accurate idea of its physical condition and historical worth. It will also suggest practical ways to restore the building and offer technical services such as paint and mortar analyses and x-ray studies of concealed areas. The principal in the firm, Allen Charles Hill, has specialized in historic preservation since 1972. Pictured here is the firm's exterior restoration of Stoodley's Tavern at Strawbery Banke in Portsmouth, New Hampshire.

Literature available.

Allen Charles Hill,
Historic Preservation & Architecture
25 Englewood Rd.
Winchester, MA 01890
(617) 729-0784

Oehrlein & Associates

Detailed and expert analysis is required for proper restoration work on any important building. This firm, headed by Mary Oehrlein, AIA, has the in-depth know-how, hands-on experience, and critical perspective needed to tackle very ambitious projects. Gallery Row, illustrated here, is but one of a number of major restorations which Ms. Oehrlein directed in her former position with Building Conservation Technology. This series of four buildings in Washington, D.C.'s Pennsylvania

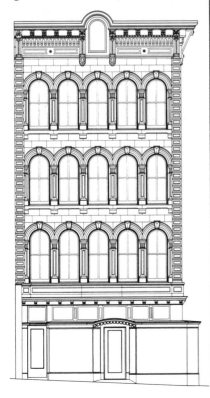

Avenue historic area, has been adapted for commercial re-use with considerable success. But this goal was not attained until the four buildings were studied from all historical and structural angles, drawn, and photographed. Eventually, only the facade was retained, a new structural frame having been built behind the old. Many of the projects undertaken by the new firm, however, are not quite so extensive or costly. Paint analysis; consulting on the preservation, restoration, or proper replacement of building materials; and the design of new historic elements are among the principal services offered by Oehrlein & Assocaites. In addition to the director, there is a staff of three architects and an architectural historian.

Information sheet available.

Oehrlein & Associates
1555 Connecticut Ave., N.W.
Washington, D.C. 20036
(202) 387-8040

Preservation Associates

Preservation Associates has now turned from contractor and supplier to consultant. Douglas and Paula Stoner Reed have had superb training in building technology of the past, and are very much attuned to today's needs. They can help guide the owner of an old building from the first tentative steps of historical documentation through the actual rehabilitation work to be performed by the contractor. They are concerned about making a building a useful structure, in cost effectiveness, and in technically and historically accurate work which will meet all Federal and state standards. They also work with nonprofit organizations and architectural firms in developing rehabilitation plans.

Brochure available.

Preservation Associates, Inc.
207 S. Potomac St.
Hagerstown, MD 21740
(301) 791-7880

The Renovation Source

Rob Raffel continues as one of the principal Chicago-area restoration consultants and suppliers of building materials. Whether you need construction drawings or something as simple as advice on how to insulate a mid-Victorian town house with 14-foot ceilings, Renovation Source can be of considerable help.

Literature available.

The Renovation Source, Inc.
3512-14 N. Southport
Chicago, IL 60657
(312) 327-1250

Society for the Preservation of New England Antiquities

SPNEA is one of the world's leading architectural preservation societies and over the years has achieved notable success in restoring and administering historic properties throughout New England. Based in Boston, this nonprofit organization has now assumed a new role as a consultant to private home owners, private and public organizations, and government agencies. The Consulting Services department of SPNEA offers the expertise of conservators, researchers, and draftsmen. Among the specific services performed are structural and historical surveys of buildings, advice on and supervision of restoration work, preparation of National Register of Historic Places forms, paint analysis, and studies of cleaning and painting early masonry buildings. Consulting Services also sponsors courses and lectures on building conservation.

For information on the programs and services available to the public, contact:

Sara B. Chase, Director
Consulting Services
SPNEA
Harrison Gray Otis House
141 Cambridge St.
Boston, MA 02114
(617) 227-3956

William J. Warren & Son

Prospective old-house owners in the Rocky Mountain states will find the inspection services of the Warren firm especially helpful. William Warren, a contractor, is very familiar with the types of problems that are likely to be encountered when a house is restored or adapted for new uses. His firm logically suggests its inspection services before a building is bought, not after. It will also supply, at no charge, brochures entitled, "A Roof Job Right," "Inspect Before You Buy," "Professional Home Inspections," and "Tips for Buying a Good Older Home."

For further information, contact:

William J. Warren & Son, Inc.
PO Box 9614
Fort Collins, CO 80525
(303) 482-1976

Contractors

Builders with the skills necessary to execute restoration or renovation work successfully can be difficult to find. Nearly every area of North America, however, has at least a few of these talented individuals. In addition to basic construction techniques, the old-house contractor must be very familiar with various period styles, old-fashioned building methods, and the types of materials which can be appropriately used. How to locate such a history-sensitive contractor? The listings that follow will be helpful, and, if one individual cannot help you, he may be able to lead you to another who can assist. The best recommendation, however, is still a house that has been successfully restored or renovated. If possible, visit a few of these homes, and find out by whom the work was done.

Anderson Building Restoration

Anderson has helped to bring sense and sensibility to the cleaning of historic masonry structures. Until recent years, the facades of such buildings were often indiscriminately sandblasted, thus pitting and nearly destroying the stone or brick surface. Anderson makes use of only the products of Diedrich Chemicals Restoration Technologies—safe, effective cleaners and paint removers. In addition, Anderson's masons are expert at matching old mortar formulas and joint treatments. As this photograph shows, no job is too big for the firm to undertake. Projects are accepted principally in the Midwest.

For further information, contact:

Anderson Building Restoration
923 Marion Ave.
Cincinnati, OH 45229
(513) 281-5258

For information on Diedrich restoration products, contact:

Diedrich Chemicals Restoration Technologies, Inc.
300A E. Oak St.
Milwaukee, WI 53154
(800) 323-3565

Architectural Reclamation

The business of this Ohio-based family firm consists of general contracting work on older buildings. During the past eight years, projects have included a variety of historic structures—Victorian balloon-frame, timber-frame, masonry, and log buildings. The exterior work that will be undertaken encompasses just about everything from the foundation to the roof. Inside the house, the company is equipped to replicate moldings and trim, handle all electrical and plumbing work, and even construct custom period kitchens and baths. Salvaged materials are used whenever possible. Architectural Reclamation can handle large, complete jobs or the smaller project that the do-it-yourselfer can't quite manage.

For further information, contact:

Architectural Reclamation, Inc.
312 S. River St.
Franklin, OH 45005
(513) 746-8964

ART, Inc.

A group of skilled artists and sculptors, ART, Inc. specializes in fabricating architectural detail for historic buildings. Work is executed in numerous materials, including stone, plaster and fiberglass. The list of restoration projects is extensive and includes fabricating replacement terra-cotta and stone facade ornamentation for Old Westbury Gardens on Long Island, Harvard University, and the White House. ART, Inc.'s capabilities are geared to large jobs, but the group will take on smaller-scale projects as well.

Free brochure available.

ART, Inc.
315 N. Washington Ave.
Moorestown, NJ 08057
(609) 866-0536

Richard W. Babcock

Richard Babcock has elevated the business of saving old barns, moving them, and reassembling them, to an art form. He is already well known for some of his major projects, including the barns at Wolf Trap Performing Arts Center, Virginia; the Dutch barn at Phillipsburg Manor, Tarrytown, New York; and his own Barn Museum in Hancock, Massachusetts. If you are interested in converting a barn as a residence, Babcock may have the one that suits your needs. Once a choice is made, the barn is dismantled piece by piece and restored in Babcock's workshop. Finally, the frame is reassembled on the owner's site.

Color brochure, $7; brochure on the barns at Wolf Trap, $10; Barn Museum brochure, $1.50.

Richard W. Babcock, Inc.
Box 484
Williamstown, MA 01267
(413) 738-5639

The Barn People

Not everyone can find the old house of his dreams, nor does every dream site come complete with the perfect old house. For those with a love of old structures, an empty building site, and an aversion to the basic modern split level, Barn People has a solution. This Vermont company skillfully dismantles old post and beam barns, preserving and restoring the timber framing. The frame is then taken to the client's building site and reassembled,

using wooden fastening pegs and the original construction methods. The company has a large and constantly changing inventory of barns to choose from. In addition, a design team works with the client to develop a personalized floor plan, designed to turn this very special structure into a very special home.

Literature available.

The Barn People
South Woodstock, VT 05071
(802) 457-3943

Beta Timber Restoration/ Dell Corporation

The Dell Corporation, a general restoration contractor in the Washington Baltimore area, is also the North American distributor for the Beta system of timber restoration, a method devised in Europe. When a building requires structural strengthening, each deteriorated section is removed and a reinforcement rod is inserted. The cavity is then filled with a synthetic resin cement and bonded with epoxy. When a timber is put back in place, the repair is virtually invisible. The Beta system has been used successfully on historic buildings throughout Europe. The Dell Corporation will

provide the name or names of contractors who have licensed the system in a prospective client's area.

For further informatoin, contact:

Dell Corporation
Box 1462
Rockville, MD 20850
(301) 279-2612

Biltmore, Campbell, Smith

The amazing decorative painting and restoration skills of this American branch of an established English firm are discussed in detail in chapter 7. In addition to painting and gilding, Biltmore craftsmen can expertly handle all types of stonework cleaning, woodwork refinishing, and allied services such as plastering, metalwork, cloth and paper hanging, wood and stone carving, and stained-glass repair. Among the major projects they have undertaken are Biltmore House—the Vanderbilt mansion in Asheville, North Carolina—and San Francisco Plantation in Louisiana.

Brochure available.

Biltmore, Campbell, Smith
Restorations, Inc.
1 Biltmore Plaza
Asheville, NC 28804
(704) 274-1776

Breakfast Woodworks

Louis Mackall and Partner, Architects, and Breakfast Wood-

works, Inc., both brainchildren of architect Louis Mackall, offer a

50 soup-to-nuts renovation service which includes inspection, design, specification drawings, millwork fabrication and installation, as well as on-site construction supervision. Mackall is prepared to tackle projects as small as a cornice molding or as large as a 20,000-square-foot renovation, and has executed numerous residential, commercial, and historic preservation projects in the New England area. Illustrated here is a recent project, Wokl House, which is used as actors' housing for the Goodspeed Opera House in East Haddam, Connecticut.

Literature available.

Breakfast Woodworks, Inc.
50 Maple Street
Branford, CT 06405
(203) 488-8364

Campbellsville Industries

This Kentucky-based firm fabricates steeples, cupolas, balustrades, and other architectural elements from aluminum, and some of the designs are suitable for period structures. Each piece is custom-produced and Campbellsville will provide installation as well. The pieces can be painted or sheathed in such a covering as copper. The photograph illustrates one of many restoration projects, the Adair County Courthouse in Columbia, Kentucky, for which a clock tower, balustrades, and cornices were supplied. The company's work can be seen on public buildings throughout the country, including churches in almost every state. While not many other houses require such elaborate facade work, a few do cry out for it. The more elaborate the old house type, the more likely it is to require substantial restoration.

For further information, contact:

Campbellsville Industries, Inc.
Box 278, Taylor Blvd.
Campbellsville, KY 42718
(502) 465-8135

CK Constructions

The San Francisco area probably boasts more well-restored Victorian buildings than any other area in North America. At the center of much of this restoration work is CK Constructions. As general contractors, the firm comes highly recommended. It is involved in all phases of commercial and residential restoration work—from estimating (usually free of charge) and structural foundation work to the interior design and finish. CK will also take on the construction of additions as well as totally new buildings in either reproduction or contemporary styles.

For further information, contact:

CK Constructions
2565 3rd St., Suite 203
San Francisco, CA 94107
(415) 647-5140

Custom Carpentry

This company, established in 1974, provides general carpentry, masonry and exterior detail work such as column and capital replacement, foundation repairs, and reproduction woodwork. The Rice House, one of the most recent custom projects, is shown here, near completion. This Second Empire row house required almost total reconstruction. Custom Carpentry rebuilt the porch, repaired the slate roof, and reproduced the ornamental hoods over the third-story windows. Other fine examples of this team's work are the exterior restoration of the Bellamy Homestead in Chicopee, Massachusetts, and the gazebo in Springfield, Massachusetts's Forest Park. Knowing that much of Custom Carpentry's work is done under the aegis of the Springfield Preservation Trust and the Massachusetts Historical Commission should inspire and reassure the most finicky of old-house owners.

For further information, contact:

Custom Carpentry
263 Union Street
Springfield, MA 01105
(413) 788-0396

Dodge, Adams & Roy

Restoration work is a way of life in historic Portsmouth, New Hampshire, and Dodge, Adams & Roy offers a wide range of building services in this area, including masonry, plaster work, timber framing, and finish carpentry. The staff of specialists is skilled, as well, in cabinetry, copper and slate roofing, mold making and casting, custom wood carving, architectural drawings, and even landscaping. The firm's projects range from the reconstruction of a 100-year-old timber dam to the construction of a new barn for an 18th-century farm. A number of projects have been undertaken for the Society for the Preservation of New England Antiquities, a high recommendation indeed. Dodge, Adams & Roy also builds reproduction houses, using traditional construction methods.

In addition to its building services, the firm undertakes consulting jobs. This type of work can include any one or all of the following services: an on-site building inspection and report, historical research, asssistance with National Register of Historic Places nomination forms, and the development of general construction plans and specifications or plans for the restoration of specific features.

Brochure available.

Dodge, Adams & Roy, Ltd.
Stoodley's Tavern, Hancock St.
Portsmouth, NH 03801
(603) 436-6424

Downstate Restorations

Since 1978, Downstate has been providing restoration services in the Midwest. The firm is skilled in careful masonry cleaning and paint removal, interior and exterior painting, and the repair and reconstruction of ornamental cornices. Each project is preceded by meticulous testing and research to insure the use of the best methods and materials to preserve the historical accuracy and beauty of the original structure.

Brochure available.

Downstate Restorations
Box 276
Macomb, IL 61455
(309) 456-3633 or (312) 929-5588

Housejoiner, Ltd.

Townsend Anderson has earned just acclaim for his meticulous and imaginative restoration projects. One of his recent jobs, the 1805 Federal-style John Warren House in Middlebury, Vermont, won him the 1984 Preservation Trust of Vermont Award for "outstanding work in preserving Vermont's architecture," as well as the 1984 National Trust for Historic Preservation Honor Award. Using detailed research, a thorough knowledge of traditional construction methods, and creative problem solving, he restores a period structure to its former splendor and illuminates the beauty of long-neglected interior and exterior details. Working with his partner (and wife), Jodee, Anderson gets to the very heart of an old house. Structural problems are solved, architectural details are repaired or rebuilt, and decorative elements are lovingly recreated.

For further information, contact:

Housejoiner, Ltd.
RD 1, Box 860
Moretown, VT 05660
(802) 244-5095

Tom Moore's Steeple People

While not, strictly speaking, restoration contractors, Steeple People provides a hard-to-find and much-needed service. This firm specializes in high-area work such as steeples, roofs, and bell towers. Steeple People has undertaken extensive restoration work on historical churches and town halls and has the expert skills needed to restore slate, copper, and metal roofs; metal ceilings; and gold leaf. For those faced with the problems of crumbling cupolas, faded gilt ceiling friezes, or perhaps just sagging roof overhangs three-stories high, Steeple People may be able to help. The firm's services are available nationwide, although most projects are carried out in New England.

Written estimates available at no cost.

Tom Moore's Steeple People
21 Janine St.
Chicopee, MA 01013
(413) 533-9515

New Jersey Barn

This firm, extensively covered in chapter 10, is—despite its name—much more than a supplier of antique barns. In storage now is a 1740 frame house and a log house that Elric Endersby dismantled before they could be destroyed in the name of "progress." The firm has transported and reassembled the frames of some of its saved structures on new sites in New England and New York State, and is willing to make even longer moves. New Jersey Barn will help with design plans and specifications, but the actual finishing of the building is left to the new owner and his contractor.

Brochure available.

The New Jersey Barn Co.
PO Box 702
Princeton, NJ 08542
(609) 924-8480

Restorations Unlimited

Because James and Elizabeth Facinelli have done so for themselves, they are admirably qualified to help others plan and execute home restoration projects. The Facinellis are master craftsmen and work with others similarly skilled in traditional craftsmanship. Kitchens are a specialty, but the Facinellis will also undertake other aspects of a renovation project such as tin and slate roofing, brick and stone masonry, decorative glass work, floor refinishing, stenciling, and plastering. If it's only advice that you need, they can provide that, too, in abundance. They will plan color schemes, lay out floor plans, work up budgets and feasibility studies, and handle historic certification procedures and papers, Restorations Unlimited works primarily in the mid-Atlantic area.

Literature available.

Restorations Unlimited, Inc.
24 W. Main St.
Elizabethville, PA 17023
(717) 362-3477

River City Restorations

This Missouri firm can handle most phases of building restoration, including masonry cleaning and the repair of such elements as chimneys. River City's masons will also duplicate original mortar and find replacement bricks to match existing facades. The firm can also construct or repair everything from front porches and kitchens to millwork details. And it is also skilled in the finish work that many contractors avoid— including stenciling, painting, plastering, and floor refinishing.

Brochure available.

River City Restorations
200 S. Seventh St.
Hannibal, MO 63401
(314) 248-0733

Donald Stryker

For dedication and sheer attention to detail, not many restoration carpenter/contractors can match Donald Stryker. Highly recommended in previous editions of this catalogue, he continues to provide New Jersey old-house owners with meticulous finish carpentry as well as detailed house inspection services and consultation. In addition, he offers guidance for the do-it-yourselfer who needs help in doing it himself.

Stryker asks that prospective clients include a phone number in letters of inquiry.

For further information, contact:

Donald Stryker Restorations
154 Commercial Ave.
New Brunswick, NJ 08901
(201) 828-7022

Swallow Woodworks

Timothy Barker best explains the goals of his company as an attempt "to maintain an eye for detail and respect for the joinery that has proven itself for many years. Our desire is to change only that which will benefit in terms of longevity." Barker was trained to execute woodwork in the styles of colonial New England, but has been working primarily on Victorian structures for the past six years. He maintains a shop capable of reproducing almost any type of period architectural woodwork. Details from two of his recent restoration projects in Little Rock are illustrated here.

For further information, contact:

Swallow Woodworks
324 N. Schiller St.
Litte Rock, AR 72205
(501) 375-2551

Victorian Interior Restoration

Stressing that it handles only restoration, not remodeling or rehabilitation projects, this Ohio company places itself firmly among the old-house purists. Offered is a full range of structural and decorative restoration services for 19th- and early 20th-century buildings, both residential and commercial. The photograph illustrates a recent project—the restoration of an 1890 kitchen. We've seen the "before" picture and can attest to the attention to detail and craftsmanship brought to the job. Victorian Interior's im-

pressive list of projects includes museum facilities, commercial buildings, and private homes.

Literature available.

Victorian Interior Restoration
6374 Waterloo Rd.
Atwater, OH 44201
(216) 947-3385

Reproduction Period Houses

Many people have neither the time nor the inclination to bring an old house back to life. But, still, there is a strong desire to live in a house which is designed and built along the lines of the old. Until recent years, only Colonial homes were reproduced; now, various types of Victorian buildings are being copied. Contrac- *tors specializing in period reproductions faithful in form to the past, but thoroughly modern in other respects, are described in the following listings. Included with these listings are additional ones for suppliers of traditional building designs and floor plans which have been adapted to suit new needs.*

Entwood Construction Fraternity

For fifteen years, Entwood has been building timber-framed structures, using traditional post-and-beam construction methods and handcrafted joinery. Although it will build to suit the client's needs, Entwood excels at building homes and barns based on Colonial models from the 17th and 18th centuries and handsome replicas of French country houses of various historic periods. If the client wishes, the firm can construct these homes incorporating modern passive solar technology. Entwood claims that it will travel anywhere for an interesting project and has ventured as far as the West Indies, where it pioneered in the study and replication of early framed Caribbean houses.

Brochure available.

Entwood Construction Fraternity
R.R. #1
Wolcott, VT 05680
(802) 253-9013

Historical Replications

Not everyone building a house today is interested in glass and concrete structures or solar and rammed-earth technology. For those who prefer the homelier styles of the past, Historical Replications offers a portfolio of Victorian house plans ranging from the stately to the humble. Each set of designs contains a foundation plan; floor plans with electrical and plumbing diagrams; elevations; window, door, and cabinetry details; and framing diagrams. Plan C3350, shown on the opposite page, is adapted from a late-Victorian home built in 1908 in Monticello, Georgia. Plan G2430, below, a good choice for a narrow lot, is adapted from

George F. Barber's *The College Souvenir #2*, published in 1890. Historical Replications offers these and a wide range of styles in between.

Portfolio of plans, $10.

Historical Replications, Inc.
Box 31198, Dept. OHC/4
Jackson, MS 39206
(601) 981-8743

Campbell Center

The Campbell Center for Historic Preservation Studies is devoted exclusively to offering short courses in restoration and preservation. The school, located in rural northwestern Illinois, was founded in 1979 on the historic campus of the defunct Shimer College. Practicing professionals serve as faculty, and hands-on experience is stressed. Workshops, which convene from two days to two weeks, are offered in four "tracks": conservation of wooden buildings, architectural preservation, care of museum objects, and furniture conservation. Each sequence of classes runs for six to eight weeks, but individual classes may be taken. While a number of courses are best suited for professional conservationists in the arts and architecture, many are applicable to serious home restorers.

Donald M. Parrish, Inc.

Donald Parrish's first love is researching old buildings and designing appropriate historic elements. The period doorway shown, copied from the main entrance of the Dwight Barnard House in Deerfield, Massachusetts, is illustrative of the fine work he undertakes. Although Parrish's principal business is the construction of reproduction houses in the 18th-century manner in the central Michigan area, he is a good man to consult if you are seeking help anywhere in North America, especially if you want to build a new old house of true historic character. He will provide drawings and can arrange for the delivery of hard-to-find building materials. He'll also work with you or your builder during every phase of construction.

Parrish offers a starter set of more than fifteen pictures and plans to help prospective clients make a

preliminary selection of the type of historic house they would like replicated. It is available, C.O.D., for $15 plus postage.

Literature available.

Donald M. Parrish, Inc.
3997 Holden Dr.
Ann Arbor, MI 48103
(313) 994-5371

Brochure available.

Campbell Center
Box 66
Mount Carroll, IL 61053
(815) 244-1173

Cornerstones

Cornerstones, a house-building "learning center" in Brunswick, Maine, was founded by physicist Charles Wing in 1972 as an outgrowth of a course he was teaching at Bowdoin College on "The Art of the House." Courses are taught at a variety of levels: for professionals, serious home remodelers, even for those who

Schools and Study

Courses and workshops in traditional building methods, architectural styles, and the interior design of

period buildings are very popular. These educational programs are especially useful to the do-it-

have "never picked up a hammer." Of the many programs offered, a course in energy-efficient renovation and solar retrofit is of particular interest to old-house renovators. This two-week program meets in morning classroom sessions and afternoon field work on a retrofit project. Cornerstones also offers courses in house building, toolmaking, and blacksmithing. There are special programs for women in carpentry, house building, and handywork. Cornerstone faculty members have held programs out of state where strong local interest has been shown, and now they are offering a unique idea for a vacation: a one-week cruise while you learn about contracting for your home.

Catalogue, $2.

Cornerstones
54 Cumberland St.
Brunswick, ME 04011
(207) 729-6701

Eastfield Village

Students attending Eastfield Village get to learn not only traditional American home-building skills, but experience firsthand what life was like in the early 19th century by living in a restored village. Eastfield, situated between Albany, New York, and Pittsfield, Massachusetts, consists of twenty-seven reconstructed buildings where workshops employing period methods and tools are held. Directed by Donald Carpentier, a master of many historic trades, including woodworking and blacksmithing, courses are all led by people who are both practitioners and historians of their fields. Programs in the techniques of restoration carpentry, historic lighting, blacksmithing, window perservation, moldings, and early American fabrics and wallpapers are among those offered.

Brochure available.

Eastfield Village
Box 145
East Nassau, NY 12062
(518) 766-2422

Heartwood

Heartwood, in the hills of western Massachusetts, offers summer workshops in a camplike setting. A five-day course in renovation calls for participants to bring photos, floor plans, sketches, and measurements of their projects so that they, together with faculty, can learn from each other. Another course deals with being your own contractor: estimating costs, ordering materials, scheduling, hiring subcontractors, and developing an "eye" for quality work. A hands-on workshop on cabinetmaking teaches basic skills and techniques. Limited to six participants, the workshop is offered three times a season . Participants are required to have previous carpentry experience. In addition to these shorter workshops, Heartwood offers a three-week house-building program, with an emphasis on energy efficiency, which would be suited for those planning a major renovation or planning to build a new structure that is compatible with an old house, such as a barn.

Brochure available.

Heartwood
Johnson Rd.
Washington, MA 01235
(413) 623-6677

RESTORE

RESTORE is a restoration-skills training program oriented to people in the building industry. The objective of Restore is to update and upgrade the restoration and preservation knowledge of those in the construction industry who are actively engaged in building maintenance and restoration. There are two components of the educational program: one is a nine-month evening course taught in New York City; the other is a series of intensive five-day workshops that are held in various locations in the country. Both entail lectures, laboratory demonstrations, and field sessions. Participants learn how to analyze and resolve preservation maintenance problems. The curriculum provides basic information about the chemical and physical properties of masonry materials and an analysis of deterioration processes, cleaning procedures, and repair and replacement techniques. The goal of the program is to enable contractors and craftsmen to participate in decisions about restoration through history of their own trade and a basic knowledge of the related trades.

For further information, contact:

Jan C. K. Anderson, Executive
*   Director*
RESTORE
19 W. 44th St., Suite 1701
New York, NY 10036
(212) 382-2570

Smithsonian Institution

The Smithsonian's Office of Museum Programs offers for loan or sale various audiovisual materials that would be of interest to many old-house enthusiasts. A twenty-seven-minute black-and-white videotape, entitled "The Morse-Libby House: Restoration of The Cornices," deals with the preservation of the famous Victorian mansion in Maine. A slide program, "Preservation and Urban Revitalization," documents the social and economic benefits from historic preservation in four successfully rehabilitated historic districts. Another slide program, "Preservation and Energy Conservation," deals with the savings in "energy cost" that can be derived from building restoration. A video program, "On Guard: Protection Is Everybody's Business," discusses threats to cultural properties and feasible protection programs.

Brochure available.

Smithsonian Institution
Audiovisual Loan Program
Office of Museum Programs
2235 Arts and Industries Building
Washington, DC 20560
(202) 357-3101

Society for the Preservation of New England Antiquities

SPNEA, founded in 1910, is the nation's largest private preservation organization. Its educational programs are designed to encourage the use of modern strategies for historic preservation, promote sound techniques for building conservation, and expand appreciation and understanding of New England's architectural heritage and decorative arts. Building conservation workshops, with an emphasis on exploring the use of various materials to solve architectural problems, are held at the Lyman Estate in Waltham, Massachusetts. SPNEA also offers workshops on such crafts as wall stenciling and architectural rubbings, and sponsors annual lectures on various topics of interst to home renovators.

Brochure available.

Society for the Preservation of New
England Antiquities
Harrison Gray Otis House
141 Cambridge St.
Boston, MA 02114
(617) 227-3956

Yestermorrow

Yestermorrow, located in Warren, Vermont, has been offering intensive two-week programs in designing and building private homes since 1979. The curriculum has been expanded to include a basic remodeling, renovation, and restoration course. Each participant is encouraged to bring his own project—a complete restoration, an adaptive re-use, or a simple addition—and develop a compatible, practical, and good-looking design of it. A hands-on remodeling or renovation project at the school teaches basic skills, techniques, and methodology. The pros and cons of different kinds of building materials and components, from windows to downspouts, are discussed. All alumni can call for advice from home if they subsequently run into a snag in working on their projects. Furthermore, they can attend future classes for free if space permits.

Brochure available.

Yestermorrow
Box 76 A
Warren, VT 05674
(802) 496-5545

Other Suppliers of Structural Products and Services

Consult List of Suppliers for addresses.

Architectural Salvage

Advance Lumber and Wrecking
Architectural Antiques (Montreal)
Architectural Salvage of Santa Barbara
Art Directions
A. W. Baker
ByGone Era
Canal Co.
Great American Salvage
David Howard, Inc.
Kensington Historical Co.
Joe Ley Antiques
Materials Unlimited
North Fields Restorations
Olde Theatre Architectural Salvage Co.
Pelnick Wrecking Co.
Rejuvenation House Parts
Renovation Source
Greg Spiess Building Materials
United House Wrecking
Westlake Architectural Antiques
The Wrecking Bar (Atlanta)

Brick and Stone

Cathedral Stone Co.
Colonial Brick Co.
Victor Cushwa & Sons Brick Co.
Delaware Quarries, Inc.
Espinosa Stone Co.
Gruber Building, Cleaning, & Restoration, Inc.
Mason's Masonry Supply Ltd.
Old Carolina Brick
Kensington Historical Co.
Rex Building Materials

Ceilings

Architectural Paneling, Inc.
Ceilings, Walls and More, Inc.
Cumberland Woodcraft Co., Inc.
Designer Resource
Hi-Art East
Quality Woodworks, Inc.

Doors and Windows

Architectural Emphasis
Bel-Air Door Co.
The Door Store Ltd.
Gargoyles, Ltd.
The House Carpenters
Al Levitan
E. A. Nord Co.
Quaker City Manufacturing Co.
Silverton Victorian Millworks
Somerset Door & Column Co.
Spanish Pueblo Doors

Lumber

Carlisle Restoration Lumber
Albert Constantine & Son, Inc.
Churchill Forest Products, Inc.
Depot Woodworking
Hardwick Rafter Mfg.
Period Pine
Southington Specialty Wood Co.
Weird Wood
Wigen Restorations

Roofing

Berridge Manufacturing Co.
Conklin Tin Plate & Metal Co.
Ludowici-Celadon Co.
W. B. Maske Sheetmetal Work
San Francisco Victoriana
Shakertown Corp.

Stairs

Cooper Stair Co.
Mansion Industries, Inc.
Midwest Spiral Stair
Stair Specialist
Stairways, Inc.

Consultants and Architects

The Acquisition and Restoration Corp.
A. W. Baker
Guardian National House Inspection, Inc.
W. R. Hasbrouck
Historic Boulevard Services
Murrel Dee Hobt
International Consultants, Inc.
Howard Lieberman
The Preservation Partnership
Preservation Resource Group

Restoration Contractors

The Acquisition and Restoration Corp.
A. W. Baker
John Conti
Douglas Gest Co.
Historic Boulevard Services
W. Harley Miller
The Rambusch Co.
Skyline Engineers, Inc.

Reproduction Period Houses

Cape Cod Cupola
David Howard, Inc.
The House Carpenters
Roger L. Hulton
Sun Designs

Schools and Study

Minnesota Trailbound School of Log Building
Owner-Builder Center of Berkeley
River Bend Timber Framing

2.

Architectural Decoration

Next to a house's structure, its applied ornamentation is the most basic element of a building's "look." Its effect is like that of a frame to a picture; it should enhance and accentuate without overpowering what it surrounds. Different periods are noted for their particular styles of ornamentation, and, in fact, architectural decoration can become a signature of the period. Think, for example, of the elaborate gingerbread fretwork of the Victorian period or the classic broken pediment over a Federal period entryway.

The modern building age brought with it a trend towards unadorned surfaces and stark corners that saw the end of fine details like beaded chair rails and leaded-glass transom lights. In fact, part of the lure of an old house is the potentiality for intricate cornice moldings, delicate plaster ceiling medallions, or ornately carved marble hearths and mantels.

Luckily for restorers and renovators, there are today many craftsmen who work in a variety of materials to create the kind of decorative elements an old-house owner can be proud of. In the field of glass, for instance, studios are creating handsome stained-glass panels, beveled Art Deco mirrors, and decorative windows and doors in all shapes and styles. Metalworkers are producing lacy wrought-iron grillwork in the 19th-century New Orleans style and meticulously molded cast iron for various styles of gates and fences. Cabinetmakers and woodworkers can create wall panels or window trim of the same high quality, and often with the same methods, as artisans of earlier times. And if your tastes are more eclectic and less strictly purist, firms and craftsmen in all fields are turning out unique and original designs that are often just as appropriate to period decor as they are to contemporary spaces. A counter top of hand-crafted tile or a fanlight in an original leaded-glass design can often be an effective counterpoint to the structure of an older building. What is most important is the quality of the workmanship and the way a piece of ornamentation complements the whole. The companies and craftsmen described in this chapter are adept at the kind of repair and new work that show particular attention to these values.

Detail, reproduction 1790 pine mantel, Calvin Shewmaker III, Harrodsburg, Kentucky.

Glass

Trying to find someone who will repair a broken window these days is difficult enough. Imagine the difficulty encountered in replacing an etched or stained glass panel! Nothing to do with an old house is ever easy, but replacing or restoring windows and other glass panels needn't be that difficult, if only you can exercise a bit of patience. There are now a large number of firms that can repair, restore, or replace just about any type of glass. They are located in all sections of North America, and, if you plan ahead, these artisans may be able to do the work fairly quickly so that you needn't live with a plastic-covered hole in the wall.

The Beveled Edge

This Illinois studio specializes in all forms of decorative glass, including stained-glass panels; etched, sandblasted, and engraved glass; and beveled panels for windows, doors, transoms, sidelights, and fanlights. The company has recently brought out a new collection of original interpretations of beveled panels from various periods. Each of the five available designs is crafted from clear and colored glass, and the customer may specify which colors are preferred. The panels measure 2' by 3', although custom sizes are available. The two designs shown here—the symmetrical and simple Prairie and the ornate fleur-de-lis-patterned Victoria—are expert interpretations of period designs, suitable for replacing existing pieces or adding a new decorative touch. The Beveled Edge also produces custom windows in almost any size and shape.

Brochure and price list, 50¢.

The Beveled Edge
865 Hillcrest Blvd.
Hoffman Estates, IL 60195
(312) 843-8960

The Beveling Studio

Crayton Etcheson has been beveling glass in the Pacific Northwest for the past decade. He specializes in custom windows and mirrors for both commercial and residential projects. Aside from beveling and window construction, the Beveling Studio also manufactures leaded panels with a choice of lead, zinc, brass, or copper canes. Illustrated is one of Crayton Etcheson's custom windows. The firm will ship anywhere.

For further information, contact:

The Beveling Studio
15507 NE 90th
Redmond, WA 98052
(206) 885-7274

Morgan Bockius Studios

A look at this studio's brochure is enough to make one feel that a stained or leaded glass piece is exactly what a late-Victorian room needs. The craftsmen at Morgan Bockius are adept at producing vivid original glass designs to enhance any design scheme. Their work runs the gamut from residential Victorian-style windows and custom mirrors to handsome stained-glass lamps and ecclesiastical panels. They can work in leaded, beveled, carved, and stained glass, as well as in repoussé, glass-bending, and restoration. On a more prosaic level, Bockius will reglaze and repair old windows, which should come as welcome news to home restorers in the Philadelphia area.

The window shown here is an example of a stock window design.

Free brochure available.

Morgan Bockius Studios, Inc.
1412 York Rd.
Warminster, PA 18974
(215) 672-6547

Center City Stained Glass

Already known for its logo designs and other commercial projects, Center City's art glass studio is equally skilled at stained glass, sandblasted window designs, fusing, and blown-glass accessories. The studio has also recently acquired several hundred antique stained-glass panels, and if none of these meet a client's design needs, others can be custom fabricated. The double-door entryway shown here contains three sandblasted panels with Art Nouveau-style designs and is a fine example of the studio's work.

For further information, contact:

Center City Stained Glass Supply,
* Inc.*
926 Pine St.
Philadelphia, PA 19106
(215) 592-8804

Peter David

Peter David's specialty is custom art glass, both new construction and restoration. Working by commission, he makes etched, beveled, and stained-glass designs, as well as custom lamps and mirrors. In addition, he offers design and consultation services concerning the restoration and installation of art glass. One of his original designs is illustrated.

For further information, contact:

Peter David
8057 28th Ave., NW
Seattle, WA 98117
(206) 783-1731

Electric Glass

Electric Glass provides innovative and well-crafted designs in beveled-glass panels for doors, windows, and sidelights. Of its extensive selection of designs, many are appropriate for various period decors, including classic diamond-patterned designs and elaborate fleur-de-lis pat-

terns. Panels come in a range of shapes, including hard-to-find ovals, and in many sizes. The firm's Nouveau design is used here for an entryway and is also available as a window panel. Electric Glass also offers standing screens, beveled-glass pedestals, and custom panels.

Brochure, $3.

Electric Glass Co.
l E. Mellen St.
Hampton, VA 23663
(804)722-6200

Ferguson's Cut Glass Works

Practicing the art of beveling and engraving the same way it's been done since the 19th century, Cary Ferguson creates one-of-a-kind windows, panels, and mirrors. His designs echo the intricate designs of the so-called Brilliant Period of cut glass, from 1880 to 1920, and are not only appropriate, but would enhance a variety of restoration projects. The beautifully detailed window shown here is in the Russian Diamond design, a pattern from the Brilliant Period. Ferguson has handled several large-scale restoration projects and executes all types of custom work. Also offered are several standard

designs in beveled and engraved glass.

Brochure available

Ferguson's Cut Glass Works
4292 Pearl Rd.
Cleveland, OH 44109
(216) 459-2929

Great Panes Glass Works

As a less costly alternative to handcrafted sandblasted art glass, Great Panes uses a process called photo-stenciling. The design is created in black-and-white artwork, transferred to the glass by a photo process, and then sandblasted. Each reproduction is an exact replica of the original, and the company has a large library of designs from which to choose. It will also produce glass from custom artwork. The design shown

here is a relatively simple stock pattern; very elaborate motifs are also available. Sandblasted glass is produced for windows, doors, mirrors, room dividers, signs, cabinet doors, and just about anything else glass can be used for.

Brochure available.

Great Panes Glass Works, Inc.
1955 Market St.,

Denver, CO 80202
(303) 294-0927

J. & R. Lamb Studios

The J. & R. Lamb Studios have been creating and repairing stained glass since 1857. The firm has produced windows for buildings virtually all over the world and has been commissioned for countless restoration projects, including museums, churches, and historic buildings. One of Lamb's typical restoration projects included repair, cleaning, releading, and reinforcing antique stained-glass windows, as well as creating new windows to match the existing ones. All of this involves the expert craftsmanship and painstaking research for which the studio is known. The photographs shown here illustrate three of the many steps involved in a restoration project, starting with taking apart the old lead canes, cementing the panel after reglazing, and finally cleaning it. While the studio generally handles only large-scale projects, inquiries are welcome.

For further information, contact:

J. & R. Lamb Studios, Inc.
Box 291
Philmont, NY 12565
(518)672-7267

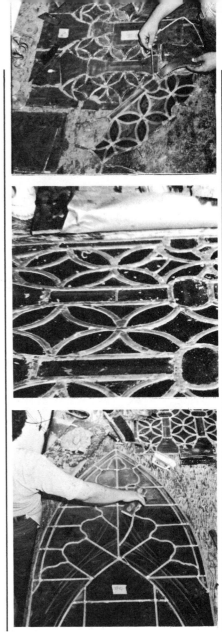

Kraatz Russell

Michael Kraatz and Susan Russell produce bull's-eye window panes in the traditional manner—from molten glass blown into a sphere and then reheated and spun to form the disc, or bull's-eye. Their panels are cut to specifications and make handsome sidelights and transoms for Colonial-style homes. The bull's-eye panes shown here were made for a transom sash from clear glass with a blue-green tinge at the edges. The studio has also started making leaded-glass panels suitable for Victorian homes. The panel shown here was made with their own handblown glass in several shades of amethyst. Kraatz Russell also handles commission work from architects, designers, and homeowners. Inquiries are invited.

 Brochure available.

Kraatz Russell Glass
RFD 1, Box 320-C, Grist Mill Hill
Canaan, NH 03741
(603) 523-4289

Lyn Hovey Studio

A staff of specialists and artisans works together at this studio to create original designs and restore even the most complex and delicate art glass. It has worked with various preservation groups on restoration projects which include Tiffany and LaFarge windows and antique European stained glass. The Water Lily mirror shown here was designed for a Victorian-Nouveau home. The mirror is created from American and German opalescents and French antique glass. It is acid-etched and plated and constructed from copper foil with a bent and welded steel bar support system.

 The-Ladies-with-Parasols doors are two of a set of an original design. They are made from French and German antique mouth-blown glass and from American opalescent glass. The intricately etched petticoats and parasols are indicative of the artistry executed by members of this studio. Both pieces illustrate Lyn Hovey's ability to create new

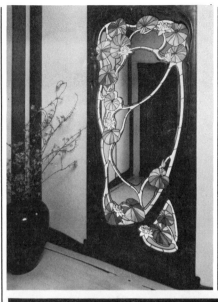

designs suitable for various period decors.

For further information, contact

Lyn Hovey Studio
266 Concord Ave.
Cambridge, MA 02138
(617) 492-6566

Pocahontas Hardware & Glass

Etched designs for entrance doors, transoms, and cabinets are the specialty of Pocahontas. The firm ships its panels all over North America. There are stock designs to choose from, such as

the example illustrated here (#230) which would be appropriate for a door panel. Double-strength glass is used for cabinet and window panels; safety sheet laminated glass is the standard for doors. In addition to the glass panels, Pocahontas is also a supplier of three different types of entrance doors in custom or stock sizes. These are made from solid sugar pine and can be supplied with applied wood carvings.

Brochure, $2.

Pocahontas Hardware & Glass
PO Box 127
Pocahontas, IL 62275
(618) 669-2880

Pompei Stained Glass

Joseph Pompei is a skilled and imaginative supplier of stained-glass windows, kitchen cabinet panels, beveled glass for doors and windows, sandblasted glass, and leaded-glass ceiling panels. He carries a traditional line of Victorian designs in stained glass such as the transom shown here. The Cabinet Door Collection is especially pleasing and includes such wonderful designs as Victorian Flower, Victorian Tulip, Victorian Diamond, and Victorian Etched. Any one of these panel designs could be effectively used for kitchen or pantry cabinets.

Catalogue, $1.

Pompei Stained Glass
455 High St.
West Medford, MA 02155
(617) 395-8867

Rambusch

No firm in North America has a better reputation for stained-glass design, fabrication, and restoration. Rambusch is simply the tops when it comes to glass artistry and craftsmanship. The company's Stained Glass Studio has been in operation since the 1890s and has handled every type of religious and secular commission. Enormous numbers of stained-glass panels were produced in the late 1800s and early 1900s for homes, churches, schools, and other public buildings. Rambusch has probably handled the repair and restoration of more of this valuable artistic legacy than any other firm.

For further information, contact:

The Rambusch Co.
40 W. 13th St.
New York, NY 10011
(212) 675-0400

J. Ring Glass Studio

Beveled-glass panels are the specialty of the Ring workshop. These decorative pieces are either custom or machine beveled on different thicknesses of clear plate glass or glue chipped plate glass; there are also various bevel widths to be considered by the buyer. As the example of Ring's work shows, the studio is also skilled at working with stained glass. Other glass products and services of the firm are abrasive and silkscreen etching, pattern glue chipping, glass bending, and glass painting.

For further information, contact:

J. Ring Stained Glass Studio, Inc.
618 N. Washington Ave.
Minneapolis, MN 55401
(612) 332-1769

Greg Spiess Stained and Leaded Glass

Spiess has expanded his architectural antiques business to include the design and fabrication of new stained leaded glass and beveled glass, as well as the restoration of the old. Many of the pieces he has salvaged, such as bars and windows, require glass repair. To be able to have this type of work done on the spot will save potential buyers considerable time and energy in tracking down a repair service.

For further information, contact:

Greg Spiess Stained and Leaded Glass
246 E. Washington St.
Joliet, IL 60433
(815)722-5639

Sunburst Stained Glass

Sunburst has grown from a workshop offering a limited number of glass designs to a full-service manufacturer and supplier of various kinds of glass products. The firm is now prepared to supply stained- and beveled-glass panels, etched glass, and clear plate and insulated glass windows. Illustrated is the Saint Charles Street transom insert panel available in beveled glass; it is one of three such designs offered in this form. Sunburst also produces similar oval door inserts, half-light door inserts, and matching sidelights.

Brochure, 75¢

Sunburst Stained Glass Co.
119 State St.
Newburgh, IN 47630
(812) 853-0460

Venturella Studios

Tom Venturella is both a skilled designer and restorer of stained glass. Illustrated is one of his recent commissions for a contemporary New York City apartment; the design would be equally at home in a 1920s or early '30s

residence. Venturella is just as adept with more traditional stained-glass pieces, whether new or antique.

Brochure available upon request.

Venturella Studios
32 Union Square, Rm. 1110
New York, NY 10003
(212) 228-4252

Williams Art Glass Studios/Sunset Antiques

Antique beveled- and stained-glass windows are the specialty of Sunset Antiques, while Williams Art Glass Studios restores the old and custom-fabricates new versions of traditional glass panels. The two firms share the same space, a convenience for prospective buyers of specialty glass. Illustrated are two of the many antique windows which Sunset has in stock.

For further information, contact:

Williams Art Glass Studios/Sunset
* Antiques*
22 N. Washington
Oxford, MI 48051
(313) 628-1111

Ornamental Metalwork

Replacing or restoring antique metalwork has become a specialty of foundries located throughout North America. Recently we watched with dismay while workmen removed the thoroughly rusted-out iron roof cresting of a Greek Revival mansion. Neither the original nor a replacement has reappeared, and the temptation is to leave a copy of this book in the mailbox, together with a note inviting the mansion's owners to "try any one of these foundries if you want to have that beautiful cresting reproduced." These same firms are perfectly set up to repair or restore other decorative elements such as fencing, gates, frieze window grilles, and railings.

Architectural Iron

The staff members of Architectural Iron consider themselves purists in the reconstruction and restoration of ornamental ironwork. Whenever possible, they employ the original methods and materials of the craft. On a typical restoration project, all existing ironwork such as fencing, fenestration, and window grilles is brought to the shop and foundry in Milford, Pennsylvania. There, as much of the original is preserved as possible and new wooden patterns are made for the parts that must be recast. Each new casting is then primed, painted, and assembled into units. The restored ironwork is reinstalled on site, often using the original method of attachment. We've seen this company's work and can say that the finished product is better than new in its meticulous adherence to the original structure and the quality of workmanship. Architectural Iron works primarily in the East, but will take on projects throughout North America.

Literature available.

Architectural Iron Co.
Box 126
Milford, PA 18337
(717) 296-7722 or (212) 243-2664

Albert Hall & Associates

Most of this Colorado company's work is custom made, although some stock items are carried. Hall's metalwork foundry specializes in producing patterns from old photographs or drawings, or reproductions from

original pieces. The firm's work, which spans the country, encompasses all sorts of ornamental metalwork, such as the casting shown here. The architectural detail was reproduced from an old photograph of the Navarre Building, now the Western Art Museum in Denver.

For further information, contact:

Albert Hall & Associates
3926 High St.
Denver, CO 80205
(303) 292-5253

Kenneth Lynch & Sons

This firm cannot be surpassed in the field of architectural ornamentation. Working in wrought iron, bronze, brass, steel, cast stone, and other metals, Lynch fabricates imposing gates, grilles, stair rails, monuments, and garden ornaments which are used throughout the world. The firm works with architects and designers to create lushly ornate and expertly crafted architectural decoration. If your project is large enough to interest this firm, you can be sure the results will be worth it.

For further information, contact:

Kenneth Lynch & Sons
78 Danbury Rd., Box 488
Wilton, CT 06897
(203) 762-8363

Nostalgia, Inc.

From Savannah and other historic cities of the South, Nostalgia has gathered patterns and authentic reproductions of cast-iron fences, gates, balcony panels, and stair parts. Aside from its large selection of stock items, Nostalgia works with craftsmen who make decorative metalwork to any specifications, working in cast iron and brass. Shown here is Nostalgia's Taylor Street panel, seen on many Savannah balconies, fences, and window guards.

Catalogue, $2.50 (refundable with purchase.)

Nostalgia, Inc.
307 Stiles Ave.
Savannah, GA 31401
(912) 236-8176

Swiss Foundry

The new facilities of Swiss Foundry are designed to make ornamental castings and to replicate antique castings. In addition, the staff can provide casting drawings, pattern design, and the preparation of special alloys. The company works in most metals, including brass, iron, and aluminum.

For further information, contact:

Swiss Foundry, Inc.
518 S. Gilmor St.
Baltimore, MD 21223
(301) 233-2000

Tennessee Fabricating

The use of ornamental cast iron is French in origin, finding its way to North America in the mid-19th century. As a decorative element for railings, balconies, doorways, and fences, cast iron found its greatest market in the French-settled lower Mississippi Valley and in New Orleans. Tennessee Fabricating offers over 100 styles of decorative metalwork, many of which are replications of authentic 19th-century designs. The Pontalba patterns, an element of which is shown here, were designed in 1848 for the Pontalba Building, one of New Orleans' noted French Quarter landmarks. Other patterns, many considerably more ornate, include Passion Flower, Bird of Paradise, Old Rose, and an extensive grouping of Victorian styles.

Catalogue, $2.50.

Tennessee Fabricating Co.
2366 Prospect St.
Memphis, TN 38106
(901) 948-3354

Wallin Forge

Located in Kentucky, Wallin Forge is a renowned hand-forged iron-work business. Approximately half of its work is on restoration projects for museums, historic buildings, and private residences, the remaining being original custom designs. Because the forge carries no stock products, it is recommended that prospective clients provide sketches or photographs of the projects for which they require an estimate.

For further information, contact:

Wallin Forge
Rte. 1, Box 65
Sparta, KY 41086
(606) 567-7201

Jonathan Dexter Whitney

This New York craftsman is involved in restoration and replication of authentic metal ornamentation. He specializes in decorative metalwork in silver, brass, and bronze, and is an expert in design, pattern-making, casting, plating, gold-leafing, and repoussé, just to list a few of his skills. The photograph shows patterns and molds used by Whitney to duplicate missing copper roof ridge ornamentation for a landmark church in Manhattan. It is also worth noting that Whitney has extended experience in projects involving mixed materials, including wood, stone, marble, and glass. Inquiries are welcome, and a visit, by appointment to his Chelsea studio, is encouraged. It would be worth a trip to see the work of this sensitive practitioner of restoration techniques and of the fine art of metalworking.

For further information, contact:

Jonathan Dexter Whitney
223 W. 19th St.
New York, NY 10011
(212) 929-2345

Plaster, Composition, and Polymer Ornamentation

Most old-house interiors are incomplete without a display of complementary moldings, ceiling ornaments, brackets, and other decorative elements. Happily, there are an increasing number of craftsmen extremely skilled in restoring and fabricating new plaster ornamentation. Many of the same imaginative craftsmen also work with compo, as the fibrous alternative to plaster of Paris is termed. Because of the high cost of such specialty work, new lightweight synthetic materials are also being used in place of plaster or composition materials. These are polymer-based products, and they are relatively easy to apply and to finish. Their use has spread even to the bastions of conservative old-house restorers.

Balmer Architectural Art

One look at Balmer's catalogue explains why this Canadian firm enjoys such high repute. The products are fabricated from non-toxic gypsum composition or fibrous plaster and are lightweight, are easy to install, and will accept any finish. Ceiling centers and panels range from simple circular designs to oversize ovals complete with swags and corner pieces. Balmer also offers Old English ceilings which have a look similar to hammered metal ceilings. These are made up of plain or ornate backgrounds, ornamental overlays, and perimeter moldings, and are available in several designs. Other Balmer products include cornices, columns, brackets, mantels, and panel moldings.

Complete catalogue, $14; ceiling centers and ornaments catalogue, $3; cornice catalogue, $3. For other brochure prices, contact:

Balmer Architectural Art, Inc.
69 Pape Ave. (rear)
Toronto, Ontario, Canada M4M 2V5
(416) 466-6306 or 466-6386

Decorators Supply

This company continues as the largest supplier of composition and plaster ornamentation in North America, supplying chiefly the decorating trade. Decorators' plaster of Paris castings are reinforced with fibre—and steel rods when necessary— and include pediments, grilles, moldings, and cornices. There is also a large selection of composition carvings in various period designs. The firm's many catalogues remain virtual encyclopedias of architectural ornamentation.

Contact the company for information about its merchandise and catalogues.

Decorators Supply Corp.
3610-12 S. Morgan St.
Chicago, IL 60609
(312) 847-6300

Dovetail

The ceiling medallions shown here are only a fraction of the plaster decoration available through Dovetail. Above is the 16-sided Anaglypta design which measures 22″ in diameter and is a Victorian adaptation of the Egyptian lotus blossom pattern. Also illustrated is Flowering Leaf (23″ in diameter) which uses the traditional acanthus leaf pattern. Dovetail carries some interesting specialty items, including a 44″ wall panel called Singing Gallery, which is a reproduction of a 15th-century Della Robbia carving. All of Dovetail's products are available by mail.

Brochure available.

Dovetail, Inc.
750 Suffolk St., Box 1569
Lowell, MA 01853-2769
(800) 344-5570
(617) 454-2944 (MA)

Focal Point

Often restorers find that reproducing ornate decorative details entails prohibitive costs. And yet they are hesitant to use modern materials, feeling that the work won't be "genuine" unless executed in the same original material. Focal Point, a leading manufacturer of polymer ornamentation, offers a happy solution. Its beautifully constructed and architecturally correct decorative elements have been used by Colonial Williamsburg, the Victorian Society in America, and by many other restorers of historic buildings. The fine product line includes cornice moldings, ceiling medallions, domes, door pieces, spandrels, mantels, and more. Shown here is the Governor's Palace fretwork molding, made for Williamsburg. It is reconstructed from an elaborate molding which originally adorned the stately Virginia builiding, built during the first decade of the 18th century. Also illustrated is the Eastlake molding. The stylized flowers, carved borders, and geometric shapes of this segmental cornice, which was taken from the 1887 Thomas Arnett House, clearly

Like many other master craftsmen, the Giannetti brothers learned the art of plasterwork from their father. One look at their plaster ornamentation makes it clear that they learned well. The vast inventory of stock moldings and medallions includes styles from virtually every period, all intricately detailed and beautifully crafted. They are fabricated from hard casting plaster with fiber reinforcement and are easily installed on drywall or plaster. The photograph shows some of their custom work, including mantel, cornices, doorheads, and wall panels. Giannetti Studios' work can be seen in private residences and historic buildings throughout the country, including the White House.

Brochures, $3.

Giannetti Studios
3806 38th St.
Brentwood, MD 20722
(301) 927-0033

show the influence of Charles Locke Eastlake.

Catalogue, $3.

Focal Point, Inc.
2005 Marietta Rd., NW
Atlanta, GA 30318
(404) 351-0820

Fypon, Inc.

From large dentil moldings to a small chair rail, Fypon moldings feature a wide variety of designs. The company's "molded millwork" parts are made of high-density polymer that won't warp or rot. They can be nailed, drilled, sawn, and painted as if they were wood. Fypon products include window trim, entranceways, decorative moldings, and pediments, among many others. Shown here is arched exterior window trim which is available in virtually any size. Sample sections of moldings are sent at no cost; Fypon will also consider custom designs.

Catalogue available.

Fypon Inc.
22 W. Pennsylvania Ave.
Stewartstown, PA 17363
(717) 993-2593

Giannetti Studios

Frank Mangione

Anyone who has ever had to have a decorative plaster ceiling repaired or elaborate cornices replicated knows that ornamental plasterwork is fast becoming a lost art. It is, therefore, especially heartening to find a master craftsman like Frank Mangione. He learned his skills from his father and is now passing along the same trade secrets to his son. One of his recent projects involved replacing badly damaged moldings on the ceiling of the Lockwood-Mathews Mansion Museum in Norwalk. This involved making his own shaping tools and patterns, as well as scaffold work that would have daunted Michaelangelo. The photograph shows a deceptively simple-looking plaster molding that Mangione created to match the tile seen in the lower left. No literature is available, but inquiries are encouraged.

For further information, contact:

Frank J. Mangione
21 John St.
Saugerties, NY 12477
(914) 246-9863

Nostalgia

Nostalgia has its decorative plaster moldings and ornaments hand-crafted in England from fibrous plaster. Hundreds of items are available and these are supplied with installation instructions. The company offers an unusual array of plaster capitals in classic Greek and Roman styles. These are suitable for decorative bases or stands, and can be used indoor or outdoors with columns.

Catalogue, $2.50

Nostalgia, Inc.
307 Stiles Ave.
Savannah, GA 31401
(912) 236-8176

Michael Piazza

Michael Piazza's specialty is decorative plasterwork that uses old-world methods, original tools, and traditional materials. He is adept at restoration and will, upon request, use authentic 19th-century molds or run his own molding to replicate existing work. He has undertaken restoration work for designers, preservation societies, and residential clients. Inquiries are welcome.

For further information, contact:

Michael Piazza
540 80th St.,
Brooklyn, NY 11209
(212) 745-6111

Russell Restoration

Dean Russell began his career as a plasterer by working on new construction. But, before long, he started to specialize in traditional methods of decorative plasterwork that he learned from masters of the trade. Now he can restore all types of ornamental plasterwork. He will run moldings and decorative detailing on site (the old-fashioned way) and do custom casting and mold-making in his shop. He and his crew can also produce moldings, niches, domes, and other elements to specification.

Brochure, 75¢

Russell Restoration of Suffolk
Rte. 1, Box 243A
Mattituck, NY 11952
(516) 765-2481

San Francisco Victoriana

SFV's unique selection of plaster ornamentation is hand-cast and

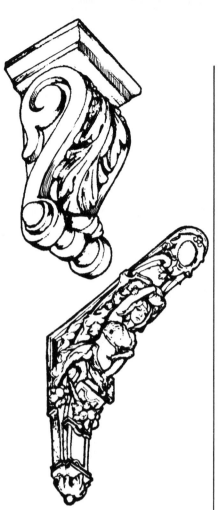

reinforced with fibre by expert craftsmen. As with most products from this company, customers can be sure of quality workmanship and authentic detailing. Shown here are ornamental brackets, ranging in design from the relative simplicity of Acanthus to the highly ornate Lorelei. Ceiling centers, cornices, capitals, picture rails, and many other elements are also available from this outstanding supplier.

Catalogue, $3.

San Francisco Victoriana
2245 Palou Ave.
San Francisco, CA 94124
(415) 648-0313

Steptoe & Wife

This Canadian company, well-known for its iron staircases, now offers a selection of plaster ornaments to the do-it-yourself market. The firm's cornice moldings and ceiling medallions come in many traditional styles from Colonial to Victorian and beyond. Steptoe also offers three frieze patterns and four highly decorative corbels which are best used to define archways and stairwells or as support brackets for small shelves.

Literature available.

Steptoe & Wife Antiques Ltd.
3626 Victoria Park Ave.
Willowdale, Ontario, Canada M2H 3B2
(416) 497-2989

Victorian Collectibles

We describe Florence Schroeder's well-known collection of antique wallpapers and Victorian rugs elsewhere in this book. But she also carries a selection of sculptured plaster moldings which complement other Victorian Collectibles merchandise. The moldings shown here are designs created from wallpaper borders, and each is a marvel of meticulous detailing. The pattern, top left, is Nouvelle Floral and is also offered in a curved shape. The other design is Grape Leaves, seen here in both flat and curved forms. These and other patterns are available in 54" lengths.

For further information, contact:

Victorian Collectibles, Ltd.
845 E. Glenbrook Rd.
Milwaukee, WI 53217
(414) 352-6910

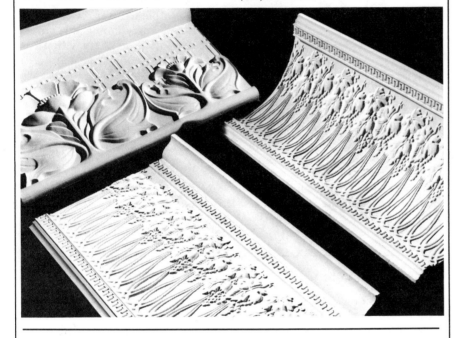

J. P. Weaver

Since 1914, J. P. Weaver has been fabricating architectural ornamen-tation from a composition material in use since the mid 1700s, and in recent years dubbed "compo." It is flexible and self-bonding and may be finished with the same methods used for wood. This California company carries all types of ornamentation—scrolls, rosettes, swags, pieces for corbels, capitals, moldings, medallions—in short, almost any conceivable decorative piece. These items are meant to be used together to create designs for ceilings, wall panels, and other ornamental elements. Aside from its enormous inventory of stock items, J. P. Weaver also executes custom work and recently completed restoration on the California State Capitol building.

Catalogue, $1.

J. P. Weaver & Co.
2301 W. Victory Blvd.
Burbank, CA 91506
(818) 841-5700

W. T. Weaver & Sons

This company continues to offer fine moldings and medallions produced from lightweight styrene. The details are delicate enough to be mistaken for plaster, with the added bonus of easier installation and lower cost. Weaver offers a line of decorative moldings, composed of swags and ribbons ornate enough for the most fanciful cornice, mantel, or doorway.

Catalogue, $2.50

W. T. Weaver & Sons, Inc.
1208 Wisconsin Ave., NW
Washington, D.C. 20007
(202) 333-4200

Stone and Brickwork

The repair and restoration of masonry is one of the most demanding and important phases of old-house restoration. Sources of stone and brick are given in chapter 1 along with some information regarding contractors who specialize in masonry work. In the following listings, the emphasis is on individuals and firms that will undertake difficult cleaning and restoration jobs and on suppliers of ornamental stone for sinks, mantels, window sills, and counters. Now that synthetic oil-based building products have become so expensive, it may be time to reconsider using natural materials for decorative as well as practical purposes.

Jamie C. Clark

A fellow craftsman told us about the stone restoration work done by Jamie Clark, and we're glad to pass the information along. He has undertaken all types of masonry work including the repair of dry stone walls, repointing, foundation work, and the matching of existing stonework

and mortar. The log house chimney in the photograph is a good example of his expert restoration work.

For further information, contact:

Jamie C. Clark
Jackson Pike
Harrodsburg, KY 40330
(606) 734-9587

Haines Construction

Since 1936 Haines has been known throughout the state of Indiana as a highly reputable masonry cleaning and repair firm. Among the superb restorations the company has completed are the James Whitcomb Riley House Museum and the Indiana Theater, both in Indianapolis. In the case of the brick Riley residence, 100% of the mortar joints were cut out by hand and tuck-pointed. Spalled brick was replaced, a chimney rebuilt, and the whole facade was chemically and hot-water cleaned.

Haines is also known for flue and chimney repairs as well as for firebox rebuilding.

For further information, contact:

Haines Construction Co.
11717 E. 42nd St.
Indianapolis, IN 46236
(317) 547-5531

Duncan Morgan

Restoration is the specialty of this third-generation stonemason and bricklayer. Working in Natchez, a city known for its wealth of historic buildings, has given Duncan Morgan plenty of experience in matching old brickwork and mortar by using the same basic materials as the original. In fact, he was recently honored with an award of merit from the Mississippi Historical Society for outstanding masonry restoration. Unfortunately for those of us in the rest of the old-house world, Morgan limits his projects to those in the wider Natchez area.

For further information, contact:

Duncan M. Morgan
21 Concord Ave.
Natchez, MS 39120
(601) 442-7702

New York Marble Works

This family business, founded in the early 1900s, has long been known for marble restoration, repair, and design. New York Marble Works supplies imported and domestic marble, cut to order, for mantels, counters, table tops, and whatever else a client wants. One of the firm's specialties is marble restoration, and projects have been carried out for Sotheby's, the Metropolitan Museum of Art, other galleries, and private customers. For an estimate, bring the object to be restored or a photo of it to the shop. Clients may also write, describing the project and enclosing a self-addressed stamped envelope.

New York Marble Works, Inc.
1399 Park Avenue
New York, NY 10029
(212) 534-2242

Vermont Marble Company

This company fabricates its products from the finest domestic marble and makes, among other objects, sills and saddles from white Danby marble in a variety of standard sizes. The window sills are available in ¾" thickness with a polished finish on the face and edge. Vermont Marble also makes sink tops in virtually any size and in many varieties of marble. Its marble tile for floors and walls comes in ⅜" thickness and in several standard sizes and types.

Literature available.

Vermont Marble Co.
61 Main St.
Proctor, VT 05765
(802) 459-3311

Vermont Soapstone

Soapstone is one of nature's wonder materials. It is soft enough to carve and yet amazingly durable. In addition, it is easy to maintain and is uniquely capable of absorbing and retaining heat. Vermont Soapstone Company produces everything, from griddles and bedwarmers to sinks and mantels. The sink illustrated here is a fine example of the company's custom work and would complement the decor of any country kitchen.

Literature available.

Vermont Soapstone Company, Inc.
RR1, Box 514
Perkinsville, VT 05151
(802) 263-5404

Applied Wood Ornamentation

Such ornamental items as moldings, brackets, finials, columns, spindles, newel posts, and railings lie very much at the heart of period interior and exterior decoration. Depending on the style of your old house, at least several of these elements will come into play. Door and window casings, of course, are standard items in every old building; it is only in recent times that these openings have been left as unadorned holes in the wall. Such casings in old houses are usually comprised of a series of handsome moldings and panels. Moldings similarly make up and define paneled doors and may delineate ceilings from walls, and walls from floors. There are thousands of types of moldings and decorative ornaments that can be used in a period room or outside the house on a porch or to embellish entryways, windows, gables, and roof lines. Producers of period millwork are found everywhere in North America, and what they can not supply from stock they will custom manufacture.

American Wood Column

Classical columns play an important part in both Colonial and Victorian architecture. We often think of their use being limited to Georgian Colonial, Greek Revival, or Colonial Revival buildings, but such is far from the case. Columns in the form of flat pilasters are used in Federal-style buildings, and other column forms are commonly found in Italianate and Queen Anne homes of the mid- to late-1800s. American Wood Column is a superb supplier of just about any type of column, capital, pedestal, or wood turning that you could possibly need. The columns are of lock-joint staved construction and are manufactured in any diameter or height.

Literature available.

American Wood Column Corp.
913 Grand St.
Brooklyn, NY 11211
(212) 782-3163

Bendix Mouldings

Bendix has been supplying carved and embossed wood moldings for many years. Those which are carved out of hardwood, as illustrated here, are of the highest quality, but lower-cost embossed moldings of pine may be as suitable in design and composition as the more expensive. It all depends on what you are looking for. And Bendix offers well over 100 designs, including beaded, dentil, scalloped, overlay, bolection, and crown moldings. These are sold in random lengths ranging from 3' to 15'; beaded moldings are available in 2½' to 3' sections only. As the photograph of a small portion of its stock shows, Bendix is also a major supplier of embossed and carved wood ornamentation.

Wood molding and ornament catalogue, $2.

Bendix Mouldings, Inc.
235 Pegasus Ave.
Northvale, NJ 07647
(201) 767-8888

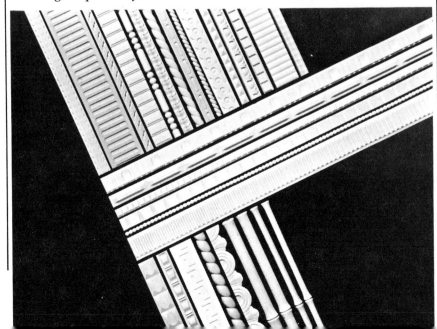

Classic Architectural Specialties

Formerly known as Renovation Products, this firm offers a very wide variety of materials to the home restorer or renovator. Many of these products are manufactured by other firms and appear elsewhere in *The Fourth Old House Catalogue*, but Classic also manufactures and offers its own line of wood architectural ornamentation. These are such exterior pieces as gable end trim, roof finials, porch gingerbread, as well as brackets, corbels, and fretwork spandrels which can be used inside or out.

Catalogue, $2.

Classic Architectural Specialties
5302 Junius
Dallas, TX 75214
(214) 827-5111

Crawford's Old House Store

Crawford's is a most convenient

supplier of such basic old-house materials as hardware, bathroom fixtures and fittings, and lighting fixtures which simply don't turn up at your local home center. Now Crawford has added a piece of decorative trim which most millwork suppliers have forgotten even existed—the corner bead. This is a notched turning—47½" long—which will fit over any 90-degree outside corner wall. Made of oak or pine, it is supplied unfinished for staining or painting. A corner bead was once commonly used to protect an interior wall at its most vulnerable point from scratches and scrapes. Its usefulness is still undeniable today.

Catalogue, $1.75 (refundable with first purchase).

Crawford's Old House Store
301 McCall St.
Waukesha, WI 53186
(414) 542-0685

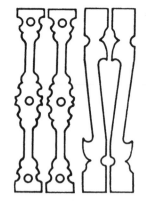

Victorian gingerbread, as it is invariably termed in Texas, is excellent and includes brackets, fretwork grilles, gable trim, newel posts, corbels, running trim, spindle trim, ball and dowel trim, and, as illustrated, porch balusters. Whether your need is for exterior or interior trim, you are likely to find an appropriate design among The Emporium's offerings. The company ships throughout the United States and Canada.

Catalogue, $2.

The Emporium
2515 Morse St.
Houston, TX 77019
(713) 528-3808

Cumberland Woodcraft

A new line of oak and poplar ornamental carvings has just been introduced by Cumberland. These may be used inside or outside a house as brackets, corbels, or applied ornaments. The Victorian designs are well documented. Cumberland is also a major supplier of Victorian-period moldings, fretwork grilles, gable-end treatments, balustrades, and rails.

Full-color catalogue, $3.75.

Cumberland Woodcraft Co., Inc.
P.O. Drawer 609
Carlisle, PA 17013
(717) 243-0063

Frenzel Specialty Molding

When you simply cannot match a particular type of molding with the offerings in a major manufacturer's catalogue, it is time to turn to a craftsman such as George Frenzel. He will produce any kind of molding or antique trim that you require. All you need do is send him an existing piece, or enough of a fragment, so that the profile is clearly delineated. Frenzel will reproduce the molding in whatever wood you specify.

For further information, contact:

Frenzel Specialty Molding Co.
4911 Ringer Rd.
St. Louis, MO 63129
(314) 892-3292

Albert Hall & Associates

Albert Hall & Associates is a general restoration firm with a millwork shop specializing in the replacement of Victorian and Georgian Colonial ornamentation. Old photographs or drawings are often used in reproduction pat-

Driwood Moulding

Driwood regularly offers several hundred different styles of interior embossed moldings. These stock designs are created out of poplar; such other woods as walnut, oak, or cherry can be substituted on a special-order basis. The firm will also undertake other types of custom millwork, including the especially heavy and durable type of millwork required for exterior use.

Moldings catalogue available, $3.

Driwood Moulding Co.
P. O. Box 1729
Florence, SC 29503
(803) 662-0541, 669-2478, or
*   669-2479*

The Emporium

Quality white pine is used for all the decorative trim made by Anthony and Son, woodworkers, for The Emporium. The selection of

terns that are one-of-a-kind or extremely rare. All of the woodwork is produced on a custom-order basis. The company has undertaken projects from coast to coast.

Prices and information available on request.

Albert Hall & Associates
3926 High St.
Denver, CO 80205
(303) 292-5253

Island City Wood Working

John Weber has had considerable success in rejuvenating the Island City firm, first established in 1908. He and his associates work with old belt-driven machines to turn out custom-ordered shutters, moldings, exterior and interior trim of all sorts, porch columns, and other turnings. The mill possesses an extraordinary collection of molding knives from which nearly any kind of Victorian trim can be reproduced; Weber grinds custom knives for those rare one-of-a-kind exceptions. Red tidewater cypress is used for the majority of pieces, although oak, walnut, ash or poplar can be substituted.

Brochure available.

Island City Wood Working Co.
1801 Mechanic St.
Galveston, TX 77550
(409) 765-5727

Mark A. Knudsen

This craftsman has more than won his restoration credentials on such projects as the Supreme Court wing of the Iowa State Capitol and numerous residential commissions in the Sherman Hill historic district of Des Moines. He is an expert in turning out finials, newel posts, balusters, pediments, porch posts, column bases, capitals, and other types of ornamental millwork. His work is either hand-turned or machine-turned, depending on the customer's needs and pocketbook.

Literature available.

Mark A. Knudsen
1100 E. County Line Rd.
Des Moines, IA 50320
(515) 285-6112

Mad River Woodworks

Mad River is a leading West Coast producer of Victorian decorative woodwork. California redwood and other fine hardwoods are used in reproduction fretwork, balustrades, large turned posts, brackets and corbels, moldings, and ornamental running trim. Illustrated is a selection of the firm's outstanding work. Mad River is also a supplier of such special items as fence pickets, screen doors, redwood window sash, ornamental shingles, and wood gutters. All-heart redwood is probably the best possible material for exterior millwork and is hard to beat for interior purposes as well.

Catalogue available.

Mad River Woodworks
4935 Boyd Rd., P. O. Box 163
Arcata, CA 95521
(707) 826-0629 or 822-2155

Mountain Lumber

Mountain Lumber is best known as a supplier of recycled longleaf heart pine, probably the finest grade lumber produced in America for construction purposes. It is from this exceptionally durable and beautifully grained wood that Mountain Lumber's millworkers assemble stair treads, risers, mantels, doors, various types of moldings—including baseboard and shoe, chair rail, landing nosing, and crown—and other custom pieces. The company will supply any type of special millwork items required to the customer's specifications.

Brochure and price list available.

Mountain Lumber
1327 Carlton Ave.
Charlottesville, VA 22901
(804) 295-1922 or 295-1757

Nelson-Johnson Wood Products

Custom millwork of almost any type is turned out by the artisans of Nelson-Johnson. Among the standard items produced are embossed wod ornaments and moldings, carved moldings, galley rail spindles and rails, and turned spindles, rails, newel posts, and balusters. Although not strictly a reproduction millwork supplier, the firm is perfectly able to copy old-fashioned work.

For further information, contact:

Nelson-Johnson Wood Products
4326 Lyndale Ave. N.
Minneapolis, MN 55412
(612) 529-2771

Renovation Source

Renovation Source is a general supplier of antique and reproduction old-house building materials, some of which is also manufactured by the firm. Included in the millwork offerings are oak interior fretwork spandrels and finials, and crown and picture moldings of oak, pine, or poplar. For exterior use, Renovation Source supplies pine porch trimmings such as columns, posts, spindles, and railings as well as brackets and spandrels of poplar.

Literature available.

The Renovation Source Inc.
3512-14 N. Southport
Chicago, IL 60657
(312) 327-1250

Rowe & Giles Millwork

As a custom producer of millwork, Rowe & Giles can reproduce just about any type of molding profile. Architects and designers seeking reproduction woodwork often turn to the firm for assistance, and the same service is available to homeowners involved in restoration or renovation projects. Rowe & Giles will reproduce one piece or ten thousand of the same design.

For further information, contact:

Rowe & Giles Millwork, Inc.
16740 Park Circle Dr., P. O. Box 210
Chagrin Falls, OH 44022
(216) 543-9852

Somerset Door & Column

Somerset has long been known for its finely crafted wood stave columns and pilasters, and composition capitals. The staves are assembled with standard tongue-and-groove joinery, a special aviation type casein glue being used for additional reinforcement. Clear Northern white pine, clear heart redwood, Sterling Idaho white pine, Pennsylvania sound knotty white pine, and poplar are among the woods that can be specified. All work is custom ordered, and columns can be built as long as 40' and with a diameter as great as 40". There are seven

standard designs to choose from; custom designs are also executed by the company. If an ornamental capital is desired, the buyer can choose from six different styles ranging from the relatively simple Roman and Greek Ionic capitals to the intricate Roman Corinthian. Plinths of cast aluminum are regularly supplied.

Brochure available.

Somerset Door & Column Co.
P. O. Box 328
Somerset, PA 15501
(814) 445-9608

Sunshine Architectural Woodworks

Sunshine is an imaginative and resourceful producer of traditional millwork for Colonial or Victorian homes. Its moldings are usually made up from kiln-dried poplar, but walnut, cherry, mahogany, or oak may be specified. There are at least fifty different moldings to choose from, some of which, of course, can be used in various combinations to form intricate cornices. Illustrated are four of Sunshine's chair rail and wainscot cap molding designs.

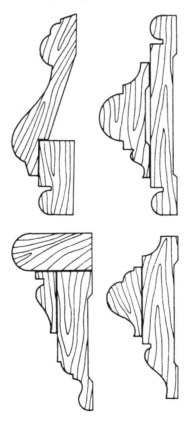

Moldings brochure available.

Sunshine Architectural Woodworks
Rte. 2, Box 434
Fayetteville, AR 72701
(501) 521-4329

Turncraft

Turncraft is best known for its standard wood columns of ponderosa and/or sugar pine, and spindles and newel posts of kiln-dried hemlock. These are not custom-crafted items, but stock products that are therefore extremely reasonable in price. As illustrated, there are four column styles and these may range from 8' to 20' high and from 6" to 20" in diameter. The spindle and newel post designs are also limited in number, most of the traditional styles readily available in lengths of 36" to 96".

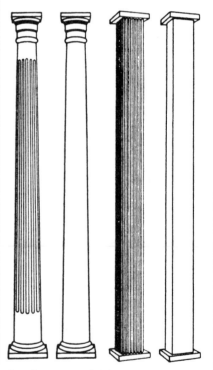

Catalogue available.

Turncraft
P. O. Box 2429
White City, OR 97503
(503) 826-2911

Vintage Wood Works

The decorative millwork available from Vintage has a snap and substance to it which is often missing from reproduction woodwork. Illustrated are six of the fanciful regular brackets of solid pine which can be used inside or outside the house. There are other bracket designs available as well as corbels, headers—decorative trim useful over doors or windows—spandrels, gable decorations, spindles, posts, finials, railings, and a particularly attractive selection of rectangular cutwork grilles.

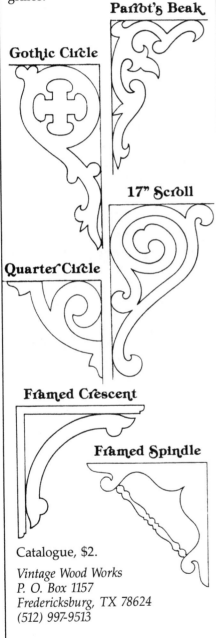

Parrot's Beak

Gothic Circle

17" Scroll

Quarter Circle

Framed Crescent

Framed Spindle

Catalogue, $2.

*Vintage Wood Works
P. O. Box 1157
Fredericksburg, TX 78624
(512) 997-9513*

Walbrook Mill & Lumber

"Goods of the Woods" is the motto of this sixty-year-old Baltimore millwork dealer and manufacturer. In a city that has undergone as much extensive renovation and restoration as Baltimore, such a firm has gained valuable experience. No wonder Walbrook claims that its "complete mill is capable of reproducing anything in wood." Anything includes windows, moldings, doors, cornices, turnings, shutters, and stair parts. Walbrook will even undertake difficult curved and circular work.

For further information, contact:

*Walbrook Mill & Lumber Co., Inc.
2636 W. North Ave.
Baltimore, MD 21216
(301) 462-2200*

Williams & Hussey

This New Hampshire firm manufactures high-quality tools for professional woodworkers and skilled do-it-yourself home craftsmen. Among the supplies regularly offered is one publication, Western Pine Club's 1955 edition of the 8,000 Series Mouldings catalogue, a classic compilation that is instructive for anyone trying his hand at such work. It is available for $6.

Brochure and price sheets available.

*Williams & Hussey Machine Co.
Milford, NH 03055
(603) 673-3446*

Wood Mouldings & Millwork Producers Association

Anyone not familiar with the use of wood mouldings and other types of classic architectural decoration will find some of the literature offered by this trade association informative and useful. These are pamphlets which offer either ideas on how moldings can be used or "how-to" information on applying them. Titles of interest to old-house restorers or renovators are:

"From Tree to Trim," a history of moldings, $2.

"American Colonial," sketches of Colonial molding profiles, and their use, 50¢.

"How to Work with Lattice," uses for lattice wood molding, 75¢.

"How to Finish Wood Mouldings," 40¢.

"How to Work with Wood Mouldings," a step-by-step preparation and installation guide, 40¢.

"How to Install Interior Jambs & Exterior Door Frames," 40¢.

All of these brochures are available from:

*Wood Moulding & Millwork
Producers Association
P. O. Box 25278
Portland, OR 97225
(503) 292-9288*

The Woodworkers' Store

The Woodworkers' Store is a convenient supplier of a limited selection of traditional spindles and finials, simple trim molding, carved wood trim, embossed moldings, and fiber ornamental carvings. For the home craftsman, Woodworkers' Store also supplies turning and carving stock of basswood, sugar pine, walnut, hard maple, or butternut in maximum lengths of 48".

These materials are available through the mail or directly from one of the four Woodworkers' Store outlets. For addresses, see the List of Suppliers.

Catalogue, $1.

*The Woodworkers' Store
21801 Industrial Blvd.
Rogers, MN 55374
(612) 428-4101*

Cabinetry

Finding a craftsman who can execute traditional cabinetry such as bookcases, cupboards, chimney breasts and mantels, and room ends is not as difficult as it used to be. Ten or fifteen years ago, one nearly had to kidnap an old-fashioned carpenter from a rest home. Some of these octogenarians, however, passed down their skills to a new generation of woodworkers, and these artisans have inspired yet others. They are found in nearly every North American town and village, working quietly in their shops on furniture and millwork, and reproducing one-of-a-kind traditional cabinetry pieces. Included here are also suppliers of materials for do-it-yourself projects. For further leads to professionals who can produce cabinetwork for you, consult chapter 9 on furniture, chapter 5 on heating and cooking for suppliers of mantels, and the preceding section of this chapter on applied wood ornamentation.

Breakfast Woodworks

Breakfast Woodworks is an architect's dream come true. In this case, the architect is Louis Mackall, a post-modern practitioner with some important restorations to his credit, including the Goodspeed Opera House actor's housing in East Haddam, Connecticut (see chapter 1), and the Davies Inn in New Haven, an immense project still in progress. Breakfast Woodworks is the millwork side of the design business and is operated by Mackall and Kenneth Field. The extremely fine cabinetwork executed by the staff of five joiners has to be seen to be fully appreciated. Kitchens are a special area of expertise.

For further information, contact:

Breakfast Woodworks Inc.
50 Maple St.
Branford, CT 06405
(203) 488-8364

Marion H. Campbell

Most old-house owners would like to be able to hire Marion Campbell on a permanent basis to do all the special projects they've had in mind for years such as bookcases, a proper fireplace mantel, cornice moldings, and chair rails. Unfortunately, there just isn't any way most individuals can afford a live-in craftsman, at least not one as talented as Campbell. Fortunately for him, Campbell has no difficulty in finding work. Illustrated are two fine examples of projects he has recently completed—the reproduction of a Federal-style mantel and a set of raised panel cabinets for an 18th-century interior. Campbell is also an expert furniture maker, and an example of his work is shown in chapter 9.

Brochure, 50¢.

Marion H. Campbell
39 Wall St.

Bethlehem, PA 18018
(215) 865-2522 (shop) or 865-3292
(home)

Albert Constantine and Son

The kinds of veneers that furniture makers find useful can also be employed in period cabinetwork. Constantine is one of the leading suppliers of such materials, including figured matched veneer faces of quartered striped walnut, diamond matched striped mahogany, fancy figured walnut, and Carpathian elm burl face. In addition to these stock faces in 15" by 30" sizes, Constantine markets the line of Monarch Veneers, the sheets of which run approximately 9" wide by 7' long. Nearly every kind of fine wood veneer is available. There are also special 50' square and 100' square packets.

Catalogue, $1.

Albert Constantine and Son, Inc.
2050 Eastchester Rd.
Bronx, NY 10461
(800) 223-8087
(212) 792-1600 (NY)

Chip LaPointe, Cabinet-maker

LaPointe is an old-fashioned woodworker who likes nothing better than meticulously reproducing old-house details in fine hardwoods. He will execute mantels, cabinets, shutters, and doors on a custom basis. Illustrated is a portion of a wall unit that blends right in with the adjoining wainscoting. This unit of oak includes a tambour-front storage cabinet.

For further information, contact:

Chip LaPointe, Cabinetmaker
186 Emerson Pl.
Brooklyn, NY 11205
(212) 857-8594

Mountain Lumber

Custom cabinetry, including mantels of Mountain's superb prime-grade longleaf heart pine, is regularly designed and executed by members of this firm. They are experts at creating traditional designs that will fit a particular situation, and in bringing out all of the warmth and richness of the recycled lumber. In addition to custom designs, Mountain Lumber regularly stocks one style of fireplace mantel suitable for many Colonial period interiors and dressed timbers that are

ready for use as fireplace cross-beams or "trees."

Brochure and price list available.

Mountain Lumber
1327 Carlton Ave.
Charlottesville, VA 22901
(804) 295-1922 or 295-1757

Old Colony Crafts

Old Colony is a convenient supplier of detailed plans for the do-it-yourself cabinetmaker. Among the projects offered is the bookcase-cabinet shown here which can be built in or left freestanding. The plans can be easily adjusted so that the unit can be expanded and/or built around windows or doors. The design of the unit is straightforward enough to fit in practically any Colonial or country setting.

Catalogue of furniture and cabinetry projects available.

Old Colony Crafts
Box 155
Liberty, ME 04949
(207) 993-2552

Calvin M. Shewmaker

Calvin Shewmaker's experience in cabinetmaking includes an apprenticeship at Colonial Williamsburg, work for Shakertown at Pleasant Hill, Kentucky, and restoration work on Georgian and Federal houses. Illustrated here and at the beginning of the chapter is an example of one of his beautifully detailed chimney

breasts. All of Shewmaker's work is done by hand in his old-fashioned workshop. As he states, "the work is slower than large firms, but the results are most rewarding."

For further information, contact:

Calvin M. Shewmaker III, Cabinet-maker
606 Cane Run
Harrodsburg, KY 40330
(606) 734-9926

Sunshine Architectural Woodworks

The principals of this quality millwork firm have intelligently put together a handsome collection of mantel and chimney breast designs which they produce on a custom-order basis. Shown is one of six chimney breast designs, this model (110FW) standing 95" high and 78" wide, with a firebox opening 39¼" high and 50" wide. Kiln-dried poplar is used for most of the designs, but they are also available in walnut, cherry, mahogany, oak, white pine, birch, maple, or other domestic woods. Sunshine also offers four basic wood mantel designs appropriate for Colonial and early 19th-century interiors.

Literature available.

Sunshine Architectural Woodworks
Rte. 2, Box 434
Fayetteville, AR 72701
(501) 521-4329

The Woodworkers' Store

Specialty veneers of every type are stocked by The Woodworkers' Store for the home craftsman. There are flexible veneers in 24" by 24", 24" by 96", and 36" by 96" sizes, and dimension veneers with straight parallel edges in 36" and 48" lengths and 6", 8", or 10" widths. Both types are especially useful for cabinetwork. The firm also carries a good inventory of face grade veneers as well as burl veneers; widths available vary according to the species selected and lengths are usually 36".

These products are available through the mail or directly from one of the four Woodworkers' Store outlets. For addresses see the List of Suppliers.

Catalogue, $2.

The Woodworkers' Store
21801 Industrial Blvd.
Rogers, MN 55374
(612) 428-4101

Paneling

Paneled walls and wainscoting are among the most handsome features of many old houses. Colonial interiors often feature paneled room ends which incorporate a fireplace and closets on each side. Victorian interiors are more likely to make use of wainscoting, generally in that space defined by a baseboard below and a chair rail above, the section of a wall technically termed the dado. Talented home craftsmen can duplicate such paneling using specially milled lumber or veneer, supplies of which are noted in the following listings. Renovators or restorers seeking professional help can turn to a number of specialsts for supplies, design
assistance, and construction. Many of the craftsmen and suppliers noted in the section on applied wood ornamentation will also assist with paneling projects.

Artistry in Veneers

If you can't stand the pressed fiber board available locally or aren't about to spend a fortune on solid walnut paneling, you might want to consider using architectural grade veneer over plywood. Artistry in Veneers specializes in 7-foot lengths and longer. There is an excellent selection of such traditional woods as mahogany, oak, walnut, yellow pine, ash, and cherry, as well as more exotic types. One word of caution, however. Unless you have worked successfully with such paneling material, turn to a professional to do the job. Applying veneer to a table top is one thing; using it effectively on walls is quite another.

Catalogue, $1.50.

Artistry in Veneers
450 Oak Tree Ave.
South Plainfield, NJ 07080
(201) 668-1430

L. J. Bernard & Son

Leo John Bernard and his father represent the third and fourth generations of woodworking craftsmen in their family. Their small custom shop specializes in reproduction Colonial and Victorian millwork, including wall paneling, moldings, and fireplace mantels. The Bernards are also experts in bulding curved and straight stairways and supplying stair parts. In all their work, the highest quality woods are used.

Brochure available.

L. J. Bernard & Son Woodshop, Inc.
Rte. 3, Box 92A
Nixa, MO 65714
(417) 725-1449

Cumberland Woodcraft

In addition to its line of Victorian ornamental millwork, Cumberland custom executes wall and wainscoting treatments, partitions, and screens. The firm's experience has been mainly in the design and construction of Victorian-style restaurants and bars. The work and the design, however, are of the quality and type that allow for residential adaptation. For built-in cabinetry and wall treatments suitable for a grand high-Victorian dining salon or even a butler's pantry, Cumberland would be an excellent choice.

Catalogue, $3.75.

Cumberland Woodcraft Co., Inc.
P. O. Drawer 609
Carlisle, PA 17013
(717) 243-0063

Depot Woodworking

Depot is a major supplier of solid-hardwood paneling, wainscoting, and trim such as baseboards, window and door casings, and chair rails. All of these materials are marketed under the trade name of Vermont Floors and Paneling. The paneling comes in $7/16$" or $3/4$" thickness and is available in several patterns; the wainscoting is offered in many patterns. Depot will also custom match just about any type of millwork or paneling.

Literature available.

Depot Woodworking Inc.
683 Pine St.
Burlington, VT 05401
(802) 658-5670 (local calls)
(800) 322-7300 (VT residents)
(800) 343-8787 (out-of-state residents)

Driwood Moulding

In addition to their extensive line of moldings, Driwood's craftsmen can supply authentically-designed and architecturally-correct raised-panel wall sections and other types of architectural woodwork. These are most appropriately used in late Colonial-style interiors, but are also found in late 19th-century Colonial Revival and Beaux Arts mansions. Driwood's custom craftsmen make "on-site" measurements and drawings, execute the work in their South Carolina quarters, and then supervise the installation at the job site.

Custom work catalogue, $3.

Driwood Moulding Co.
P. O. Box 1729
Florence, SC 29503
(803) 669-2478

San Francisco Victoriana

As a manufacturer and supplier of wainscoting, San Francisco Victoriana is hard to beat. The firm's three basic patterns—batten, paneled, and beaded wainscoting—fairly well cover the standard Victorian treatments found throughout the country. In addition to the paneling, San Francisco Victoriana can also supply many different types of baseboard, base cap, chair rail, plate rail, and wainscot cap. Clear pine is used for the stock items; red oak, fir, poplar, mahogany, redwood, and walnut can be substituted.

Catalogue, $3.

San Francisco Victoriana
2245 Palou Ave.
San Francisco, CA 94124
(415) 648-0313

Sunshine Architectural Woodworks

Sunshine's standard wainscot sections are of raised panel design—as shown here—and are admirably suited for most Colonial or early 19th-century interiors. Sunshine will also supply the baseboard and wainscot cap moldings

necessary. There are four panels per section, and each is manufactured in two grades—paint and stain grade—of kiln-dried poplar. . Walnut, cherry, mahogany, oak, white pine, birch, or maple may be substituted.

Literature available.

Sunshine Architectural Woodworks
Rte. 2, Box 434
Fayetteville, AR 72701
(501) 521-4329

Tiresias

Tiresias's main product is flooring of longleaf heart pine which has been carefully remilled from massive old timbers saved from doomed warehouses, wharves, and other commercial and industrial buildings. The flooring is just as appropriate for paneling and is available from Tiresias in three standard patterns—tongue and groove, V-joint, and shiplap. The thickness of the boards is ¾″ or 1¼″, with widths of 4″, 6″, 8″, or 10″. Lengths range from 8′ to 16′, with 80% of any shipment consisting of 10′ to 14′ widths. There is one grade only, with approximately 20% of the lumber being clear. A supply of clear boards only is available on request.

Literature available.

Tiresias, Inc.
P. O. Box 1864
Orangeburg, SC 29116
(803) 534-8478 or 534-3445

Tile Ornamentation

Don't despair if you've just made your first trip to a ceramic tile supplier and discovered that everything on display is either speckled or tinted in a sickly pastel. Unless you are a complete defeatist, you will be ready to search further for tile that is truly attractive and fitting for an old-house interior.

In chapter 3 some of the leading suppliers of handsome floor tiles are described. Many of these same firms produce decorative tiles which can be used effectively for fireplace surrounds, hearths, kitchen and pantry counters, and as splashboards.

American Olean

American Olean is the largest ceramic tile manufacturer in North America and is well known for the variety of tiles it has available in a multitude of colors, finishes, and shapes. The Primitive Encore tile, illustrated here in a redecorated 1924 kitchen, is offered in a wide range of neutral colors in an assortment of surface/glaze combinations. These tiles are offered in 8″ by 8″ and 4″ by 4″ squares, 8″ by 4″ rectangles, and 8″ hexagons. Also of interest are quarry tiles in natural colors and small ceramic mosaic tiles in traditional patterns.

There are American Olean showrooms in most major cities.

Brochure available, 50¢.

American Olean Tile Co.
1000 Cannon Ave., Box 271
Lansdale, PA 19446
(215) 855-1111

Laura Ashley

Traditional tiles, boldly printed with rich colors, are made for Ashley in Italy, and are as suitable for walls as they are for floors. Twenty designs are available, including solids and two- and three-color square tiles. The Quatrefoil design tiles, which come in navy or terra cotta on a cream background, are reminiscent of late-Victorian ceramic tiles which were used for fireplace surrounds and hearths. Today they might be used as effectively as splashboards and counter tiles in a Victorian-style kitchen or pantry.

All of the Ashley tiles are sold in packs of twenty-five for the 7¾" by 7¾" size or twenty-two for the 6" by 6" size.

Home furnishings catalogue, $3.50.

Laura Ashley
Box 5308
Melville, NY 17114
(800) 367-2000

Berkshire Porcelain Studios

Berkshire Porcelain Studios specializes in decorative, custom-designed tiling. The firm is best-known for its "environments," large murals in which the smallest detailing is not omitted. Shown here is "Lady Slippers" by Ann Morris, a detail of a 36" by 60" hand-painted tile mural depicting a woodland in full bloom. Colors reflect the subtle hues of nature. Berkshire will paint designs on tiles supplied by customers or on imported bisque tiles.

For further information, contact:

Berkshire Porcelain Studios, Ltd.
Deerfield Ave.
Shelburne Falls, MA 01370
(413) 625-9447

Swampwitch Tile

Swampwitch Tile specializes in custom-made hand-painted tile. All painting is fired onto or under the glaze depending on customer preference. Swampwitch will follow customer designs or provide its own for contertops, splashboards, tub surrounds, flooring, and hearths. The naturalistic scene shown here is comprised of 6" by 6" bisque tiles brought together to form an 18" by 30" panel that can be used as a splashboard or wall mural.

Literature available. Send SASE.

Swampwitch Tile
1414 Elmhurst
Canton, MI 48187
(313) 455-5306

Taos Clay Products

Taos Clay Products manufactures tiles in geometric designs as well as more traditional styles. Its custom tiling, which can be used in both interior and exterior settings, utilizes bas relief, hand painting, and slip casting. Shown here is Penrose Parallelograms, a tiling designed and patented by noted geometer Roger Penrose of Oxford University. It is composed of two rhombuses that may be assembled in an orderly or random manner. The tiling is most effective using three colors, one

color for the 5-pointed stars, another for the narrow rhombuses, and a third for the bands. The rhombuses here are 1½", but size can be varied. A sample module of Penrose Parallelograms is available for $5.

Taos utilizes native clay body mixed with commercial clay in the production of its tiles. Glazes also contain native materials. A sample set of solid glaze colors on stoneware tile ($25) shows both glossy and matte finishes. The brighter glossy tiles are suitable for walls and countertops, while the more muted matte glazes are best for high-traffic floors. The stoneware squares are available in nineteen colors in 3" by 3", 4" by 4", 6" by 6", and 8" by 8" sizes.

Literature available.

Taos Clay Products, Inc.
Box 15
Taos, NM 87571
(505) 758-9513

Terra Designs

Tiles offered by Terra Designs are created by American artists and potters. The Buttermold series, designed by Anna Salibello, with its folksy country reliefs of such traditional items as pineapples, sheaves of wheat, and hearts, is based on wooden Colonial buttermold patterns. The tiles are available in 6" by 6" and 4" by 4" sizes with thicknesses of ⅜" or ½". Tiles come in three unglazed colors or can be glazed. The designs are deeply cut and, especially in the unglazed state, have the feel and appearance of primitive stoneware. The tiles are suitable for kitchen walls.

Terra Designs' tiles are sold nationwide in ceramic tile stores.

Catalogue, $1.

Terra Designs, Inc.
4 John St.
Morristown, NJ 07960
(201) 766-3577

Helen Williams/Rare Tiles

Helen Williams has recently expanded her collection of rare tiles to include Art Nouveau and limited quantities of antique Minton tiles, Victorian designs produced by one of the foremost English porcelain and pottery firms of the 19th century. These squares were once widely used in fashionable American homes and public buildings for fireplace facings and flooring.

Available, as always, is a very large selection of tin-glazed antique Delft tiles, in the traditional blue and white as well as manganese brown. These are approximately 5" square in size.

Literature available. Send SASE.

Helen Williams/Rare Tiles
12643 Hortense St.
North Hollywood, CA 91604
(818) 761-2756

Other Suppliers of Architectural Decoration

Consult List of Suppliers for addresses.

Glass

Sandra Brauer
Century Glass, Inc.
Cherry Creek Enterprises, Inc.
Conrad Schmitt Studios
Ice Nine Designs
Louisville Art Glass Studio
Manor Art Glass Studio
Master's Stained & Etched Glass Studio
Meredith Stained Glass Studios
Walton Stained Glass

Ornamental Metalwork

Bernadini Iron Works, Inc.
Greensboro Art Foundry & Machine Co.
Rejuvenation House Parts
Robinson Iron Corp.
Schwartz's Forge & Metalworks

Plaster, Composition, and Polymer Ornamentation

L. Biagiotti
Vernon M. Cassell & Sons,Inc.
Cichello and Son Plastering
Crawford's Old House Store
Crown Restorations
Entol Industries
Felber, Inc.
Harne Plastering Co.
David Flaherty
Albert Lachin and Assoc., Inc.
Edward K. Perry Co.
Renovation Concepts

Stone and Brickwork

Art, Inc.
Bragunier Masonry Contractors, Inc.
Chester Granite Co.
Custom Carpentry
Espinosa Stone Co.
Shaw Marble & Tile Co., Inc.

Applied Wood Ornamentation

Anderson & McQuaid Co.
Boston Turning Works
Classic Moldings
Haas Wood and Ivory Works
Hallelujah Redwood Products
Humberstone Woodworking
Iberia Millwork
Klise Manufacturing Co.
Maurer & Shepherd, Joyners
Maine Architectural Millwork
Old World Moulding
Walter E. Phelps
Silverton Victorian Millworks
Thorn Lumber Co.
Victorian Reproduction Enterprises, Inc.

Cabinetry

Fine Woodworking Co.
Haas Wood and Ivory Works
House Joiner, Ltd.
Maine Architectural Millwork
Maurer & Shepherd, Joyners
Simon Newby
Walter E. Phelps
Restoration Fraternity

Paneling

Amherst Wood Working & Supply
Architectural Components
Architectural Paneling, Inc.
Art Directions
The 18th Century Hardware Co.
Kensington Historical Co.
Maurer & Shepherd, Joyners
Simon Newby
Period Pine
Dennis Paul Robillard
The Woodstone Co.

Tile Ornamentation

Amsterdam Corp.
Architectural Terra Cotta and Tile Ltd.
Country Floors
Wm. H. Jackson
W. D. Virtue

3.

Floors and Floor Coverings

Often, the chief virtue of an old house's interior will be the richly mellowed wooden floors, whether the random-width planks in an 18th-century farmhouse or the elaborate inlay designs of a Victorian parlor. Sometimes the floors need no more than hard cleaning, but all too often they require refinishing to remove years of paint and grime, repair gouges, and protect them from further damage. In almost all cases, the effort will be worth it.

If a new floor is needed, there are many sources for all types of wood flooring, including solid planks, parquet, and laminated pre-finished strips. Some of these floors are designed to be put down easily by the homeowner.

Some stately older houses come equipped with only fragments of their original marble or stone floors. These are more difficult to repair, but can be replaced with newly available thin marble tile, which can be every bit as suitable as the existing floor. The cost of natural materials such as marble, stone, and slate is often less than you would expect, and the choices in these materials are wide-ranging in both color and finish.

The modern homeowner wishing to duplicate or suggest the look of antique floor coverings has many choices, limited only by style and price. From expensive imported silk and woolen rugs to more modest hooked and woven ones to painted sheets of canvas, floor coverings are available in designs limited only by the skill and imagination of the maker. Painted floors, of course, were as popular during the 18th and 19th centuries as the floor coverings just described, and progressed in complexity from stenciled or freehand designs to such decorative techniques as *faux* marble or splatterwork. Some floor coverings were a matter of convenience, such as the thick linoleum tiles which revolutionized kitchen maintenance or even the sand that was raked over wooden floors in the 16th and 17th centuries.

In spite of the proliferation of "no-wax" floors, sheet vinyl, flake tiles, and other contemporary "easy care" materials, there are many sources for the old-fashioned coverings mentioned here. Rugs and floorcloths produced by today's artisans offer almost limitless styles and designs suitable for period homes. Painted floors are often a reasonable alternative to extensive repair and refinishing and can frequently be done by a homeowner with a small flair for interior design. And, of course, a gleaming wooden floor looks good in almost any room and is well worth its initial investment.

Jacquard Wilton weave carpeting, Langhorne Carpets, Penndel, Pennsylvania.

Flooring

American Olean Tile

American Olean, one of the last of the major U.S. manufacturers of ceramic tiles, continues to expand its fine line. Along with ceramic tiles for walls and counters, the company offers a good selection of glazed and unglazed tiles for floors. The firm's Quarry tile, which comes in many shapes and a variety of earth shades, is suitable for interior and exterior floors and has the advantage of being warm in winter and cool in summer. For baths, American Olean carries an extensive line of coordinates, with textured or matte-surface tiles for floors. The Primitive Encore series, described in chapter 2, is offered with the Ultra Power series in complementary neutral tones and a slip-resistant surface.

Brochure, 50¢. For information regarding outlets for American Olean products, contact:

American Olean Tile Co.
1000 Cannon Ave., Box 271
Lansdale, PA 19446
(215) 855-1111

Laura Ashley

Laura Ashley is so well-known for fabrics that it comes as a surprise to learn about the firm's very handsome solid-color and decorated ceramic tiles from Italy. Aside from their ornamental use on walls and counters, these tiles are also appropriate for flooring. The solids are available in colors that complement Ashley's home furnishings collection, but will also harmonize with other types of country-style furnishings. Ashley's decorated tiles in designs similar to the firm's small-print fabrics and papers are also adaptable for use with non-Ashley furnishings. Tiles are available in two sizes: 7¾" by 7¾" or 6" by 6". Only the larger size is recommended for floors.

Yearly catalogue, $3.50, available by mail or at an Ashley outlet. See List of Suppliers for locations.

Mail order:

Laura Ashley
Box 5308
Melville, NY 17114
(800) 367-2000

Bruce Hardwood Floors

Bruce is a leading supplier of flooring for both new and old houses. The firm's solid plank flooring is still one of the best choices for older structures. Also offered is a wonderful selection of solid-oak parquets. The Jeffersonian, for example, is a 10" unit consisting of a 6" center square and 2" side strips. Each piece is beveled to create a look that would be right at home in a grand Federal-style estate house or a turn-of-the century town house. It is one of many interesting and appropriate parquets the company has available.

Bruce Hardwood floors are available from many retail sources. If you need assistance in locating a supplier, contact:

Bruce Hardwood Floors
16803 Dallas Pkwy.
Dallas, TX 75248
(214) 931-3000

Harris-Tarkett

This manufacturer offers a great variety of hardwood floors, many suitable for period homes. Of special interest is its selection of plank flooring, which is available in random widths or in patterns.

Shown here is the Frontier line of solid plank flooring. It is offered in red oak with tongue-and-groove ends and beveled sides, and comes unfinished. For those less inclined to the difficult work of floor finishing, Harris also makes pre-finished laminate flooring which is easy to install and is less costly than a solid-wood floor. The firm's Longstrip Plank laminated flooring is available in oak, ash, pine, kambala, beech, and merbau.

Suppliers of Harris-Tarkett flooring are located throughout North America. If you need information regarding outlets, contact:

Harris-Tarkett, Inc.
383 Maple St.
Johnson City, TN 37601
(615) 928-3122

Hartco Flooring

Hartco produces a variety of wood flooring, including solid-oak parquet, acrylic-impregnated parquet, and Pattern Plus random-length narrow strips. Of special interest to us is its Heritage Finish solid-oak parquet, since Hartco uses a sealer that leaves no gloss or shine. It is practically invisible, but still resistant to scuffs and stains. The Appalachian oak is sealed and waxed in the factory, so there is no on-site finishing. This flooring should be a great boon to those of us who yearn for the classic look of a waxed wood floor, but can't spare a lifetime or so to keep it looking good.

Hartco Flooring is available through retail outlets in the U.S. and Canada. If assistance is needed in locating a supplier, contact:

Hartco, Inc.
Oneida, TN 37841
(615) 569-8526

Kentucky Wood Floors

Kentucky offers several types of ready-to-install wood floors as well as custom flooring. Its solid plank floors are available in random or specified widths with either bevelled or square edges.

Plugs of matching or contrasting wood are also available. The firm's

Tony Lauria

Over the years, linoleum has certainly gotten a bad name with the increasing turn to "natural" materials. But for some early 20th-century rooms an old-fashioned *real* linoleum floor would be perfect, if only it were available. Tony Lauria offers authentic battleship linoleum—newly manufactured and made of all natural materials including linseed oil, pine resins, wood flour, and jute. It is available in nine colors: brown, beige, light or dark green, blue, gold, terra cotta, gray, and black. It can be purchased in almost any length and in widths up to 6'6".

Samples available. Send SASE to:

Tony Lauria
RD 2, Box 253B
Landenberg, PA 19350
(215) 268-3441

Lebanon Oak Flooring

This Kentucky firm specializes in oak flooring and manufactures a variety of styles. Its random-width plank is available in several grades of red or white oak and in 5/16" thickness. They also offer square-edge strips in 2" widths that are

pre-finished parquet is sealed and finished with either wax or polyurethane. The squares glue down for easy installation. For more affordable parquet flooring, Kentucky sells unfinished parquet which the do-it-yourselfer can sand and finish on site. Kentucky flooring is available in a variety of woods, including oak, walnut, cherry, teak, and ash. Shown here is a custom floor designed for the oval office of the White House and crafted in quartered oak and walnut.

The names of local distributors are available by calling or writing the company.

Kentucky Wood Floors
4200 Reservoir Ave.
Louisville, KY 40213
(502) 451-6024

ideal for use in narrow-strip or parquet flooring. These are available in most grades and in several species of oak.

For information regarding Lebanon Oak retail suppliers, contact:

Lebanon Oak Flooring Co.
Box 669
Lebanon, KY 40033
(502) 692-2128

Tiresias

One of the nice things about Tiresias is the firm's utter commitment to the reuse of heart pine. Its millwork products are salvaged from massive old timbers and have a glow and patina that can only come with age. Now a finite resource, heart pine particularly lends itself to use in restored buildings. Tiresias flooring ranges in color from light honey to dark reddish brown, with deep graining. It is available in widths of from 4" to 10" and thickness of 3/4" or 1 1/4".

Brochure available.

Tiresias, Inc.
Box 1864
Orangeburg, SC 29116
(803) 534-8478

Vermont Marble

Vermont Marble has developed a thin tile suitable for use as flooring. It is offered in a uniform ⅜" thickness and in three sizes: 12" by 12", 12" by 5⅞", and 5⅞" by 5⅞". The color selection ranges from pure white to deeply veined green to black. Warm-toned russet is particularly suited to period rooms or to such heavily-traveled areas as entrance halls. Shown here is the Danby marble tile in a residential bathroom. These thin marble tiles offer the beauty of stone with the reduced weight load and ease of installation of ceramic tile.

Brochure available.

Vermont Marble Co.
61 Main St.
Proctor, VT 05765
(802) 459-3311

Carpets will also accept orders for custom colors. Custom designs will also be executed.

Catalogue, $1 (deductible from purchase).

Mail order:
Canvas Carpets
Box 181
S. Egremont, MA 01258
(413) 528-4267

Retail shop:
292 Main St.
Great Barrington, MA 01230
(413) 528-3231

Floor Coverings

Canvas Carpets

Marilyn Orner's canvas carpets are made of heavy cotton canvas, stenciled with either traditional or contemporary designs, and finished with a hard varnish. The company offers a large choice of designs and colors, and each floorcloth is made to meet the client's particular requirements. To help in the selection, Ms. Orner will send a 12" by 18" placemat showing a portion of the design in specified colors for only $10. Shown here are two popular designs, each 2' by 3'. The Gameboard design is available with any border motif, including the Heart Vine border shown. Stars and Stripes is offered in combinations of two or three colors. The many stock colors should satisfy any taste, but Canvas

Country Braid House

For many years this small New Hampshire firm has made custom braided rugs which are all hand-laced and reversible. It also sells rug kits containing all the necessary do-it-yourself materials, including thread and a lacing needles, and will even lace the first few rows to get you started. Estimates on custom rugs are available if you specify size, style, type of braid, and color choices.

Literature available.

Country Braid House
RFD #2, Box 29, Clark Rd.
Tilton, NH 03276
(603) 286-4511

Floorcloths by Ingrid

Started in 1981, this small family mail-order business specializes in hand-stenciled floorcloths. The canvas rugs come in a wide variety of traditional and new designs, all most appropriate for 18th- and early 19th-century rooms. All of Ingrid's floorcloths are available in a large selection of stock colors, or you can select special colors if you wish.

Brochure available.

Floorcloths by Ingrid
8 Randall Rd.
Rochester, MA 02770
(617) 763-8721

The Gazebo

The Gazebo is one of those tantalizing stores—chock full of a dazzling array of rugs, quilts, pillows, and wicker—and impossible to pass without walking in.

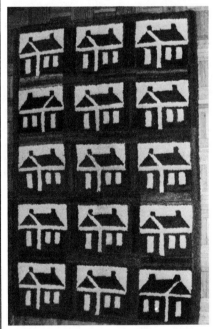

Luckily for those who do not live in the New York area, the Gazebo's merchandise is also available through the mail. Aside from its enormous stock of striped and solid-cotton rag rugs, it offers a selection of 100% wool, hand-crafted hooked rugs. The rugs in stock are based on traditional quilt patterns, but custom rugs can be ordered in other shapes, patterns, and colors. Shown here

are two popular designs: School House and Rose Cross. As with all Gazebo's hooked rugs, these are priced by the square foot.

Full-color catalogue, $4.50.

The Gazebo
660 Madison Avenue
New York, NY 10021
(800) 221-3130
(212) 832-7077 (NY, AK, HI)

Good Stenciling

Nancy Good Cayford and Philip Cayford continue to create colorful and authentic stenciled floorcloths and have increased their selection of stair runners. Shown here is a new stair runner design, "Philip," in navy, brick, and putty. It is available in a 2' width and in any length, and in several color combinations. Recently, the Cayfords have done many museum and historical house projects, including a wonderful marbleized floorcloth for the Salisbury Mansion in Worcester, Massachusetts. We're pleased to note that these marbleized patterns are now being offered to the public. Although the Cayfords' catalogue is quite extensive, they also accept orders for custom floorcloths.

Catalogue, $2. Color photos of a specific design, 50¢.

Mail order:
Good Stenciling
Box 387
Dublin, NH 03444
(603) 563-8021

Retail Store:
Carriage Depot, Rte. 101A
Amherst, NH 03031
(603) 880-3480

Import Specialists

This wholesale company is offering a new selection of charming floor rugs. Called "stencil dhurries," they are handwoven in India

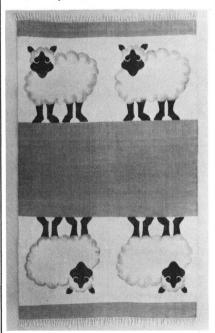

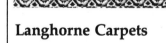

Langhorne Carpeting Co.
Box 175
Penndel, PA 19047
(215) 757-5155

Mulberry Street Rugs

from 100% cotton and stenciled by hand in custom designs. They are currently available in nineteen patterns of animals and old-fashioned geometric motifs and are offered in two sizes: 2' by 3' and 4' by 6'. Shown here are Bringing in the Flock and three floral designs: Double Dutch, in rose, heather, and blue; Posies, in spice accented with blue; and last, And Flowers, in shades of pink and soft greens—all on parchment-colored backgrounds. Import Specialists is happy to answer inquiries regarding the retail availability of its rugs.

For further information, contact:

Import Specialists, Inc.
82 Wall Street, 9th Floor
New York, NY 10005
(800) 334-4044
(212) 709-9633 (NY, AK, HI)

All Mulberry Street rugs are handmade from heavy-weight 100% wool. The braided rugs are quadruple folded, hand-laced, and hand-braided in six different designs. The woven rugs, also offered in six patterns, are hand-loomed using Irish linen warp. All are completely reversible. Custom rugs are also available.

Information packets, $1.

Mulberry Street Rugs
871 Via de la Paz
Pacific Palisades, CA 90272
(213) 454-3995

Langhorne Carpets

Langhorne is one of the few North American firms supplying custom Wilton carpeting for historic restoration projects. The work of preparing and weaving reproduction designs is very complicated and time-consuming. The two carpets pictured here are Wilton weaves of 100% wool and are good examples of some of Langhorne's Victorian designs.

They also illustrate the firm's extraordinary craftsmanship and eye for aesthetic detail. Langhorne also produces standard residential carpeting in a number of different designs which may suit the needs of the average buyer.

For information regarding custom work and suppliers of Langhorne's standard carpeting, contact:

Rastetter Woolen Mill

Tim and Maureen Rastetter are continuing a long tradition in producing hand-woven rugs and carpets. The Rastetter family has been in the wool weaving business since the 1860s and moved to this rural Ohio location in 1939.

The Rastetters continue to weave coverlets in traditional patterns, but the bulk of their business is in throw rugs of either 100% wool or cotton and wool strips which can be sewn together to make wall-to-wall carpeting. The weaves are very handsome; one known as the Smithsonian Brick & Block pattern was woven at the famous Washington, D.C., institution and features a design of multicolor stripes and checkerboard squares. The Rastetters are invited each year to transport their loom to Washington for the annual craft show sponsored by the Women's Committee of the Smithsonian.

Over 1,000 braided and woven rugs are in stock at any given time and may be orderd by mail or purchased at the mill. Runners in sizes ranging from 6' to 15' are also available. As mentioned previously, the firm will sew woven strips together to form carpeting. An extra heavy warp is used for this type of floor covering. The two basic widths of the woven rugs and runners are 27" and 36". All of the braided and woven rugs are offered in a wide variety of colors, lengths, and designs.

Free brochures available.

Rastetter Woolen Mill
Star Rte., Box 42
Millersburg, OH 44654
(216) 674-2103

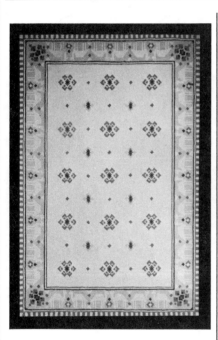

Scalamandré

This world-famous firm has long been known for its high-quality custom rugs and carpets. Many of the designs are specifically made for historic restoration projects, both for museums and private residents. The four 6' by 9' rugs shown here are from the new Studio collection, which is adapted from some of Scalamandré's fabrics and papers. They are all domestically made and of 100% wool. Each rug is offered in a large selection of stock colors or custom dyes. A client can choose from either group of colors. The rugs illustrated (*counterclockwise from left*) are Sudan, Floral Lace, French Paisley, and Summer Carnival.

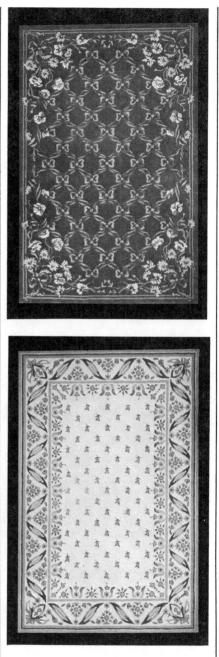

Scalamandré carpets are available only through interior designers or the decorating departments of select stores. For further information about sources, contact:

Scalamandré, Inc.
950 Third Ave.
New York, NY 10022
(212) 980-3888

moss, brown, and wine borders; Frosted Lily (center) is ivory with a floral border and a medallion in soft blues, rose, deep reds, and gold; Poppy (bottom) has an Art Nouveau border in red, greens, and brick.

An information packet is available on request.

Victorian Collectibles, Ltd.
845 E. Glenbrook Rd.
Milwaukee, WI 53217
(414) 352-6910

Victorian Collectibles, Ltd.

Florence Schroeder is already well-known for her collection of antique wallcoverings, hand-painted canvas ceilings, and friezes. Now she has created a group of 100% wool area rugs to complement these decorative elements. The Brillion rug collection is produced in India. The high-relief designs are reproductions of 19th-century patterns. Six patterns are available, plus six solid-color rugs with patterned borders. All are available in two sizes: 6' by 9' and 9' by 12'. Illustrated here are three designs: Grapevine (top) has clusters of grapes in lavender and blue with

Other Suppliers of Floors and Floor Coverings

Consult List of Suppliers for addresses.

Floors

Architectural Terra Cotta & Tile, Ltd.
Bangkok Industries
Bergen Bluestone
Dale Carlisle
Castle Burlingame
Craftsman Lumber Co.
Country Floors
Delaware Quarries, Inc.
Depot Woodworking
Diamond K
Elon Inc.
Maurer & Shepherd, Joyners
Old Carolina Brick
Period Pine
Structural Slate
Taos Clay Products
Vermont Structural Slate Co.
Helen Williams/Rare Tile

Floor Coverings

Adams & Swett
Braid-Aid
Diane Jackson Cole
Conran's
Dildarian, Inc.
Floorcloths, Inc.
Heirloom Rugs
Kenmore Carpet Corp.
Marvin Kagan, Inc.
Newbury Carpets
Patterson, Flynn, & Martin, Inc.
Rosecore Carpet Co., Inc.
F. Schumacher & Co.
Stark Carpet Co.
Sunflower Studio

4.

Lighting

You may decide to forego wallpaper and curtains, cabinets, or a woodstove. You may even elect to live without furniture. But as austere as your tastes may be, you will have to put lights in the house. The problem in selecting fixtures for old houses is not the limit of choices, but the virtually endless possibilities. Antique fixtures are available, newly wired and restored. Craftsmen are turning out high-quality handcrafted designs taken from many periods. There is also an enormous market in machine-tooled reproduction fixtures. "Reproduction" does not necessarily mean shoddy materials and tacky designs. Many companies produce fixtures from top-quality materials, such as solid brass, with elegant appointments like etched ruby-glass shades or mirrored reflectors.

There are probably some people who can cook in a kitchen lit by a flickering candle in a tin sconce, but the truth is that if electricity had been harnessed at the time, the Colonists would have used it. With the availability of quality fixtures today, there is not need to sacrifice convenience for historical authenticity down to the stub of a candle. A Victorian dining room can be outfitted with a fully wired, handsome brass gasolier or a table lamp with a fringed silk lampshade. Graceful, hand-forged iron or pewter wall sconces are eminently suitable for 18th-century homes. And outdoor areas can be lit in a variety of imaginative ways, most notably with glass and metal lanterns designed to be hung, wall-mounted, or affixed to a post.

An important consideration in choosing lighting is the space and the manner in which it will be used. Candle sconces offer lively light in a dining room, until they drip wax on the random-width floorboards, overturn suddenly, or become objects of fascination to a child. Such fixtures can be fitted with electric candles and still be effective.

Hallways are often suitable for simple hanging fixtures. They are less elaborate than chandeliers and are available in a variety of period styles. Good reading lights are harder to come by, but there are simple reproduction wrought-iron table lamps modeled after candlestands or electrified candlestands themselves that are perfectly suitable in design and function.

The pages of this chapter offer many sources for reproduction, handcrafted, and antique fixtures to satisfy both the requirements of modern lighting and the harmony of period decor.

Mid-Victorian gasolier, c. 1855, Greg's Antique Lighting, Los Angeles, California.

Chandeliers

Because of its size and placement, a chandelier is usually the focal point of a room, whether hung in a spacious entry hall, over a satiny oak dining table, or as the centerpiece of a Victorian parlor. As such, the selection of the right chandelier is of paramount importance. Carefully chosen, it can tie together more disparate elements of the design scheme, while the wrong one will be as apparent a gaffe in design as a five-and-dime plastic umbrella stand placed next to a 19th-century grandfather clock.

Authentic Designs

Painstaking research in museums and universities has resulted in Authentic Designs' superb reproductions of early American chandeliers. The brass arms are individually cut, bent, and shaped by hand; candelabra sockets for small bulbs are provided in all models to simulate the warmth of the graceful tapers used in Colonial days. (Fixtures can be fitted to receive candles upon request.)

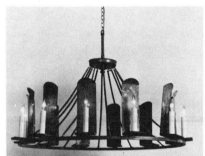

The simple design illustrated measures 19″ high and 32″ in diameter; it is supplied with two feet of solid-brass suspension chain and a ceiling canopy, as are all the company's hanging fixtures.

Catalogue, $3.

Authentic Designs
The Mill Road
West Rupert, VT 05776-0011
(802) 394-7713

Authentic Lighting

Barry Hauptman offers a variety of supplies and services to antique lighting enthusiasts: he will restore and refinish ceiling fixtures, lamps, and sconces; can reproduce a fixture from an original, photo, or blueprint you supply; and offers stock reproductions as well, among them this early gas/electric combination. Hauptman works primarily with antiques dealers and interior decorators, but his shop is open to the public as well.

For further information, contact:

Authentic Lighting
558 Grand Ave.
Englewood, NJ 07631
(201) 568-7429

The Classic Illumination

The specialty of the craftsmen at The Classic Illumination is custom design and restoration. Phil Waen, president, is an authority in the field of restoration lighting and was involved in, among other projects, the restoration of the State Capitol in Sacramento. In addition to custom work, however, the company offers a line of 19th-century-inspired chandeliers, sconces, and table lamps. All, including the eight-branch chandelier illustrated, are handcrafted of solid brass and fitted with glass shades. This particular piece, model 1890-4, was inspired by a combination gas/electric chandelier from about 1890. It is available in four standard

lengths—from 26″ to 62″—and can be fitted with a choice of shades.

The Classic Illumination
431 Grove St.
Oakland, CA 94607
(415) 465-7786

The Classic Illumination sells exclusively to the trade; mail order sales are handled by Ocean View Lighting and Home Accessories, through whom the company's full-color catalogue should be ordered.

Catalogue, $3.

Ocean View Lighting and Home
* Accessories*
1810 Fourth St.
Berkeley, CA 94710
(415) 841-2937

D'Light

The turn-of-the-century chandeliers, pendants, wall sconces, and portable lamps reproduced by D'Light are not widely available in retail shops, as the company is primarily concerned with institutional installations. Many of the careful replicas D'Light offers, however, are eminently suitable for period homes as well, and its full-color catalogue will help you make an informed choice. A late-Victorian dining table, for instance, would be beautifully illumined by this replica of a combination gas/electric chandelier.

Catalogue, $6.

D'Light
533 W. Windsor Rd.
Glendale, CA 91204
(213) 956-5656

Essex Forge

Painstakingly reproduced from an

original in a private Massachusetts collection, the Salem chandelier would look equally well in entrance hall, small dining room, or country kitchen. Its simple design would complement either the ubiquitous "country look" or a more stately Colonial home. The inverted cone supports three reinforced arms. The dimensions (12" high, 17" wide, depended from an 18" chain) make the Salem ideal for smaller rooms. Pewter or antique black finishes are offered.

Catalogue, $2.

The Essex Forge, Inc.
12 Old Dennison Rd.
Essex, CT 06426
(203) 767-1808

Metropolitan Lighting

The Art Nouveau-inspired chandelier pictured at the left in this photo (Metropolitan's model N1331) is crafted of solid brass and hand-blown Murano frosted glass. The metal is 24K gold-

plated, providing a luxurious finish which will enhance even the most elegant decor. The fixture on the right is a simpler, more sophisticated design (N1329), also featuring frosted glass and gold plating. These are among the many handsome styles Metropolitan offers; the company sells only to the trade, and is represented in most major cities by dealers. Contact Metropolitan for the dealer in your area.

For further information, contact:

Metropolitan Lighting Fixture Co.
  Inc.
1010 Third Ave.
New York, NY 10021
(212) 838-2425

Period Lighting Fixtures

Richard Scofield is justifiably proud of the exquisite reproductions he produces—so much so that many of the pieces illustrated in his catalogue are accompanied by photos of the originals which inspired them. That is the case

with both of the painstakingly hand-crafted chandeliers illustrated here: the pine and iron model, with its gracefully turned shaft and lemon drop, was first made in the latter half of the 18th

century. The original hangs in Hathaway House, Suffield, Connecticut. The six-arm painted tin chandelier is a copy of a William and Mary piece dating from c. 1710. The original illumines the Wells-Thorn House in Deerfield, Massachusetts.

Catalogue, $2.

Period Lighting Fixtures
1 Main St.
Chester, CT 06412
(203) 526-3690

Price Glover

Eighteenth-century English brass chandeliers are worth a fortune—when you can find them. Lovers of fine English craftsmanship and detailing can find solace, however, in the superb reproductions of these priceless originals available from Price Glover. One of the company's most beautiful offerings is a precisely detailed copy of an eight-branch chandelier (c. 1750). The rare swirled gadrooning on the central ball is repeated in the detailing of the stem, which is surmounted by a dove with outstretched wings. Wiring is available; purists may wish to supply the piece only with the graceful candles which adorned the original.

Brochure available.

Price Glover Inc.
817 Madison Ave.
New York, NY 10021
(212) 772-1740

St. Louis Antique Lighting

Antique Victorian chandeliers are difficult to find and expensive to restore. More reasonable, and just as beautiful, alternatives are the solid-brass reproductions available from St. Louis Antique Lighting. The company's catalogue illustrates a number of styles, among the most attractive of which is its model C4. Four graceful, upward-curving arms branch out from a polished globe; each arm is guarded by a whimsical brass cherub. If none of the

company's standard models is to your liking, proprietor Gary Behm suggests that he may be able to design one for you.

Catalogue, $3.

St. Louis Antique Lighting Co.
25 N. Sarah
St. Louis, MO 63108
(314) 535-2770

Victorian Lightcrafters Ltd.

Dean Stansfield's firm has been restoring and selling antique lighting fixtures for nearly fifteen years; in 1979 the company introduced a line of solid-brass

reproductions as well. Each piece is soldered and assembled by hand and is made to the customer's order. The gas/electric chandelier illustrated is available with either two or four arms; standard heights range from 27" to 50". The company will entertain requests for special dimensions.

Catalogue, $3.

Victorian Lightcrafters Ltd.
Box 332
Slate Hill, NY 10973
(914) 355-1300

Hanging and Ceiling Fixtures

Generally less ambitious in design than chandeliers, hanging lamps are ideal choices for dim hallways or smaller rooms where multibracketed chandeliers would be overwhelming. Ceiling fixtures, of course, are good selections for low-ceilinged rooms. Yet their more utilitarian nature is not an excuse for inferior design and workmanship, since there are handsome, well-made reproductions available to complement any decor.

Brasslight, Inc.

All lamps and fixtures made by Brasslight are, as the company's name implies, created of solid

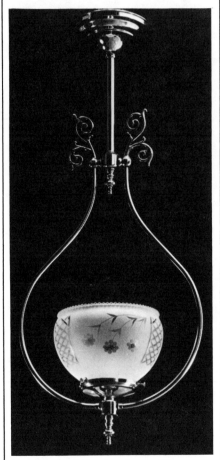

brass. The hanging lamp illustrated here, called Belle Harp, is fitted with a cut-glass shade. It is 27" tall and 12" wide and will accommodate a 150-watt bulb. Brasslight offers many reproductions of

Victorian-era hanging lamps, some with matching wall sconces.

Catalogue, $3.

Brasslight, Inc.
90 Main St.
Nyack, NY 10960
(914) 353-0567

Metropolitan Lighting

Most modern ceiling fixtures, while utilitarian, are less than satisfactory design accents, especially for lovers of the Art Nouveau and Art Deco styles. Metropolitan Lighting, however, offers some unusual fixtures that are perfect accompaniments to these styles. Model N1393, for instance, is composed of a solid-brass globe depended from a ceiling canopy. Affixed to the globe so as to hide the canopy are six frosted-glass shells, each of which diffuses the light of a 60-watt bulb. The final touch to complete this elegant fixture is the addition of 24-K gold plating to the metal.

Metropolitan sells to the trade only; it is, however, represented in major cities throughout the country, and will be glad to supply the name of a local dealer.

For further information, contact:

Metropolitan Lighting Fixture Co.
* Inc.*
1010 Third Ave.
New York, NY 10021
(212) 838-2425

Price Glover

Price Glover is a haven for those whose first love is 18th-century English design. Among the outstanding solid-brass reproductions offered by the company is a graceful hanging lantern crafted by skilled artisans who used the original antique as a guide. The brass fittings are molded with beaded detail, the glass hand-blown with folded edges. This lantern is most effective when illumined by a single wax candle;

wiring (with a three-light cluster) is available for an additional charge.

Brochure available.

Price Glover Inc.
817 Madison Ave.
New York, NY 10021
(212) 772-1740

Rejuvenation House Parts

This Oregon-based firm specializes in reproductions of turn-of-the-century fixtures. The offerings range from gas and electric shades to sconces to ceiling lights and chandeliers. Among

the simplest of the designs is the Laurelhurst, a bowl-light fixture wired for three 60-watt bulbs. The shade is etched crystal, its diameter a mere 14". The metal used is polished brass, which can be lacquered at the customer's request.

Catalogue, $3.

Rejuvenation House Parts Co.
901 N. Skidmore
Portland, OR 97217
(503) 249-0774

| ## St. Louis Antique Lighting

Among the most attractive reproductions offered by Gary Behm of St. Louis Antique Lighting is a solid-brass ceiling light, 36" long. A graceful scroll-shaped holder depends from a simple polished stem. The single glass shade is available in a variety of styles and colors. Optional finishes are polished brass and nickel-plating.

Catalogue, $3.

St. Louis Antique Lighting Co.
25 N. Sarah
St. Louis, MO 63108
(314) 535-2770

Victorian Lightcrafters

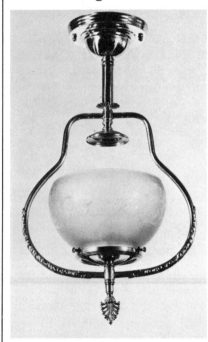

Gas-style hanging lamps such as the one pictured here were ubiquitous in many Victorian homes. Yet originals, carefully restored and wired for electricity, are difficult to find. Why not, then, select a superb solid-brass reproduction such as this one? Victorian Lightcrafters makes all such fixtures to order, enabling the customer to specify length. A variety of cut-glass, etched, and pressed-glass shades is available

to suit individual taste. The imported French shade illustrated is an etched design with satin finish and measures 4½" by 7".

Catalogue, $3.

Victorian Lightcrafters Ltd.
Box 332
Slate Hill, NY 10973
(914) 355-1300

Lt. Moses Willard & Company

Lt. Moses Willard manufactures the Colonial Tin Craft line familiar to readers of previous editions of *The Old House Catalogue*. Each of the company's lighting fixtures is handmade, following the traditions of the early tinsmiths, and replicates styles of the 17th, 18th, and 19th centuries. Among the many hanging lamps offered are a pierced-tin shade 15" wide and 12" high; a simple lantern with four glass sides; a conical 12½"-wide pierced shade; and a hooded fixture which can be fitted for either electric light or a simple taper.

Catalogue, $2.

Lt. Moses Willard & Company
7805 Railroad Ave.
Cincinnati, OH 45243
(513) 561-3942

Gates Moore

The distressed tin fixture illustrated here is handmade by Gates Moore to simulate an antique lamp. It is supplied, as are all the company's hanging fixtures, with a ceiling canopy, crossbar, hook and handmade chain, or hollow hook in any length to suit individual specifications. Gates Moore will finish any fixture in an authenticated Colonial paint color, from brown-on-red to black, or will paint to match your color sample. Any of its metal fixtures are available in brass as well. This particular lantern style can be ordered in two sizes: 4⅝" wide by 9½" high, or 6" by 15½". Gates Moore will also restore and electrify antique fixtures.

Catalogue, $2.

Gates Moore
River Rd., Silvermine
Norwalk, CT 06850
(203) 847-3231

Wall Fixtures

With the exception of simple candle sconces which require just a nail or two to install, wall fixtures seem to have been ignored recently in favor of table and floor lamps—and with good reason. It's rare to find an old house with junction boxes already in place in just the right locations; installing electric (or gas) hookups in pre-existing walls can be a costly expense. But if the connection is already there, you'll find the selection of appropriate fixtures more than ample.

Authentic Designs

Painstaking reproductions of early American wall sconces are made by the original, centuries-old methods at Authentic Designs. Solid-brass arms are individually cut, bent, and shaped; maple wood turnings are made by hand. Authentic Designs offers a wide variety of beautiful wall sconces, many illustrated in the firm's catalogue. All are available in original natural brass finish or in an antique pewter plating which is applied to the brass. The maple is stained and hand rubbed with paste wax.

Catalogue, $3.

Authentic Designs
The Mill Road,
West Rupert, VT 05776-0011
(802) 394-7713

Essex Forge

Hand-wrought iron and tin fixtures reproducing early American pieces are the specialty of this Connecticut firm. One of the classic designs offered is the Winthrop, a lovely oval sconce with a traditional pie-crust border. It measures 10" by 6" and extends a mere 4" from the wall, making it ideal for hard-to-light hallways and staircases where space is often at a premium.

Catalogue, $2.

The Essex Forge, Inc.
12 Old Dennison Rd.
Essex, CT 06426
(203) 767-1808

Federal Street Lighthouse

This retail shop specializes in 18th- and early 19th-century reproductions of American and European chandeliers, sconces

(such as the handsome scalloped one illustrated), and lanterns. In addition, you will find accessories such as shades, mirrors, and hardware. Materials used include brass and pewter, tin, wood, and iron. Proprietor Cheryl B. Smith welcomes inquiries on custom work as well.

For further information, contact:

Federal Street Lighthouse
38 Market Square
Newburyport, MA 01950
(617) 462-6333

Metropolitan Lighting

The Art Nouveau and Art Deco styles are enjoying a resurgence of popularity; what's difficult is finding the right fixtures to complement interiors decorated in one or the other style. Metropolitan Lighting has a wide selection of such reproductions, of which two are illustrated here. Number 1359 is constructed of polished brass with clear accents and clear glass rods. It measures 16" by 6½" and projects a mere 3" from the wall.

A fantasy of frosted glass and cast brass, Metropolitan's model 1382 measures 11½" by 5½" with a 6"-projection. Both fixtures accommodate standard 60-watt bulbs. Metropolitan sells directly to the trade only; the company is represented in most major cities, however, and will be happy to suggest a dealer near you.

For further information, contact:

Metropolitan Lighting Fixture Co.
Inc.
1010 Third Ave.
New York, NY 10021
(212) TE 8-2425

Period Lighting Fixtures

A dozen wall sconces such as the one illustrated at the top of this grouping were believed to have been in place when the first Continental Congress met at Carpenter's Hall in Philadelphia in 1774. Only two of the originals

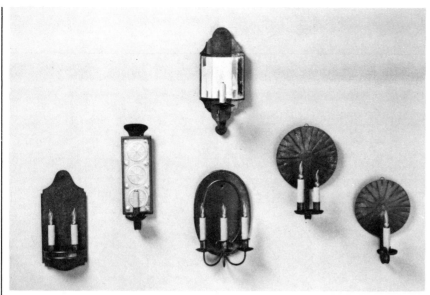

remain, but superb reproductions are available from Richard Scofield at Period Lighting. Each of his sconces is handcrafted according to the most exacting standards, and his concern for verisimilitude is evident, for he takes pains—and space—in his catalogue to explain proper selection and installation of each piece.

Among the finishes used on his sconces are pewter, aged tin, and paint (he will send a packet of samples to aid your choice).

Catalogue, $2.

Period Lighting Fixtures
1 Main Street
Chester, CT 06412
(203) 526-3690

fabrics which will blend well with any decor. The standard finish used is dull black; turnings and spinnings are solid brass; and each fixture accommodates a standard bulb.

Catalogue available.

The Village Forge
Box 1148
Smithfield, NC 27577
(919) 934-2581

W. T. Weaver

Washington's Georgetown section contains some of the most beautifully preserved examples of late-18th and early 19th-century residential architecture to be found anywhere in the country. W. T. Weaver has been supplying hardware to the owners of these landmarks since 1889. But in addition to its extensive line of hardware and supplies (see chapter 6), the firm offers a variety of handsome lighting fixtures. Among the most attractive are its wall sconces—four different early American designs crafted of brass and available with either polished brass or antique pewter finishes—which accommodate from one to three wax candles depending on the style. One, the Unicorn, can be wired for electricity—if you insist.

Catalogue, $2.50

W. T. Weaver & Sons, Inc.
1208 Wisconsin Ave., N.W.
Washington, DC 20007
(202) 333-4200

Rejuvenation House Parts

Lovers of turn-of-the-century Victoriana can be somewhat dismayed by the prospect of cleaning the pieces they cherish: most Victorian lighting fixtures, for instance, are ornate, elaborately molded pieces which look beautiful but are extraordinarily difficult to maintain in shining order. There are, however, exceptions. Rejuvenation House Parts specializes in carefully crafted reproductions of late-Victorian fixtures. Among them is its model WD1E1G, a gas/electric sconce which is surprising for its simplicity of design. A single brass arm extends from the wall plate; from it are mounted two fluted glass shades, nonetheless effective for their lack of ornamentation.

Catalogue, $3.

Rejuvenation House Parts Co.
901 N. Skidmore
Portland, OR 97217
(503) 249-0774

The Village Forge

Wrought-iron lighting designs inspired by the work of pre-Revolutionary blacksmiths are the specialty of the Village Forge, as they have been for more than a decade.

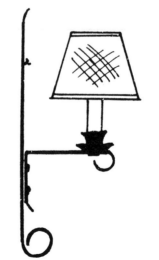

All lamps, including the simple model illustrated, are supplied with shades of the appropriate size in basic, natural-colored

Table and Floor Lamps

We have said before that it's not easy to find well-designed and executed table and floor lamps for the period home— and it's still true. The situation is improving, however, as reputable craftsmen and manufacturers recognize the gap and strive to fill it. And when all else fails, you might consider one of the handsome lanterns illustrated in the following section.

Catalogue, $3.

Brasslight, Inc.
90 Main St.
Nyack, NY 10960
(914) 353-0567

The Classic Illumination

Each fixture offered by The Classic Illumination is hand-crafted from solid brass and accompanied by a complementary glass shade. The scroll desk lamp, for example (model #15), is fitted with a holophane-style pressed-crystal shade with fluted edge.

The Classic Illumination
431 Grove St.
Oakland, CA 94607
(415) 465-7786

The Classic Illumination sells exclusively to the trade; mail order sales are handled by Ocean View Lighting and Home Accessories, through whom the company's full-color catalogue should be ordered.

Catalogue, $3.

Ocean View Lighting and Home
Accessories
1810 Fourth St.
Berkeley, CA 94710
(415) 841-2937

Brasslight, Inc.

Among the table and floor lamps offered by this lamp company, all constructed of solid brass, are the Station Light table lamp and Main Street floor model, both illustrated here. Standard heights are 21″ and 53½″ respectively; both can be ordered in custom sizes to suit individual requirements. The finish on each is polished and lacquered brass; other finishes can be specified by the customer. The Station Light swivels at its base, the Main Street model at its shade. Both accommodate standard bulbs.

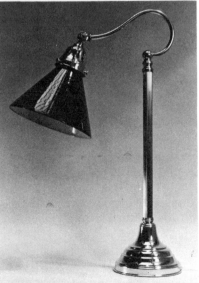

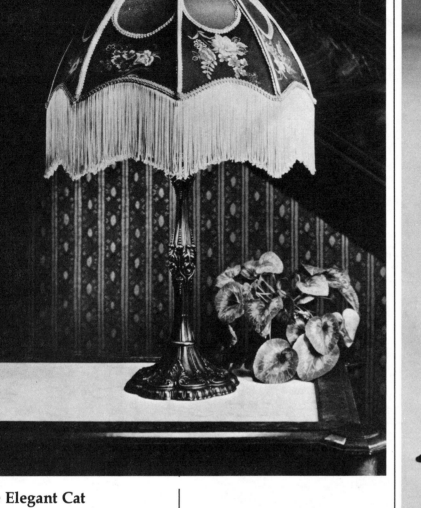

The Elegant Cat

Authentic Art Nouveau lamps are extraordinarily expensive and thus out of the reach of most of us mortals. If your budget won't stretch to accommodate the real thing, you might want to consider a reasonable facsimile. The Elegant Cat offers several different shade designs and various bases for both table and floor models. The shade pictured here can be used on either type of lamp; the company will entertain requests for custom color combinations in fabrics, as well.

Brochure available.

The Elegant Cat
1440 B St.
Eureka, CA 95501
(707) 445-0051

Essex Forge

This copy of an 18th-century candle stand (electrified, of course) will provide a flexible light source for your period room. The harp moves up and down on its 52"-high wrought-iron spindle and turns a full 360 degrees, providing illumination exactly where you need it. The burlap shade is included; finish is antique black.

Catalogue, $2.

The Essex Forge, Inc.
12 Old Dennison Rd.
Essex, CT 06426
(203) 767-1808

Lyn Hovey Studio

Lyn Hovey is that rarest of combinations—both artist and craftsman. His skills with stained glass are such that he and his associates have been called upon to handle delicate restoration work, not only on windows by most of America's famous studios (including Tiffany and LaFarge) but on early European panels as well. Admirers of Tiffany's extraordinary lampshades need not pine

over the scarcity of his work to-day: they can contact Hovey for one of his own (signed) original designs, any one of which even Tiffany might envy. Two are pictured here: if one of Hovey's current creations is not appropriate, he will entertain commissions for shades of individual design and color.

Catalogue, $2.

Lyn Hovey Studio, Inc.
266 Concord Ave.
Cambridge, MA 02138
(617) 492-6566

Hurley Patentee Lighting

The artisans responsible for the superb, handwrought reproduction lighting fixtures of Hurley Patentee need not travel far for inspiration: the company is affiliated with an historic house museum of the same name in New York's beautiful Catskill Mountains. Hurley Patentee Manor, a National Historic Landmark, dates from 1696; among its collections is one of the finest arrays of antique lighting to be found in America. The diminutive (6″) brass oil lamp illustrated is a copy of one from the early 1800s; the iron whaler's lamp, with its swinging circular cage and weighted base, would be at home on a weekend sailor's 20th-century craft.

The formal floor lamp illustrated

(also available in a desk model) dates from the early 1700s. Every fixture, whether crafted of wood, tin, or brass (as is the handsome desk lamp), is handmade using the original techniques of soldering and fitting. Reproductions of designs originally meant to hold candles are available with candlebase sockets to maintain as much authenticity as possible without sacrificing utility; standard sockets can be ordered as well.

Catalogue, $2.

Hurley Patentee Lighting
R.D. 7, Box 98A
Kingston, NY 12401
(914) 331-5414

or green shades. All are fashioned of solid brass and accommodate standard bulbs.

Spivak's designs include sconces, chandeliers, and table lamps—all fitted with glass shades and reminiscent of the best of Victorian, Art Nouveau, and Art Deco styling.

Catalogue available.

Roland Spivak's Custom Lighting
Pendulum Shop
424 South St.
Philadelphia, PA 19147
(215) 925-4014

Lundberg Studios

If you have found just the right Victorian lamp base for just the right corner, but can't find an appropriate shade to complete it, Lundberg Studios may be the place for you. James Lundberg and his brother, Steven, create superb pieces in the manner of Tiffany and Steuben. They offer many sizes and styles of shades, and hand-blown bases are available as well. The company will entertain special projects—it has undertaken restoration work for major landmarks such as Frank Lloyd Wright's Arizona Biltmore Hotel and "The Old Ebbit" in Washington, D.C.

Catalogue, $3.

Lundberg Studios
131 Marineview Ave., Box C
Davenport, CA 95017
(408) 423-2532

St. Louis Antique Lighting

This Missouri-based company began more than a decade ago as antique lighting restoration experts. Proprietor Gary Behm still maintains a stock of original fixtures, but has developed a line of solid-brass reproductions as well. He offers nine separate styles of

table lamps, ranging from gas to early electric models (all electrified), along with a selection of glass shades to match.

Catalogue, $3.

St. Louis Antique Lighting Co.
25 N. Sarah
St. Louis, MO 63108
(314) 535-2770

Roland Spivak's Custom Lighting

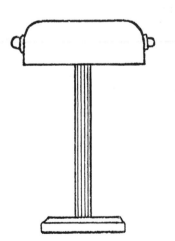

All of the fixtures created by Roland Spivak are his own designs and are available exclusively through his shop. Some styles, such as the library lamp illustrated, are available with either frosted white, white-cased, amber,

Lt. Moses Willard & Company

The pierced-tin Willow lamp base pictured here is handmade by the craftsmen at Lt. Moses Willard and is indicative of the quality and attention to detail for which the company is noted. It is available in a choice of tin finishes and wired for a standard bulb on top and a candelabra bulb inside the base (a three-way switch allows top and bottom bulbs to operate independently). A matching tin shade (not shown) is available. The Willow lamp measures 27" high and 16" wide with shade.

Catalogue, $2.

Lt. Moses Willard & Company
7805 Railroad Ave.
Cincinnati, OH 45243
(513) 561-3942

Lanterns

The original lanterns were nothing more than candles with some sort of protective shield—made of oiled paper, tin, or glass—to guard the flame from sudden gusts of wind. As such, they are one of the earliest, and still among the most attractive, forms of lighting, as is obvious from the following examples. Whether used indoors or out, on a wall or on a table, a lantern can add immeasurably to the charm and warmth of a period home.

A. J. P. Coppersmith

This suburban Boston firm specializes in reproductions of early American lighting fixtures, primarily lanterns, sconces, and chandeliers. The Salem lantern il-

lustrated is available in a wide range of models, with either one, two, or three lights and with candelabra or standard sockets. Its utility is further enhanced because it can be mounted on a wall or hung from an appropriate hook. Each lantern is crafted of copper and is available in either antique copper or brass finish.

Clear glass panes are generally furnished, though special requests—plexiglass, amber or opaque glass, or marine glass—will be honored.

Catalogue available.

A. J. P. Coppersmith
34 Broadway
Wakefield, MA 01880
(617) 245-1216

Essex Forge

The onion globe lantern, probably the most traditional style of the early 18th century, can be found in the collections of many New England museums and illuminates the entrance of many a restored home. Essex Forge reproduces it in copper, with a solid-copper wire frame enclosing the globe. It measures 13″ by 8″ and extends 10″ from the wall.

The onion globe is only one of the painstaking, hand-wrought lanterns available from Essex Forge, many suitable for either exterior or interior use.

Catalogue, $2.

The Essex Forge, Inc.
12 Old Dennison Rd.
Essex, CT 06426
(203) 767-1808

The simple copper lantern illustrated here would look equally well on a post or mounted on a wall. Gates Moore handcrafts the piece in copper; it is available in either oxidized or flat black finish, and comes in two sizes: 6″ by 10″ by 15″ and 8″ by 11¾″ by 18″. Other reproductions of lanterns used in Colonial Boston and Philadelphia are available, as are redwood posts, predrilled to accommodate wiring, which the company recommends be set on 2″ iron pipe and firmly cemented in the ground.

Catalogue, $2.

Gates Moore
River Rd., Silvermine
Norwalk, CT 06850
(203) 847-3231

Lehman Hardware

Among the thousands of unusual items offered in Lehman's eighty-eight page catalogue is the buggy light, a practical kerosene lantern which, as pictured, comes with a red "bull's-eye" conversion kit and mounting bracket. It's easy to think of lots of uses for this utilitarian lantern. Keep it nearby when blizzards or thunderstorms threaten power failure; have one handy on the back stoop for midnight forays to ill-lit parts of the

yard; use it in unelectrified out-buildings—you'll think of dozens more.

Catalogue, $2.

Lehman Hardware & Appliances, Inc.
Box 41
Kidron, OH 44636
(216) 857-5441

Period Lighting Fixtures

Richard Scofield, proprietor of Period Lighting, cautions the uninitiated on the proper selection of a wall lantern—especially when it is to be used out-of-doors.

He suggests that such fixtures are rarely too large, as the facade of the house and the openness of the setting combine to dwarf them. He also recommends that the proper height (especially for a pair of lanterns meant to illuminate the front entrance) be level with the top of the door, or within a foot below it. For instance, the New England barn

lantern illustrated, with its optional pewter reflector, is more than 17" tall; the bracket lantern is 26". Each is hand wrought of copper to insure years of wear and is available in oxidized copper, natural, or flat black finish.

Catalogue, $2.

Period Lighting Fixtures
1 Main St.
Chester, CT 06412
(203) 526-3690

E. G. Washburne & Co.

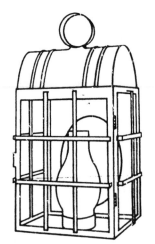

Handmade reproductions of antique lanterns are a specialty at Washburne. The model shown, the firm's number L-60, is available in copper and brass and comes with clear glass pane and frosted chimney. It can be ordered in several forms: for use as a wall lantern, a post light, or to stand

on a complementary table. Available finishes are natural copper, coppertone, antique copper, and flat black. Protective bars can be specified in either "H" or "X" configuration.

Brochures available.

E. G. Washburne & Co.
85 Andover St. - Rt. 114
Danvers, MA 01923
(617) 774-3645

The Washington Copper Works

Serge Miller welcomes visitors to his showroom in the Berkshire foothills; he is justly proud of the workmanship and beauty of all of the lights he and his apprentices create. Each of his copper fixtures is handmade down to its hinges and can be stained, if requested, in a variety of hues from light brown to nearly black. Miller, however, recommends leaving the copper untreated because of the lovely patina it acquires with age.

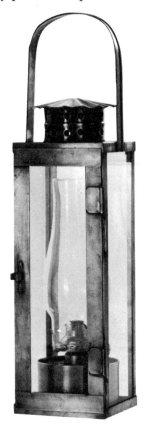

The handsome kerosene lantern illustrated can be carried about when necessary—the handle remains cool—and Miller guarantees the light won't blow out, no matter how fierce the gale. All Washington Copper Works fixtures are approved by Underwriters Laboratories.

Catalogue, $2.

The Washington Copper Works
Washington, CT 06793
(203) 868-7527

Catalogue $2. (Brochure free.)

City Lights
2226 Massachusetts Ave.
Cambridge, MA 02140
(617) 547-1490

Antique Lighting Devices

True period lighting fixtures of an early age are the province of fine antiques dealers and collectors. Rushlights, crusies, Argand lamps, and Sandwich glass whale oil lamp bases command very high prices. They are not, however, impossible to find or to use. Some of these fixtures can be electrified; others only make sense as candle- or oil-burning vessels. Somewhat easier to locate are the kerosene lamps, gas fixtures, combination gas and electric chandeliers, and early electric lamps. Some second-hand dealers have specialized in their retrieval from doomed structures and effectively recycled them for new use. Increasingly, however, such later fixtures are being handled by special dealers. In those parts of the country where Victorian architecture is the norm and does not play second fiddle to Colonial, they are somewhat easier to come by. But renewed interest in Victorian decor is driving the prices up for all but the most mundane pieces.

Greg's Antique Lighting

Brass Light of Historic Walker's Point

Stephen Kaniewski, proprietor of Brass Light, specializes in finding and restoring superb Victorian and later gas, electric, and combination gas/electric chandeliers and sconces. He also has a wide selection of table and floor lamps from the same era. If nothing but an original will do, call or write Brass Light for photos and descriptions of the type of fixture you have in mind.

For further information, contact:

Brass Light of Historic Walker's Point
719 S. 5th St.
Milwaukee, WI 53204
(414) 383-0675

Citybarn Antiques

Connoisseurs of lighting from the period 1850 to 1920 will want to contact this shop. It routinely carries a stock of between 100 and 150 Victorian chandeliers and wall lights and is happy to entertain requests for specific styles and types of fixtures. Photos and descriptions of antique fixtures are available to prospective customers.

For further information, contact:

Citybarn Antiques
362 Atlantic Ave.
Brooklyn, NY 11217
(212) 855-8566

City Lights

City Lights sells only fully restored antique lighting (mostly brass). Christopher Osborne is so proud of the painstaking work he does to bring a piece back to life that he explains the process in his brochure. First, the fixture is dismantled and all necessary repairs are made, including soldering, straightening, and replacement of parts as needed (from his stock of antique pieces). Next the components are submerged in a chemical bath to strip the metal bare, then burnished, cleaned, lacquered, and reassembled (they are electrified at this point). Last, the piece is outfitted with complementary (and original) glass shades. Among the hard-to-find lights usually available here are floor lamps—in a wide variety of styles and sizes.

Greg Davidson carries a comprehensive selection of lighting fixtures, wall sconces, and table and floor lamps, primarily of American origin, which cover various styles and periods from 1850 to 1930. As most of his offerings are one-of-a-kind, he does not produce a catalogue, but can send photos in response to specific inquiries received by mail or telephone. Pictured here are two of his recent finds. The first, a gracefully designed gas wall light (c. 1855), displays its original ruby glass shades with gold veins. The second, a combination gas/electric chandelier which dates from about 1895 and features ornate detailing on the arms and pendant.

Since Greg's has the largest stock of antique fixtures on the West Coast, an appointment to visit

this first-rate supplier would be well worth your while.

For further information, contact:

Greg's Antique Lighting
12005 Wilshire Blvd.
W. Los Angeles, CA 90025
(213) 478-5475

Half Moon Antiques

When only an original will do, the old-house enthusiast might contact Half Moon Antiques, as the company carries only antique lighting fixtures with the original glass shades. It specializes in devices made between 1870 and 1930; each is expertly restored and rewired and the brass polished and lacquered. The ever-changing selection includes chandeliers, ceiling pendants, wall sconces, table and floor lamps, and hard-to-find ceiling fixtures for low-ceilinged rooms. Half Moon exhibits at antiques shows throughout the country; proprietors Lee & Lynne Roberts will be happy to send show schedules or to see customers by appointment at their Red Bank, New Jersey, showroom. The two chandeliers illustrated here are indicative of the selection Half Moon maintains: a combination electric/gas fixture (c. 1895) with clear pressed-glass shades, and a brass model with hand-painted milk-glass shades which dates from about 1925.

For further information, contact:

Half Moon Antiques
Box 141
Fair Haven, NJ 07701
(201) 842-1863

The Old Lamplighter Shop

The Old Lamplighter specializes in restoring antique lighting fixtures; many of them are available for sale, or they'll fix yours for you. If you are a do-it-yourselfer, they can supply the parts you need. The shop carries a full selection of glass shades in every size to suit every lamp. Custom-painted china shades can be ordered to suit. It it's a glass chimney you need, you can choose from fifty-two sizes—in both clear and frosted styles.

Brochure available.

The Lamplighter Shop
Route 12-B
Deansboro, NY 13328
(315) 841-8774

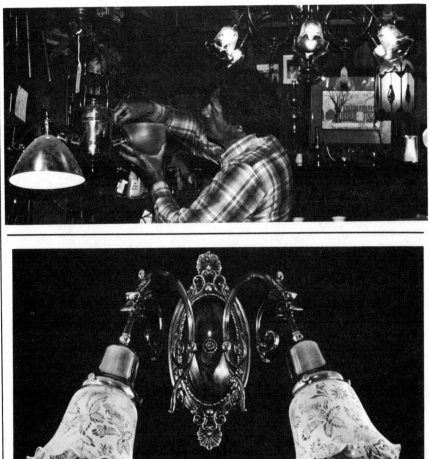

Readers of past *Old House Catalogues* are familiar with the wide variety of antique lighting fixtures offered by Bill Sweeney and his two sons. Both their workshop and adjacent three-story barn are filled with such pieces, each of which is lovingly restored, wired, and refurbished. Chandeliers, table lamps, and wall sconces are present in abundance, but the turnover is much too great to permit the recreation of a comprehensive catalogue. The Yankee craftsmen welcome inquiries and are happy to supply photos and detailed information to meet the precise needs of prospective customers. They take special pride in creating one-of-a-kind pieces from antique lamp parts.

For further information, contact:

Yankee Craftsman
357 Commonwealth Rd.
Wayland, MA 01778
(617) 653-0031

Roy Electric Co.

Brooklyn is chock-a-block with 19th-century brownstones. Many neighborhoods of this New York borough have been the targets of massive restoration drives in recent years. Roy and Roz Greenstein have taken advantage of the refurbishment of their native borough to collect, restore, and rewire (or electrify) thousand of antique fixtures. The two ornate Victorian wall sconces pictured here give only a rudimentary idea of the variety of the fixtures they offer. In addition to original lighting devices, the Greensteins also offer a fine line of exact reproductions.

Catalogue, $3.

Roy Electric Co., Inc.
1054 Coney Island Avenue
Brooklyn, NY 11230
(212) 339-6311 or 761-7905

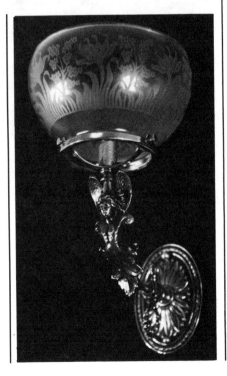

Outdoor Lighting Fixtures

It makes little sense to spend years—not to mention dollars—restoring and refurbishing the interior of a period home only to neglect its exterior appointments. Unfortunately, however, the senseless often occurs. The aisles of building-supply stores and lighting shops are filled with "rustic" horrors that can easily destroy the appearance of an old house. But there are also postlights, doorway lanterns, and even garden lamps to dispel the gloom of contemporary bad taste. Besides lighting the way to the door, these handsome fixtures provide a cheerful welcome to the night visitor. As an alternative to the floodlit look of a prison yard, increasingly common in these security-conscious days, the delightful period fixtures that follow are definitely to be preferred.

| # A. J. P. Coopersmith

Visitors to Boston will probably have noticed that the city has been outfitted with countless reproductions of Colonial streetlights. A. J. P. Coopersmith crafts them of heavy-gauge copper with thick glass and heavy-duty wiring. The firm's Boston Street Light Special, as it's called, is suitable as well for a post light outside a period home. It measures 48" tall and 15½" wide and can be mounted easily on a standard 3" post fitter. Coppersmith hand-fashions other early American designs as well. All are made of either copper or brass and are finished in a hand-rubbed antique patina. Exterior fixtures are also available in a lead-coated copper finish designed to reflect the look of aged pewter.

Catalogue available.

A. J. P. Coppersmith
34 Broadway
Wakefield, MA 01880
(617) 245-1216

Spring City Electrical

This venerable company began as a manufacturer of cast-iron stoves in 1843; it has remained under the ownership of the same family for more than sixty years. As one might expect, therefore, the array of cast-iron lampposts it offers is wide indeed. Each, from the sleek Franklin (designed by Benjamin himself) to designs introduced in the 1920s and '30s, has been historically validated. All posts are made to order, so that the type of light source desired—incandescent, mercury vapor, metal halide, or high-pressure sodium—can be accommodated. Heights range from 6' 11" to more than 23' depending on style (some come in several lengths).

Full-color catalogue, $3 (refundable with purchase).

Spring City Electrical Mfg. Co.
Drawer A
Spring City, PA 19475
(215) 948-4000

E. G. Washburne & Co.

While even the most intrepid antique-hunter might have difficulty finding an authentic gas streetlight of the type used in the Boston area more than a century ago, superb replicas, such as the lantern illustrated here, are readily available from Washburne. Model L-136 is crafted in copper, with clear glass and a frosted chimney. The bell- and ball-topped post lantern can be ordered in 24", 30" or 36" heights and in any of four finishes: Natural Copper, Coppertone, Antique Copper, or Flat Black. Washburne suggests that the lantern looks best if it's chosen in a size at least one-third the height of the post. The original of the 36" model, for instance, was meant to be used on a post at least 7' high.

Free brochures available.

E. G. Washburne & Co.
85 Andover St., Rt. 114
Danvers, MA 01923
(617) 774-3645

The Washington Copper Works

The exquisite, classic candleholder shown on the opposite page, would look equally well in an 18th-century stone manor house or a modern city apartment and would enhance any patio, porch, or dining room table you place them on. They are even practical —that is, if you take a tip from Serge Miller, proprietor of Washington Copper Works. No need to scrape the melted wax from the bottom: merely stick them in the freeezer for a couple of hours, then turn them upside down and give them a few good whacks. (The copper carpet tack remains to hold your next candle.)

Another beautiful, handmade copper fixture from Miller's Berkshires studio that will serve equally well indoors or out is the Gunnery Wall Light, a compact (7" x 7" x 14½"), weatherproof model that accommodates a standard electric bulb.

Catalogue, $2.

The Washington Copper Works
Washington, CT 06793
(203) 868-7527

Winterthur

It would be sad, indeed, if you spent months or years planning and executing a superb early American garden to complement your period home and then ruin the effect with inappropriate outdoor lighting. But that needn't happen. The experts at the Winterthur Museum have selected just the right patio lights to scatter throughout the garden, line a path, or illuminate a set of steps. The glass reservoir (for kerosene or lamp oil) fits snugly into a steel base; the base is decorated with acanthus leaves of the sort found as motifs on much late-Federal furniture in Winterthur's collection. The fittings are solid brass, the globe hand-blown glass. Overall height (including the steel shaft which slips easily into the ground) is 42"; the globe is 2½" wide. Specify Wintherthur order number 13-324.

Catalogue available.

Direct Mail Marketing Office
Winterthur Museum and Gardens
Winterthur, DE 19735
(800) 441-8229
(302) 656-8591 in DE

Supplies and Services

While many of us wouldn't hesitate to tackle painting, repapering, and furniture refinishing, we tend to freeze when confronted with a faulty light cord. What, then, do we do with the Victorian sconce just purchased at auction, which is perfect save for the fact that it hasn't been converted from gas to electricity? The solution is a relatively simple one. Many of the craftsmen who sell antique and reproduction fixtures will also undertake the restoration and rewiring. Others can supply missing parts— shades, finials, drops, globes—for a variety of fixtures as well.

Bradford Consultants

There could be nothing less appropriate than a vintage 1980s electric light bulb illuminating a vintage 1920 fixture. For that special early 20th-century lamp (even when visibility is an issue), Bradford Consultants can supply classic bulbs first introduced between 1909 and 1930. These are Edison-type carbon loop filament bulbs which recreate the soft, mellow light of the early electric age. Bradford offers three different models, ranging in subtle brightness from eight to sixteen candlepower.

Brochure available.

Bradford Consultants
16 E. Homestead Ave.
Collingswood, NJ 08108
(609) 854-1404

Campbell Lamps

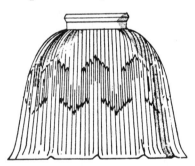

If the authentic turn-of-the-century fixture picked up for a song at the flea market is minus its shade, don't despair. Chances are that Campbell Lamps has just the right one. The company carries a vast assortment of glass shades for both gas and electric fixtures, in a rainbow of colors and patterns. In addition, it offers brass globe holders and back plates, finials, arm backs, and much more: the offerings are so extensive that its catalogue doesn't hold them all. Campbell Lamps suggests a visit to its suburban Philadelphia showroom and welcomes inquiries about hard-to-find items.

Catalogue, $2.

Campbell Lamps
Dept. 26, 1108 Pottstown Pike
West Chester, PA 19380
(215) 696-8070

Crawford's Old House Store

Hard-to-find crystal prisms for chandeliers are a specialty of Crawford's; its catalogue illustrates seven different styles, ranging in length from 1½" to 4". Discounts are offered for orders of a dozen or more. Replacement gas/electric shades for Victorian wall sconces and ceiling lights are also offered, as are brass shade holders and carbon filament bulbs. Crawford's also has a small selection of inexpensive reproductions of Victorian chandeliers and wall sconces, in both gas and electric styles.

Catalogue, $1.75.

Crawford's Old House Store
301 McCall
Waukesha, WI 53186
(414) 542-0685

The Arden Forge

Peter Renzetti and his staff have become so adept at restoring antique metal work—from hinges and fireplace accessories to weather vanes and copper lanterns—that they are often called upon by museums, antiques dealers, and major private collectors to return old pieces to life. If you have a treasured antique post light that needs expert care, you couldn't find a more knowledgeable doctor than Renzetti. If the piece is beyond help, he may be willing to produce an exact copy for you.

The Arden Forge Co.
301 Brintons Bridge Rd.
West Chester, PA 19380
(215) 399-1530

Elcanco

Once you've chosen just the right candelabra-based lantern, sconce, or chandelier, you may have problems finding enough electric candles to illuminate it. Not only are the candles themselves sometimes difficult to find, but modern ones tend to spoil the effect of a period fixture. Elcanco has a variety of electric candles

and flame-like bulbs to fit nearly every light. The company also offers beeswax covers with hand-applied wax drippings that can be slipped over conventional wired sockets.

Brochure available.

Elcanco
60 Chelmsford St.
Chelmsford, MA 01824
(617) 256-8809 or 256-9972

Kyp-Go

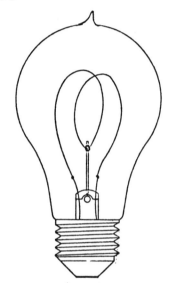

Early carbon-filament incandescent bulbs, first developed in teh late 1870s by Sir Joseph Swan and Thomas Alva Edison, and improved during the last years of the 19th century, emitted a soft glow that looked particularly attractive when reflected in the etched-glass shades used in early fixtures. Kyp-Go has been manufacturing such bulbs for twenty years; while its process is, of course, more efficient than Edison's, the result produces a warm, mellow glow missing in modern lighting and the carbon filament lasts far longer than its 1980s equivalents. Kyp-Go's bulb is a perfect complement to the turn-of-the-century chandelier, whether authentic or reproduction, which illuminates your dining room.

Brochure available.

Kyp-Go, Inc.
Box 147
Naperville, IL 60540
(312) 584-8181

E. W. Pyfer

Whether you want to have a period lamp rewired, think that great-grandma's flower vase would make a perfect lighting centerpiece for the kitchen table, need a part for the oil lantern you just purchased at auction, or have an art glass shade that needs repair, E. W. Pyfer can help. He specializes in giving new life to old lights and asks only that you call or write for an appointment or for detailed information.

E. W. Pyfer
218 N. Foley
Freeport, IL 61032
(815) 232-8968

The Shade Tree

Gail Teller, whose intricately wrought cut and pierced lamp shades of parchment paper were once featured among the offerings of Connecticut's Lamplighter Shoppe, has now opened her own business. Her shades are still designed, executed, and finished with minute attention to detail; she offers a brochure explaining the various patterns and options available. Three different types of

cut and pierced shades are made: Empire (standard), Hexagon, and Flame (candle clip). The Flame shades are also available with stencil designs on paper or muslin. Illustrated are two of the Empire designs. All shades are lined with paper or fabric in white or special colors, and are trimmed with grosgrain and velvet.

Brochure, $1.

The Shade Tree
6 Half-King Dr.
Burlington, CT 06013
(203) 673-9358

Squaw Alley

No matter what you need to complete the restoration work on an old table lamp, you'll probably find the pieces at Squaw Alley. From shades to sockets, canopies to chimneys, this retail shop stocks a staggering assortment of reproduction—and antique—hardware and fixtures. If your talents don't run to wiring or restoring that precious antique, Squaw Alley can do it for you.

Catalogue, $3.

Squaw Alley, Inc.
401 S. Main St.
Naperville, IL 60540
(312) 357-0200

Other Suppliers of Lighting

Consult List of Suppliers for addresses.

Chandeliers

Arrowhead Forge
Dutch Products & Supply Co.
Greene's Lighting Fixtures Inc.
Hubbardton Forge and Wood Corp.
King's Chandelier Co.
Luigi Crystal
Nowell's Inc.
The Old Lamp Shop
The Rambusch Co.
The Saltbox
Turn of the Century Lighting
Victorian Reproduction Lighting Co.

Hanging and Ceiling Fixtures

Ball & Ball
Colonial Williamsburg
Heritage Lanterns
MarLe Co.
Matthew Richardson
The Old Lamp Shop
The Saltbox
Sturbridge Yankee Workshop
Turn of the Century Lighting

Wall Fixtures

Alcon Lightcraft Co.
Baldwin Hardware
Gates Moore
Nowell's Inc.
The Rambusch Co.
The Saltbox
Victorian Lighting Works

Table and Floor Lamps

The Blacksmith Shop (Orleans, MA)
Newton Millham
Royal Windyne Ltd.
Victorian Reproduction Enterprises
  Inc.
Welsbach

Lanterns

Heritage Lanterns
Mewstamp Lighting Co.
The Saltbox
Village Lanterns
Wrightsville Hardware

Antique Lighting Devices

Canal Co.
City Knickerbocker, Inc.
Graham's Lighting Fixtures
Illustrious Lighting
London Venturers Co.
C. Neri Antiques
The Old Lamp Shop
Sandy Springs Galleries
Stanley Galleries

Outdoor Lighting Fixtures

Antique Street Lamps
Hammerworks Ironware
Period Lighting Fixtures
Valley Iron & Steel Co.
Victorian Reproduction Enterprises
Welsbach Lighting

Services and Supplies

B & P Lamp Supply Co., Inc.
Coran-Shales Industries
Dermit X. Cotcoran Antique Services
Custom House
Old Lamplighter Shop
E. W. Pyfer
Squaw Alley
Victorian Lighcrafters

5.

Heating and Cooking

These days, when the hearth is only metaphorically the center of the home, it is often difficult to imagine the efforts our forebears devoted simply to keeping warm and to cooking their food. If you were to examine the design and appointments of a 200-year-old farmhouse, for example, it would be immediately clear that in days before central heating and electricity, buildings were designed primarily with the elements in mind. Rooms had small windows to prevent the cold from penetrating, hearths were built with slanting backs to throw heat into the room, fireplaces were placed everywhere the family gathered, and the kitchen, with its constantly burning fire, was the focus of all activities.

Today we can forego many of our ancestors' hardships, but we also lose the spirit, vigor, and homely pleasures of older times. Nonetheless, with the high cost of fuel and system maintenance, some old-fashioned ideas have a real place in modern life. A wood- or coal-burning stove, for example, can be appropriate in a house of any period. Several firms today produce reproduction models that are attractive and highly efficient. What they cost in hours of splitting wood or carrying coal, they make up in reduced fuel bills, coziness, and a touch of pioneer spirit. Fireplaces, in spite of their basic inefficiency, are too decorative to pass up and can be fitted with efficient grills to hold fuel, firebacks to reflect heat, fireboards to cover the opening when not in use, and all sorts of inserts to increase their heating power.

As for cooking, the convenience of modern appliances is indisputable. Surprisingly efficient coal and wood cookstoves are still available, however, and can be an interesting addition to period kitchens.

If you do plan to use a stove or fireplace in your old house, it is crucial to examine carefully the condition of chimney, flues, and hearths. Aside from a deteriorating flue, which is the quickest way to burn the house down, faulty roof flashing and dampers can be hazardous. Dirty flues, filled with creosote, can cause chimney fires and release dangerous gases into the room. We have therefore described in these pages many companies that can provide maintenance and design for stoves and fireplaces. Unless you are an expert in this area, these tasks are best left to the pros. In fact, many building inspectors and insurance companies will only accept work done by qualified and licensed professionals.

Glenwood Base Heater No. 3, Good Time Stove Co., Goshen, Massachusetts.

Antique Stoves

The choice of wood as an alternative fuel source in recent years has rescued many an old cast-iron monster from the junkyard. But before you buy one of these originals, beware. While an antique can be equally as warming as a reproduction, make sure that it has been expertly refurbished. A stove that isn't airtight can be just as great a fuel thief as that oil burner down in the basement, and a hundred times as dangerous.

Aetna Stove

As the picture of Aetna's storefront indicates, Aetna has been making stoves for many years. Established in 1890, it has been at the same location in Philadelphia's historic district since 1912 and is now operated by the third generation of the Markowitz family. Whatever you're looking for, be it a new or reconditioned wood or coal stove, a cast-iron floor register (Aetna has both originals and reproductions), or a hard-to-find part for the antique stove you already have, this venerable firm can probably supply it.

Brochure available.

Aetna Stove Co., Inc.
S.E. Corner 2nd and Arch Sts.
Philadelphia, PA 19106
(215) 627-2008

Agape Antiques

The parlor stoves and kitchen ranges offered by Dave and Ruth Wells of Agape are all period pieces (from the 1830s to the 1930s) that have been professionally restored. All, of course, are one-of-a-kind items. Agape also has an extensive inventory of old parts for such models that you may be restoring yourself. The shop offers new liners and wood grates for Glenwood and Crawford stoves, which are its specialties. Illustrated is a Glenwood C-model coal and wood cookstove.

Catalogue available.

Agape Antiques
Box 225
Saxtons River, VT 05154
(802) 869-2273

Good Time Stove

Many modern wood stoves, though certainly efficient, tend to be uninspired, often badly designed adjuncts to an old house. A better choice, and just as utilitarian, would be one of the many original 19th- or early 20th-century models available from Richard "Stove Black" Richardson at Good Time. As the late-Victorian cookstove illustrated demonstrates, Richardson is an expert at restoring these old beauties. He guarantees every stove he sells—whether it's a small parlor model or a gas/wood combination behemoth intended for a country kitchen. If you have an antique that needs restoration, Richardson's craftsmen will reset

the doors and hinges, reseal all seams, replace missing parts, and guarantee the result for a year.

Catalogue available.

Good Time Stove Co.
Rte. 112, Box 306
Goshen, MA 01032
(413) 268-3677

Portland Stove

In addition to selling reconditioned antique wood and coal cookstoves (most of them originally manufactured by the Atlantic Company), Portland Stove offers a wide variety of replacement parts, including grates and liners, and can restore most other makes as well. The company also manufactures, to special order, a variety of Franklin stoves, a B & M potbelly stove, and one model of the old

Atlantic box stove. All are authentic reproductions of original 19th-century designs. Illustrated is Atlantic's Princess-model cookstove, a cast-iron antique from the turn of the century.

Brochures available, $1.

Portland Stove Co.
Fickett Rd.
North Pownal, ME 04069
(207) 688-2254

West Barnstable Stove Shop

Doug Pacheco buys, restores, and sells antique wood and coal stoves. He specializes in turn-of-the-century cookstoves and parlor stoves. If foundry recasting or nickel plating of parts is required, he is skilled in the work. In addition to the changing inventory of stoves, he maintains a large stock of substitute parts, including grates. He also stocks isinglass.

Brochure, $1.

West Barnstable Stove Shop
Box 472
W. Barnstable, MA 02668
(617) 362-9913

Reproduction Stoves

Many companies have capitalized on the recent demand for wood-burning stoves by mass-producing them in record numbers. It's therefore easy to find one; what's difficult is to locate one that's handsome as well as utilitarian. The manufacturers listed in the following section have not sacrificed style for the sake of utility or profit: they offer many attractive models, some basd on 19th-century originals, in a variety of sizes and styles to suit every need.

Lehman Hardware & Appliances

If you're fortunate enough to have a luxuriously roomy old-fashioned kitchen and want a stove to match, you might consider Lehman's aptly named Enterprise Monarch, a first-rate reproduction of a late-Victorian cookstove (illustrated on the following page). This beauty is 5' tall and nearly as wide. It will accommodate either wood or coal, boasts a large oven with a tempered glass panel in the door, a warming closet, an optional 10-gallon warm water reservoir (seen to the right of the oven), and a gleaming black porcelain-enamel and nickel-plated exterior. The Monarch is shipped complete with ash scraper, shaker, poker, and lifter. At the other end of the spectrum is Lehman's compact gas hot plate (also shown on the following page). The cast-iron burners (from one to three depending on model) can be individually regulated and convert easily from propane to natural gas.

Catalogue, $2.

Lehman Hardware & Appliances, Inc.
Box 41
Kidron, OH 44636
(216) 857-5441

Upland Woodstoves

Upland's handsomely designed model 207 cast-iron stove, illustrated, will heat an area as large as 10,000 cubic feet. It is available with either a top or rear flue exit, can be ordered with an optional glass door, and can be installed in an existing fireplace if desired. Upland's three other models, all somewhat smaller than this style, range in size from 27" to 31½" in height and from 12½" to 20" in width. Since Upland has dealers throughout the country, installation and maintenance are relatively easy to arrange.

Brochure available.

Upland Woodstoves
2 Green St., Box 361
Greene, NY 13778
(607) 656-4156

Vermont Iron

The unusual rounded shape of Vermont Iron's Elm and Catalytic Elm models makes them superior to most other wood stoves, according to the company, because the design results in a hotter, more efficient fire. The Catalytic Elm model, illustrated, houses a special "Corning Catalytic Combustor" in its fluted cast-iron top. The company claims that this addition produces 20% more heat, 75% fewer pollutants, and 90% less creosote. Both models can be inserted in an existing fireplace or used free-standing as desired.

Brochure available.

Vermont Iron, Inc.
424 Prince St.
Waterbury, VT 05676
(802) 244-5254

Woodstock Soapstone

While most antique and reproduction wood stoves are made of cast iron, there is an alternative, a more efficient one, according to David Chioffi, founder of this Vermont firm. Soapstone produces gentle, even heat without the temperature fluctuations of metal; warms efficiently at low heat output; and holds coals long after the fire has died down, so rekindling from the coals is quick and easy. Chioffi manufactures his handsome soapstone stove with iron castings and double soapstone walls, in three models: the

Woodstock, patterned after a century-old New England piece; the Classic, with its solid front and glass door; and the latest and most popular, the Fireview (illustrated), with a glass front and solid door. The modified Gothic styling makes the Fireview a par-

ticularly handsome addition to a mid-Victorian room setting.

Brochures available.

Woodstock Soapstone Co.
Box 223/371, Rte. 4
Woodstock, VT 05091
(802) 672-5133

Heating Supplies

It's not particularly difficult to find floor and ceiling hot-air registers, chimney collars to hide the ugly intersection of pipe and wall, or other necessary adjuncts to the heating system. What can be frustrating, however, is finding such supplies to

complement your decor as well as to perform a useful function. The following companies have taken great care in manufacturing or stocking such accessories with form as well as utility in mind.

Hearth & Home

Once you've selected just the right wood stove and had it properly installed, you may be left with an unsightly connection where the stove pipe meets the wall. Hearth & Home can easily solve the problem. Decorative, solid-brass chimney collars are the firm's specialty. They are available in three sizes to fit 6", 7", or 8" pipe, and can be selected in either natural brass finish or with copper or nickel overlay.

Brochure available.

Hearth & Home Co.
Box 371
Brielle, NJ 08730
(201) 223-3218

Lyemance International

If your current fireplace damper is in need of replacement, or that ancient chimney never had one to begin with, consider the top-sealing damper available from Lyemance. It's easy to install on chimneys with or without flue liners, eliminates the need for a chimney cap, seals in heat and air conditioning while sealing out birds and animals, and is available in three standard sizes. Lyemance will be happy to send a list of dealers and distributors in your area.

Brochure available.

Lyemance International
Box 505
Jeffersonville, IN 47131
(812) 288-9953

Reggio Register

Rugged cast iron makes the floor registers and ceiling grilles available from Reggio virtually indestructible; careful design makes them attractive as well as utilitarian adjuncts to forced hot-air heating systems or wood-burning stoves. Illustrated is a variety of replacement floor grilles, available in various sizes, any one of which would be a handsome alternative to the plain, stamped metal grilles commonly utilized with such systems. The round cast-iron grille would be a

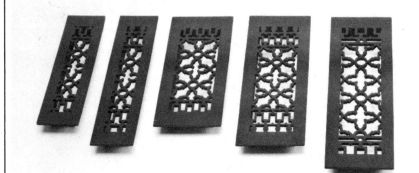

good choice if floor or wall thickness is minimal; it can also be used with 8" round duct pipe and works well with a suspended or dropped ceiling. Reggio grilles are also available in brass. The firm offers a variety of accessories as well—including fireplace tools, flexible air ducts, and register boots.

Catalogue, $1.

The Reggio Register Co.
Box 511, Dept. OHC
Ayer, MA 01432
(617) 772-3493

Mantels

If you're fortunate enough to have one or more working fireplaces, good period mantels will be of interest to you. Every fireplace should be properly "framed," in much the same way you would set off a treasured painting. The companies listed in the following section can supply antique and reproduction mantels in a variety of styles, materials, and sizes to meet every need and to suit every period decor. Other suppliers can be found in chapter 1, Structural Products and Services.

Decorators Supply

Reproduction mantels in a variety of styles—basically inspired by the Colonial period—are a specialty of Decorators Supply. Stock mantels are constructed of birch and poplar with composition ornaments applied; walnut or oak can be special ordered. Each mantel is made to the customer's specifications so that odd sizes can be accommodated easily. Illustrated is the Adam model, No. 15731.

Catalogue, $2.

Decorators Supply Corp.
3610-12 S. Morgan St.
Chicago, IL 60609
(312) 847-6300

Jerard Paul Jordan Gallery

Jerard Paul Jordan and his associate, Pat Guthman, are specialists in 18th- and early 19th-century building materials, architectural components, and hearth accessories. So if the parlor mantel in your newly acquired Colonial farmhouse is beyond repair and you can't bear the throught of replacing it with a flimsy reproduction, you might want to get in touch with the Jordan Gallery. Jordan will not only supply the proper mantel, but make sure that it is properly installed as well.

Catalogue, $4.

Jerard Paul Jordan Gallery
Box 71, Slade Rd.
Ashford, CT 06278
(203) 429-7954

Ye Olde Mantel Shoppe

Its folksy name notwithstanding, this Florida company stocks a wide variety of rare old marble and wood mantels, along with a number of quality reproductions. The handsome antique English mantel illustrated, for instance, was removed from a mansion in Essex. It dates from c. 1847 and features elaboate decorative carving. Similar handcrafted treasures are always available at this well-known shop.

Catalogue available.

Ye Olde Mantel Shoppe
3800 NE 2nd Ave.
Miami, FL 33137
(305) 576-0225

Maintenance and Design

While most owners of conventional heating systems include regular cleaning and maintenance checks in the cost of those systems, many of the same people balk at the expense involved in keeping fireplace chimneys and wood stoves in good working order. And that's unfortunate. Proper liners and clean flues are essential for efficient operation—not to mention safety; ignoring them can be very costly in the long run. Your local phone book can supply the name of a good chimney sweep; for more complicated maintenance work, you may wish to contact one of the following specialists.

Chimney Relining International

If your chimney is crumbling at the mortar joints, needs cleaning more than once a year, or if you've had a chimney fire, it may be time to reline it. Relining, however, can be costly and time-consuming. This New Hampshire company offers a safe, inexpensive method of chimney relining called Permaflu. A rubber former provides a smooth, seamless mold for the insulated masonry mix which is poured into it. When the mix has hardened, the former is removed. This method provides fully reconditioned flues in even crooked and deteriorating chimneys without costly and disruptive reconstruction. For the franchised Permaflu dealer nearest you, contact:

Chimney Relining International, Inc.
105 W. Merrimack St., Box 4035
Manchester, NH 03108
(603) 668-5195

Flue Works

Before you light the first romantic fire in the parlor hearth of your old house, check to make sure that it's safe to do so. Flue Works specializes in relining chimneys with stainless-steel pipe, clay tile, or insulating castable refractories. The company has devised a method of removing cracked and damaged clay tile liners and installing new ones without having to rebuild the whole chimney or tear out the face. If your existing 19th-century fireplace must be converted from coal or gas, Flue Works offers the patented Victorian Rumford fireplace as an efficient, safe, and attractive wood-burning masonry fireplace appropriate for such a potentially dangerous restoration.

Brochure available.

Flue Works Inc.
86 Warren St.
Columbus, OH 43215
(614) 291-6918

National Supaflu Systems

Like Permaflu, National Supaflu has developed a tested, proven way to reline a chimney without taking it apart. A pneumatic rubber former is inserted from the top, then a special aggregate mix is poured in around it. When the mix hardens, it will withstand temperatures of over 2200 degrees, exceeding UL standards. National Supaflu has franchises througout the country. Call or write for the name of the dealer nearest you.

Brochure available.

National Supaflu Systems, Inc.
Rte. 30A, Box 289
Central Bridge, NY 12035
(518) 868-4585

Preway

In this age of higher oil and natural gas prices, it has become accepted practice to enclose woodburning fireplaces so as to reduce heat loss through their chimneys. Owners of period homes may shudder at the thought of such inserts: many of them are as ugly as they are practical. Preway, however, offers several handsomely designed polished-brass or black-enamel masonry inserts with bi-fold glass doors which will solve the problem in a most attractive way. The inserts can be installed easily by even a novice; they are made to fit fireplace openings from 28″ to 42″ in width and 24″ and 29″ in height. Adjustable front-control flue dampers and combustion air vents assure an efficient burn rate; the built-in heat circulation systems draw in cool room air, heat it in a sealed chamber, and return it warmed to the room.

Brochures available.

Preway Inc.
1430 Second St. N.
Wisconsin Rapids, WI 54494
(715) 423-1100

Firebacks and Fireboards

After more than a century of virtual obscurity, firebacks and fireboards are enjoying a resurgence of popularity. It's easy to understand why. A fireback is not only a handsome addition to a period hearth, but helps to radiate heat outward into the room as well. Decorative fireboards seal the fireplace opening to prevent heat loss as the fire dies (and to block the escape of cooler air in the summer).

Adams

To complement its attractive line of fireplace accessories (andirons, screens, and lighters, to name only a few), The Adams Company offers a group of European-made firebacks. Inspired by centuries-old designs, ranging from coats of arms to provincial scenes, each is made of durable cast iron to reflect the fire's heat into the room and to help protect the stone or brick from eventual damage. There are eleven different styles to choose from and the sizes are equally varied: the smallest measures 15″ by 15″, the largest 31″ by 34″. Illustrated are the Louis XV (003) and Escutcheon with Lions (018) designs.

Brochures available.

The Adams Co.
100 E. Fourth St.
Dubuque, IA 52001
(319) 583-3591

Nostalgia

Historic old Savannah is a treasure trove of 19th-century architecture, most of it located in the central historic district, one of the largest landmark areas in the country. Housed in a Victorian building, Nostalgia is perfectly situated to capitalize on the architectural heritage of its neighborhood. All of the company's reproduction iron fire screens and surrounds, including those illustrated here, are cast from

originals found in Savannah homes. Most are available in either cast iron or aluminum; dimensions vary with the particular style selected.

Catalogue, $2.50.

Nostalgia, Inc.
307 Stiles Ave.
Savannah, GA 31401
(912) 232-2324

Helen Williams

In addition to her outstanding collection of antique Delft tiles (one of the largest in the United States), Helen Williams maintains a fine selection of 17th-century Dutch iron firebacks. A representative piece is illustrated here. Ms. Williams will be happy to send information about the other superb antiques she has available.

Brochure available. (SASE requested.)

Helen Williams/Rare Tiles
12643 Hortense St.
North Hollywood, CA 91604
(818) 761-2756

Fireplace Accessories

If you've just taken possession of the old house of your dreams and are about to purchase the first accessories for a fireplace, you'll probably want to begin with andirons, tools, and a screen. There are hundreds of styles and sizes to choose from: some of the best and most attractive are described in the following listings. After you've *taken care of those necessities, you might consider additional pieces. How about a wood box? Or a swinging crane from which to hang a cast-iron pot? Or a brass firelighter? Any of these pieces, if selected with an eye to design and workmanship, can increase your enjoyment of the fireplace for years to come.*

Adams

No wood-burning fireplace would be complete without the proper accessories—tongs, bellows, brush, shovel, poker—arrayed nearby. Adams has a wide range of such tools, each designed with both utility and aesthetic appeal in mind. The handsome cherry wood bellows illustrated, for in- stance, has a solid-brass turned spout and leather covering. The cast-iron firelighter is made up of a pot, lid, handle, and torch rod, is available in various finishes, and is 8¾" high and 5½" in diameter.

Brochures available.

The Adams Co.
100 E. Fourth St.
Dubuque, IA 52001
(319) 583-3591

Ball and Ball

In addition to its superb line of quality reproduction hardware (see chapter 6), Ball and Ball carries some unusual fireplace accessories. Among the most difficult to find are jamb hooks, intended to keep the handles of fire tongs and shovels in place while the bottoms rest on the hearth or on a special tool stone (which the company can also supply). In addition to its handsome reproduction fireplace tools, Ball and Ball generally has two or three antique fire sets on hand, carefully restored and refurbished.

Catalogue, $5.

Ball and Ball
463 W. Lincoln Hwy.
Exton, PA 19341
(215) 363-7330

The Essex Forge

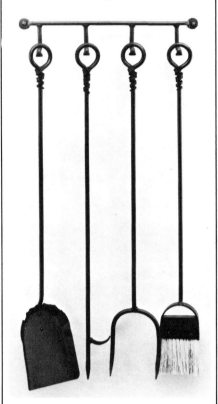

Fireplace tools must be sturdy, but they needn't be unattractive. There is little advantage in appointing a handsome Colonial kitchen hearth with a flimsy, badly designed shovel and poker. The blacksmiths at Essex Forge, inspired by museum-quality antiques, have crafted superb fireplace sets from heavy wrought iron. The model illustrated, the Standish, is available either with a wall hanger, as shown, or with a graceful, stable floor stand.

Catalogue, $2.

The Essex Forge
12 Old Dennison Rd.
Essex, CT 06426
(203) 767-1808

Pat Guthman

Pat Guthman, an associate of Jerard Paul Jordan, works out of a different location and specializes in antique hearth utensils and other furnishings that are appropriate for early kitchens and keeping rooms. Among the objects of iron, copper, brass, and tin that she regularly keeps on hand are cranes, trammels, trivets, kettles, posnets, spiders, spits, toasters, griddles, and roasters. A fine assortment of antique stoneware and treen is also offered. She has worked with museums, restoration groups, and private individuals in creating kitchen hearths that are not only attractive to view but authentic in every detail.

Catalogue, $4.

Pat Guthman
342 Pequot Ave.
Southport, CT 06490
(203) 259-5743

Hearth Realities

Coal-burning fireplaces have become a rarity, even in period homes. Because of their scarcity, there are few companies that manufacture accessories for them. Hearth Realities claims to be the only manufacturer of replacement hanging basket grates in the country. The company offers many different styles and sizes of grates, each hand cast in high-quality gray iron to insure durability. Hearth Realities warns, however, that great care in measuring is required in order to insure that the proper grate is supplied for your frame and fireplace. Illustrated are

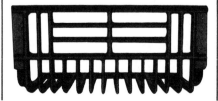

the tile hanging basket grate, so named because it was first used in fireplaces with a sloped ceramic tile embedded in the masonry above it, and a universal hanging basket grate.

Brochures available.

Hearth Realities
246 Daniel Ave. S.E.
Atlanta, GA 30317

Lemee's Fireplace Equipment

Whether you need a new cast-iron grate, a screen, andirons, a canvas log carrier, a wood basket or box, a cast-iron dutch oven or skillet, or a new poker, you'll find a wide selection in Lemee's catalogue. Even unusual items such as swinging cranes and brackets, corn brooms, and cooking grills are offered by this Massachusetts firm.

Catalogue, $1.

Lemee's Fireplace Equipment
815 Bedford St.
Bridgewater, MA 02324
(617) 697-2672

Period Furniture Hardware

Period Furniture's 120-page catalogue cannot begin to include each and every item offered by the firm. Among the pieces it does list, however, are andirons (twenty different styles), firebacks, jamb hooks, serpentine fenders, tool sets, and screens. Each accessory is made of solid brass or brass and cast iron; most are available in a choice of finishes.

Catalogue, $3.50.

Period Furniture Hardware Co., Inc.
Box 314 Charles St. Station
Boston, MA 02114
(617) 227-0758

Information

There's little point in setting aside a large portion of your yearly household budget for fuel—be it primarily oil, gas, wood, kerosene, or electricity—if you haven't taken the time to make sure that the warmth generated will stay where you want it: inside. Many old houses are notorious fuel-robbers.

They seem to leak from every pore. But there are techniques you can employ to stop the theft, many of them inexpensive. The following sources will supply information about energy conservation as well as alternative energy sources. Much of the material is available at no charge.

Conservation and Renewable Energy Inquiry and Referral Service

Known familiarly as CAREIRS, this service is operated by Solar America, Inc., and the Franklin Research Center under contract to the U.S. Department of Energy. CAREIRS is a free public service specifically designed to provide the general public with basic information about renewable sources of energy and energy conservation. It offers a wide variety of materials free of charge, among them pamphlets providing information about Federal incentive programs for energy conservation, ways to decrease energy use in older homes, insulation techniques, conversion to solar heat, and much more.

Brochures available.

CAREIRS
Box 8900
Silver Spring, MD 20907
(800) 523-2929
(800) 233-3071 (AK and HI)

State Energy Offices

Over the past decade, soaring oil and natural gas prices, not to mention escalating electric bills, have resulted in a rush to find alternative sources of fuel. The popularity of wood has given way in some measure to that of kerosene; either fuel, however, can be dangerous if improperly used. All states (and the District of Columbia) maintain specific offices where consumers can inquire about energy sources, materials, and manufacturers. Information is offered at no charge.

Other Suppliers of Heating and Cooking

Consult List of Suppliers for addresses.

Antique Stoves

Bryant Steel Works
Empire Furnace and Stove Repair Co.
Grampa's Wood Stoves
Old Mansions Co.
United House Wrecking Corp.

Reproduction Stoves

Cumberland General Store
Energy Marketing Corp.
Mohawk Industries
Schrader Wood Stoves and Fireplaces
Shenandoah Manufacturing
Vermont Castings
Washington Stove Works

Heating Supplies

A.A. Used Boiler Supply Co.
Acme Stove Co.
Cumberland General Store
Empire Furnace and Stove Repair Co.

Mantels

Marion Campbell
Chip LaPointe, Cabinetmaker
Wm. H. Jackson
Mountain Lumber
Old Colony Crafts
Old Mansions Co.
The Readybuilt Products Co.
Calvin W. Shewmaker III, Cabinetmaker
Sunshine Architectural Woodworks
Norman Vandal

Maintenance and Design

Acme Stove Co.
Dobson & Thomas Ltd.
Superior Clay Corp.
H. S. Welles Fireplace Co.

Firebacks and Fireboards

A. E. S. Firebacks
The Country Iron Foundry
Portland Willamette Co.
Steptoe & Wife Antiques Ltd.

Fireplace Accessories

The Country Loft
Hammerworks Ironware
Wm. H. Jackson
Newton Millham

6.

Hardware

As do-it-yourself magazines are always pointing out, there is something eternally fascinating about the tools and gadgets that make things work. Just walk into any crowded hardware store on a Saturday afternoon and you'll see how enthusiastic people can be about nails, hinges, locks, and such. And you can generally find a dozen of whatever you need in any such store. If you're the owner of an old house, however, beware. The hardware in any home is a detail that affects the whole, and modern fittings can be glaring anachronisms in a period room. Luckily, there are many sources of good reproduction hardware, an area of manufacture that has grown enormously in recent years because of the increasing popularity of old-house restoration and renovation. Victorian *cire perdue* or lost wax manufacturing methods, for instance, are being used once again after seventy-five years of obsolescence. A number of companies that have resurrected this method for making ornate brass hardware are listed in the pages that follow.

If it's early American hardware you need, you'll probably find that exactly the right piece can be wrought by any one of a number of working blacksmiths who can supply you with a set of strap hinges or re-create an old latch to your specifications. All you need do is allow enough time; such craftsmen generally work to custom order, and each piece is, after all, made by hand.

When it comes to kitchen and bath fixtures, you'll find that you can select a handsome reproduction to provide just the right period accent, or reconditioned antiques that work as well as any modern equivalent. And you needn't give up that old clawfoot tub merely because it has become pitted and stained. There are companies that can refinish it for you without even removing it from your home, and others that can supply appropriate shower adapters as well, so that you won't have to sacrifice convenience for the sake of style.

The one area in which modern equipment is far superior to the old is that of precision measuring equipment. Old-house restorers need well-calibrated tools, such as moisture gauges, in order to do their jobs well. A selection of such equipment is included at the end of this chapter, along with accessories like safety goggles, gloves, and coveralls which are highly recommended for most reconstruction work.

Reproduction 17th-century openwork English lock and key, Newton Millham, Star Forge, Westport, Massachusetts.

Architectural Hardware

America is blessed with a number of hardworking and imaginative architectural hardware craftsmen. Some of them are employed by a few major reproduction hardware firms that have continued over the years to produce quality work, but the majority work a forge by themselves just as blacksmiths did a hundred years ago. Because so much commercially-available hardware is shoddily made and of inferior or inappropriate design, today's old-fashioned artisan can make a good living from his craft.

Such relatively small items of iron and brass would seem to merit only passing attention on the part of the home restorer or renovator, but these are the fittings which not only hold together important structural elements, but endow them with a distinct style and character. Doorknobs, locks, latches, sash lifts, shutter dogs, door knockers, hinges of various types, bolts and hasps—all are reproduced today in a multitude of sturdy designs and forms.

The Arden Forge

Peter Renzetti, proprietor of The Arden Forge, maintains an extensive collection of hardware and delights in working with old-house owners and restorers to choose the proper pieces. He will readily reproduce early designs, using Albert H. Sonn's *Early American Wrought Iron* as a guide. In addition, Renzetti does a considerable amount of restoration work for museums, historical societies, private collectors, and antique dealers. Pictured here are two of the many pieces Renzetti has available, a drop latch which would look equally well on an old garden gate or a period front door, and a box lock.

For further information, contact:

The Arden Forge Co.
301 Brintons Bridge Rd.
West Chester, PA 19380
(215) 399-1530

Baldwin Hardware

Among the small details often overlooked when it comes time to select hardware are appropriate switch plates to cover wall outlets and light switches. While no such hardware, of course, is authentic to any period design prior to the 20th century, there is no reason to put up with the tacky plastic plates generally available at the five and dime, and even less reason to make do with the pseudo-Colonial frippery offered in some mail-order catalogues. Baldwin has several handsome, simply-designed solid forged-brass plates to accommodate single and double switches, outlets, and combinations.

Catalogue available.

Baldwin Hardware Mfg. Corp.
841 Wyomissing Blvd., Box 82
Reading, PA 19603
(215) 777-7811

Ball and Ball

Among the 1,500 items offered in Ball and Ball's comprehensive catalogue are shutter dogs and Colonial door locks and latches. Each (with a few rare exceptions) is designed and produced by the company's own craftsmen. Most pieces are fashioned of brass or cast iron, depending on style and type. In addition to its fine standard offerings, Ball and Ball also welcomes inquiries about repairs or custom reproduction work.

Catalogue, $5. (Seasonal brochure at no charge.)

Ball and Ball
463 W. Lincoln Hwy.
Exton, PA 19341
(215) 363-7330

Crawford's Old House Store

Not only does Crawford's stock a huge selection of reproduction architectural hardware, all of solid brass with appropriate fasteners supplied, but the company offers to help you find pieces that it may not have in stock. Its telephone inquiry service is available seven days a week from 9:00 a.m. to 9:00 p.m. Among the styles of door hardware Crawford's carries are the Brocade line, whose intricate detailing is typical of mid-Victorian tastes, and the English Rope style, a simpler, more elegant design inspired by hardware brought to America during the Colonial era.

Catalogue, $1.75.

Crawford's Old House Store
301 McCall St.
Waukesha, WI 53186
(414) 542-0685

Blaine Window Hardware

Whether you're searching for replacement hardware for windows, patio doors, closet doors, or security screens, Blaine can probably supply it. The company's catalogue gives only a small indication of its inventory: it carries more than 18,000 replacement parts, in all sizes and configurations for all purposes.

Catalogue, $2.50.

Blaine Window Hardware Inc.
1919 Blaine Dr., Rte. 4
Hagerstown, MD 21740
(800) 638-3042

The Brotman Forge

Harvey Brotman imports European wrought-iron door latch and handle sets, escutcheons, and hinges in a variety of intricate designs which he calls the French Country style. Each solid-iron piece is treated with a special pro-

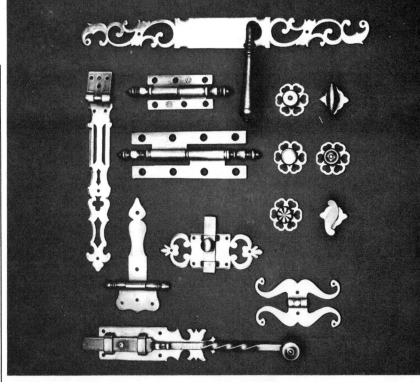

cess which adds luster and resists oxidation, and each piece is guaranteed. Brotman offers a full refund if you are unsatisfied for any reason.

Catalogue, $2.

The Brotman Forge
Box 511
Hanover, NH 03755
(802) 295-6393

Cirecast

Cirecast has supplied custom Victorian hardware for a number of famous institutions and public buildings, among them the Smithsonian Institution, the St. Francis Hotel in San Francisco, Conversation Hall in Philadelphia's City Hall, and the Georgia state capitol. It should come as no surprise, therefore, that its collection of first-quality reproduction bronze hardware—doorknobs, escutcheons, hinges, keyhole plates, and sash lifts—is among the best we've found. All hardware is reproduced from original patterns using the lost wax process, yet it has been refitted to be compatible with modern locksets and restoration methods. Illustrated here is a variety of pieces indicative of the mid- to late 19th-century designs Cirecast offers. In addition, the company does expert repair and restoration work.

Catalogue, $2.

Cirecast, Inc.
380 7th St.
San Francisco, CA 94103
(415) 863-8319

R. Hood & Co.

In addition to its line of early American hand-forged iron wall hooks, plant hangers, and hinges, Hood offers several different sizes of machine-made nails and screws with simulated forged heads. In addition, if the smallest detail must be absolutely correct, you may wish to order Hood's ½"-square leather washers, which were used in the 18th century to cushion the usually uneven base of the nail head and to take up slack between it and the hinge.

Brochure available.

R. Hood & Co.
RFD, 3 College Rd.
Meredith, NH 03253
(603) 279-8607

The Farm Forge

Blacksmith Larry Wood has been working with metals for nearly thirty years; most of the wrought-iron and tin architectural hardware and accessories he fashions is custom made. His catalogue is

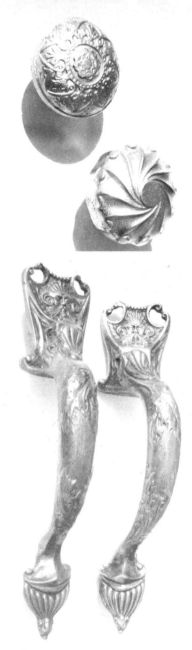

full of examples of the kinds of pieces he creates, but he cautions that it is by no means meant to be a representation of his complete line. Inquiries are welcomed with a SASE; Wood suggests that you send pictures or sketches with the basic sizes and styles required. Illustrated here are several pieces of his work: a door latch set and a shutter dog.

Catalogue, $1.

The Farm Forge
6945 Fishburg Rd.
Dayton, OH 45424
(513) 233-6751

Jerard Paul Jordan Gallery

Jordan specializes in finding and restoring 18th- and early 19th-century building materials of all sizes and shapes, from entire barns and houses to structural components and hardware. If reproduction hardware doesn't suit, therefore, Jordan may be able to supply original iron pieces such as exterior latches, strap or butterfly hinges, or door knockers.

Catalogue, $4.

Gerard Paul Jordan Gallery
Box 71, Slade Rd.
Ashford, CT 06278
(203) 429-7954

Kayne & Son

If it can be fashioned of steel, brass, or bronze, chances are that Steve Kayne and his son can make it for you. Custom work is their specialty. They will restore your old architectural hardware, make a copy of an old piece to your specifications, or provide anything else you need—from hinges and bolts to shutter dogs. Several examples of their work are pictured here: a bolt and a series of strap hinges. The Kaynes offer

two catalogues—one suggests pieces to be handcrafted of bronze and brass, the other sketches ideas for custom-forged steel pieces. We suggest that you order both, as each is full of handsome and utilitarian pieces to inspire and intrigue.

Two catalogues, $3.50 ($2 each).

Kayne & Son Custom Forged
* Hardware*
Rte. 4, Box 275A
Candler, NC 28715
(704) 667-8868

Brian F. Leo

If there's only one original doorknob remaining in your period home and you wish to duplicate it for use in other rooms as well, Brian Leo's your man. He specializes in finely wrought custom reproduction hardware and works in most any style. His catalogue illustrates just a few of the pieces that he has crafted; the two doorknobs and two handles pictured here are indicative of Leo's quality work.

Catalogue available.

Brian F. Leo
7520 Stevens Ave. S.
Richfield, MN 55423
(612) 861-1473

Litchfield House

Porcelain-china door furnishings manufactured in England are a specialty at Litchfield House. All fixtures, such as the Apple Blossom pattern illustrated, are made of solid, heavy-weight china for durability. Designs are hand-stenciled and finished in a ceramic glaze impervious to wear. Doorknobs are 2½" in diameter and are packaged complete with spindles and screws. Push plates measure 11" by 3"; matching drop keyhole escutcheons are available

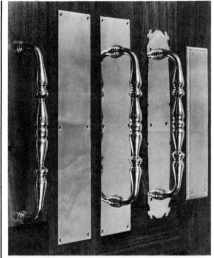

as well. Litchfield carries a number of floral patterns; if greater simplicity is preferred, the sets come in plain white, white with gold line, or black with gold line as well.

Brochure available.

Litchfield House
Church St.
Roxbury, CT 06783
(203) 355-0375

Newton Millham

All of the hardware illustrated in Newton Millham's handsome catalogue is hand-forged and finished. He pays close attention to both forging and bench work (filing, fitting, and finishing) to insure faithful reproduction of the detailing and feel of early wrought hardware. Millham specializes in early American styles of ironware—most of his designs are reproductions of pieces from the

1600s and 1700s—and will replicate most types and styles from those centuries. The openwork lock illustrated at the beginning of this chapter is indicative of this expert blacksmith's work: it is a faithful copy of one recovered from the grounds of a Rhode Island house known to have burned in 1675 and is typical of English locks of the period.

Catalogue, $1.

Newton Millham
Star Forge
672 Drift Rd.
Westport, MA 02790
(617) 636-5437

Period Furniture Hardware

Among the thousands of items offered by this Massachusetts firm is a staggering array of door fittings and locks, as well as accessories such as the brass door knockers illustrated here. Period Furniture's 120-page catalogue will give you some idea of the choices available; most pieces are made of solid brass and the company prides itself on the quality of all items it carries.

Catalogue, $3.50

Period Furniture Hardware Co., Inc.
Box 314, Charles St. Station
123 Charles St.
Boston, MA 02114
(617) 227-0758

Ship 'n' Out

If you're looking for simple brass door pulls, you might want to get in touch with this New York firm. Ship 'n' Out specializes in brass

rail and accessories; among the items offered is this fine assortment of pulls and plates.

Brochure available.

Ship 'n' Out
8 Charles St.
Pawling, NY 12564
(800) 431-8242
(914) 855-5947 (NY)

The Smithy

Robert Bourdon started working with forge, hammer, and anvil because he found the blacksmith's art to be a relaxing and rewarding hobby; he's been at it full time now for about twenty years. Most of his work, such as the exterior door latches illustrated, is in the duplication of hardware and other iron pieces necessary in the restoration of old buildings and the construction of period reproduction homes. He will duplicate a piece to your specifications and offers a variety of other objects— from chandeliers to weather vanes—as part of his extensive repertoire.

Brochure available.

Robert Bourdon
The Smithy
Wolcott, VT 05680
(802) 472-6508

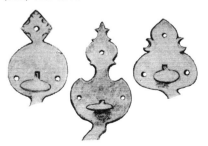

Strafford Forge

Kenneth Parrot specializes in reproductions of 17th- and 18th-century hardware; each piece is individually hand-forged and finished. His catalogue gives samples of some of the more common pieces found during the Colonial period, but his work is not restricted to those alone. Parrot will work from clear drawings, original pieces, or recognized books on the subject to recreate specific items you may have in mind. Pictured here are two ball-and-spear latches, the originals of which were common in Massachusetts during the late 1600s,

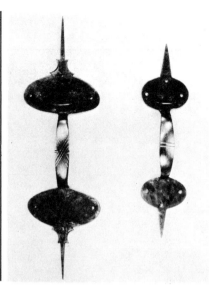

and three bolts. The rat-tail bolt was traditionally used at the top or bottom of a door, the others generally placed midway between the latch and the top of the door. Each is mounted on a wrought backplate and is available with either a mortice plate (as shown)

or a mounted staple as the keeper.

Catalague available.

Strafford Forge
Box 148
South Strafford, VT 05070
(802) 765-4455

Tremont Nail Company

Tremont, established in 1819, is the oldest nail manufacturer in the United States. The company makes twenty varieties of cut nails using the old patterns (it originated hardened steel nails on the same furnace still in use today). Send for a sample kit containing one each of the twenty patterns, historical information, and a price list ($3.75 postpaid). A catalogue of wrought-iron hardware and household accessories is available as well.

Tremont Nail Company
Dept. OHC, 8 Elm St., Box 111
Wareham, MA 02571
(617) 295-0038

Williamsburg Blacksmiths

Strap hinges, sometimes called pintles, have traditionally been used on large, heavy doors, yet the grace of their design belies their strength. Using the traditional methods and tools, Williamsburg Blacksmiths forges from heavy iron such hinges, along with a wide variety of other Colonial-style hardware. Each piece is protected by applying a bonded phosphate coating, then finished with black lacquer. (Some hardware is available with a natural iron finish as well.) An introductory brochure can be had at no charge; the catalogue, however, is probably a better choice,

as it details all items available, along with instructions for installation.

Catalogue, $3.

Williamsburg Blacksmiths
Buttonshop Rd.
Williamsburg, MA 01096
(413) 268-7341

Woodbury Blacksmith & Forge

Thumb and bar latches, strap hinges, bolts, hasps, door knockers, and shutter dogs are among the handsome wrought-iron items available from Woodbury. A pair of H/L hinges, illustrated here, is indicative of the quality of early American designs reproduced on the Woodbury forge. So, too, is the heavy iron door knocker. Woodbury offers, as well, a selection of hand-wrought nails in both rose-head and T-head styles.

Catalogue, $2.

Woodbury Blacksmith & Forge Co.
Box 268, 161 Main St.
Woodbury, CT 06798
(203) 263-5737

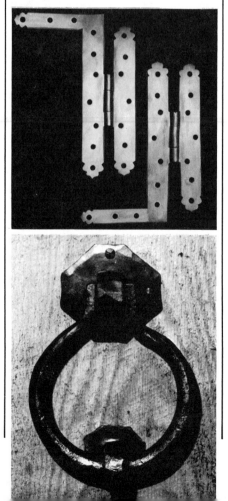

Emily Zum Brunnen

If your taste runs to the exotic, you'll want to order this firm's catalogue to see its line of brass door hardware and other accessories. Among the door knockers illustrated there, for instance, are brass lions' heads, dolphins, and cherubs. The accent is on European design in general and the French mode in particular; the pieces are not particularly suited to Victorian decor, but might be just the thing for an elegant Edwardian town house.

Catalogue, $4.

Emily Zum Brunnen Imports
5914 Fairfield Ave.
Shreveport, LA 71106
(318) 221-5540

Household Hardware

Little attention is paid to such functional pieces of hardware as curtain and drapery tiebacks, poles, and finials until they are needed. Have you tried to find well-made curtain hardware lately? You wouldn't want to hang even a piece of muslin from the flimsy plastic rods which come ready-packaged in the local hardware store. And if you have invested in quality fabrics for period window hangings, you are not going to want to draw them back with acrylic tiebacks that are more appropriate for the latest synthetic material than for lace or silk. If the prospect of standardized household hardware depresses you, then the high quality of the selections that follow will illustrate how some history-minded manufacturers are pursuing the quest for excellence and helping to dispel the gloom of contemporary mediocrity.

Baldwin Hardware

Baldwin is well known for the quality of its brass architectural hardware; the company makes superb decorative pieces as well, such as the drapery holdback shown here. What more handsome way to accent the graceful folds of window treatments in a formal room?

Brochure available.

Baldwin Hardware Mfg. Corp.
841 Wyomissing Blvd., Box 82
Reading, PA 19603
(215) 777-7811

Ball and Ball

When you want to keep curtains out of the way to admit cooling evening breezes, consider the variety of curtain tiebacks available from Ball and Ball. From ornamental circular forms to flowers and eagles, all are made of solid brass with single screw mounting stems, and all can be easily removed from the window jamb. They come with regular polished and lacquered finish or can be special-ordered in antique finish.

Catalogue, $5.

Ball and Ball
463 W. Lincoln Hwy.
Exton, PA 19341
(215) 363-7330

Gould-Mersereau

No matter how complicated your drapery hardware needs, chances are that Gould-Mersereau can meet them. The company offers a complete line of both wood and metal rods and accessories in a wide variety of standard sizes or will cut to suit unusual measurements. We find Gold-Mersereau's Sierra line of wooden traverse poles, brackets, and rings most appealing. The components come in a choice of three finishes—fruitwood or walnut stained or white-painted—or can be ordered unfinished so that you can complete them to suit your own decor.

Brochure, 25¢.

The Gould-Mersereau Co., Inc.
21-16 44th Rd.
Long Island City, NY 11101
(212) 361-8120

The Ground Floor

Because so very few drapery rod finials are appealing, The Ground Floor has designed and copyrighted fourteen unusual ones of its own. The shapes, each molded of a wood and resin composition, range from acanthus leaves and pineapples to thistles, dragonflies, and pine cones. Two are illustrated here. They may be ordered unfinished; in the shop's choice of gold/brass, pewter, bronze, or walnut/mahogany; or The Ground Floor will paint them to your specified colors (with paint chip or fabric swatch supplied). Each comes with a screw embedded in its base for easy attachment to the dowel; sizes range from 5″ to 9½″ in length.

Brochure and price list available.

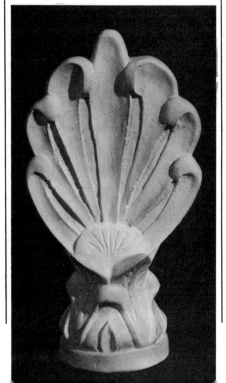

The Ground Floor
95½ Broad St.
Charleston, SC 29401
(803) 722-3576

Kayne & Son

Steve Kayne calls this handmade wrought-iron pot rack a bean rack because of its ornamentation. Whatever the appellation, it is a particularly useful piece, since the hooks are adjustable—sliding along the rack to accommodate various sizes of pots and pans. Kayne has a number of other kitchen accessories available in addition to his wide selection of hardware. All of his work is custom made, so you can suggest alterations or different designs to suit your needs. He has two catalogues chock-full of suggestions: one for hand-forged iron hardware, the other for pieces of cast bronze and brass.

Catalogues, $2 each (both for $3.50).

Kayne & Son
Rte. 4, Box 275A
Candler, NC 28715
(704) 667-8868

Period Furniture Hardware

Among the hundreds of brass items illustrated in Period Furniture's substantial catalogue are a number of handsome doorbell plates. We especially like a simple circular plate, just 1¾" in diameter, that features a double ring of beading as its sole ornamentation.

Catalogue, $3.50.

Period Furniture Hardware
Box 314, Charles St. Station
123 Charles St.
Boston, MA 02114
(617) 227-0758

Williamsburg Blacksmiths

While many essential hardware items have remained more or less unchanged in basic design and utility over the centuries, others have virtually disappeared from the modern scene. Boot scrapers are a prime example of the latter, and it's too bad. Who hasn't had to scrape off mud (or worse) from a shoe sole before entering the house? The problem becomes where to do it. (The porch steps are not recommended.) Why not order one of these sturdy and practical boot scrapers from Williamsburg Blacksmiths? Each is hand-forged; the model to the far right can be mounted in either wood or masonry as you choose. The others are meant to be implanted in masonry alone.

Catalogue, $3.

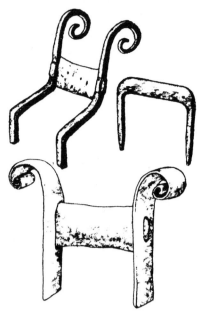

Williamsburg Blacksmiths, Inc.
Buttonshop Rd.
Williamsburg, MA 01096
(413) 268-7341

Emily Zum Brunnen

Among the cast-metal and solid-brass decorative hardware imported by this Louisiana firm are a number of ornate drapery tiebacks suitable for the most elegant and luxuriously furnished of rooms. The company specializes in European design with an accent on the French style.

Catalogue, $4.

Emily Zum Brunnen
5914 Fairfield Ave.
Shreveport, LA 71106
(318) 221-5540

Bath and Kitchen Hardware

The fixtures and fittings found in the kitchen and bath are those which are usually the first to go in any renovation. Careful thought, however, should be given to the replacement of sinks, tubs, and toilets. In many cases, it is possible to refinish these antique pieces. If that proves impossible, they can be replaced with fixtures that are at least old-fashioned in appearance. Specialty plumbing and salvage houses around the country regularly supply reconditioned and reproduction fixtures. Similarly, these dealers can supply reproduction old-style fittings such as faucet sets that can be substituted for the hopelessly corroded antique.

A-Ball Plumbing Supply

Chances are you treasure that old clawfoot tub in your master bathroom and wouldn't trade it for anything. But what to do when it needs new fittings? A-Ball can probably help. The company specializes in quality West German, American, and French fixtures and accessories for both bathroom and kitchen. Among its many offerings are solid-brass tub fill/shower combinations, high-tank toilet parts, and period accessories such as the three brass toilet tissue holders pictured here.

All of the items in A-Ball's extensive catalogue are made of quality materials—brass, china, solid oak, and white porcelain. Many of the brass plumbing fittings are available in either brass or chrome finish.

Catalogue available.

*A-Ball Plumbling Supply
1703 W. Burnside St.
Portland, OR 97209
(503) 228-0026*

Barclay Products

If you happen to be in the Chicago area, you may want to visit Barclay's display outlet, the Old House Store, for a first-hand look at the company's products. But, if you can't, send for the firm's catalogue, for Barclay has been both a manufacturer and importer of plumbing supplies for more than half a century. The company often works with architects and interior designers specifically involved in restoration work. Illustrated is one model of Barclay's Converto shower, which transforms an existing tub into a tub/shower combination. Also pictured is one of its pedestal sinks, this one in cast iron. Barclay also carries a wide variety of Chicago Faucet products which are available in styles to suit every decor.

Catalogue available.

*Barclay Products Company
424 N. Oakley Blvd.
Chicago, IL 60612
(312) 243-1444*

Heads Up

Not only is the pull-chain toilet illustrated here a welcome relief from the humdrum porcelain models of the 1980s, but it's also a water saver. This handsome oak model uses less than half the water per flush of most modern toilets. All oak surfaces, inside and out, are coated with two coats of sealer, one of stain, and two of lacquer (three coats on vanity tops). All bowls are made of high-quality vitreous china. The Bristol sink, also shown, is a wall-mounted model. It, too, is fashioned of kiln-dried Ap-

palachian red oak with a china bowl. The complementary mirror is optional. Heads Up offers a number of choices in toilets, vanities, mirrors, and medicine cabinets, all of oak with appropriate accessories.

Catalogue and price list, $1.

Heads Up
2980 E. Blue Star, Unit B
Anaheim, CA 92806
(714) 630-5402

Lehman Hardware & Appliances

Even the most rigid of old-house purists wouldn't really want to return to the days of the old icebox, which necessitated hauling unwieldy cakes of ice into the kitchen on a regular basis. But if you want to be free, at least, of depending on the electric company for every appliance you need, order Lehman's non-electric catalogue for starters. The company offers refrigerators and freezers which run on kerosene or natural gas; gas-powered washing machines (and hand wringers); and old-fashioned wall- and floor-model clothes dryers which use no energy at all (save the human energy necessary to hang the wet clothes on them).

Catalogue, $2.

Lehman Hardware & Appliances
Box 41
Kidron, OH 44636
(216) 857-5441

Nostalgia

This Savannah firm specializes in antiques and fine reproductions of architectural accessories, statuary, lighting, and more. Among its offerings are some handsome marble pedestal sinks, each a copy of a cast-iron original. The basins are available in simple oval or round shapes, or in a more elegant, scalloped pattern called the Fleur de Lis. Two styles of pedestals are offered; brass faucet sets, with or without porcelain handles, can also be ordered. Nostalgia also carries a supply of antique tubs and fittings in a wide range of sizes.

Catalogue, $2.50.

Nostalgia, Inc.
307 Stiles Ave.
Savannah, GA 31401
(912) 232-2324

Perma Ceram

If you shudder at the cost of replacing a chipped, stained, or worn tub or sink and don't really want to give up that antique anyway, Perma Ceram may have the answer for you. The company specializes in resurfacing tubs, sinks, and wall tile. All standard fixture colors are available, or you can specify a custom color if you wish.

Perma Ceram dealers are available throughout the United States. Consult your local yellow pages, or call the number below for the name of a dealer near you.

Brochures available.

Perma Ceram Enterprises, Inc.
65 Smithtown Blvd.
Smithtown, NY 11787
(800) 645-5039

Restore-A-Tub

Not only does this Louisville company specialize in refinishing sinks, tubs, and tile, as its name suggests, but it offers a line of merchandise for a complete bathroom renovation—down to the hardware, accessories, and wallpaper. Among the more tempting of Restore-A-Tub's offerings is a hydro-spa system that can convert most standard tubs into whirlpool baths.

For further information, contact:

Restore-A-Tub and Brass, Inc.
1991 Brownsboro Rd.
Brownsboro Plaza
Louisville, KY 40206
(502) 895-2912

The Sink Factory

The Sink Factory specializes in reproducing Victorian plumbing fixtures. All of the company's pedestal sinks, basins, and accessories are handmade of vitreous china. White is standard; requests for colors will be considered, as will special requests for custom fixtures not listed in the company's catalogue.

Catalogue available.

The Sink Factory
2140 San Pablo Ave.
Berkeley, CA 94702
(415) 540-8193

Steptoe & Wife

As you would expect, Steptoe & Wife specializes in staircases and other architectural items (see chapter 1). In addition, however, the firm offers a carefully selected group of reproduction faucet sets and shower sets. All are made of solid brass and are available in either polished brass or in a chrome-plated finish.

Catalogue available.

Steptoe & Wife Antiques Ltd.
3626 Victoria Park Ave.
Willowdale, Ontario, Canada
*   M2H 3B2*
(416) 497-2989

Sunrise Specialty & Salvage

Sunrise offers a large selection of original and reproduction fixtures and accessories with an accent on Victorian design. Salvage materials include original porcelain and cast-iron clawfoot tubs and pedestal sinks of the same materials or of china. Pictured here is an original clawfoot tub with brass-plated legs and a custom-made oak rim. Tubs of this type are available by special order. Also shown is one of the company's tub/hand shower units, designed for use on either a clawfoot tub or to be wall mounted on a conven-

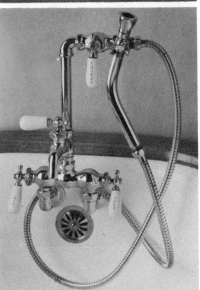

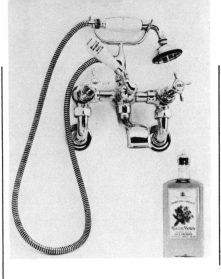

makes available in bathroom fittings and accessories. The company is represented across the country; its products must be specified or purchased by your architect, interior designer, or contractor.

Contact Watercolors for the name of the dealer nearest you.

Watercolors
Garrison-on-Hudson, NY 10524
(914) 424-3327

Furniture Hardware

Reproduction hardware of the same quality as your period furniture is made by a number of manufacturers and craftsmen. It is often difficult, however, to find exactly what you need in an old-fashioned hardware store, if one, indeed, still exists in your neighborhood. It is relatively *simple, however, to order various types of pieces such as escutcheons, keyhole plates, pulls, and ornamental brass filigree through the mail. The catalogues of the suppliers that follow are fun to read and amazingly instructive.*

tional tub. This fitting is provided with a 4' flexible hose and swivel head on the hand shower.

Catalogue, $2.

Sunrise Specialty & Salvage Co.
2210 San Pablo Ave.
Berkeley, CA 94702
(415) 845-4751

Watercolors

The mixer with hand-shower attachment shown here is part of Watercolors' Edwardian series. It is available in either a bath-mounted or wall-mounted version; can be fitted with a riser pipe and wide shower head; and is made from solid brass and gunmetal with porcelain fittings. Finishes are polished brass, chrome, nickel, and gold plating.

The Edwardian series is just one of a number of styles Watercolors

Anglo-American Brass

Solid-brass reproduction hardware is the specialty of this California manufacturer. Whether you're looking for Victorian keyholes, Chippendale-style handle sets, or old-fashioned icebox hardware, the company can probably supply it. If you don't find quite what you need in the catalogue, inquire about Anglo-American's lost wax model shop, where virtually any item can be duplicated. Illustrated here is a cast bin pull (model B-13), measuring $3\frac{3}{8}$" by $1\frac{1}{2}$", which is available in a polished finish, as are most of the company's products.

Catalogue, $1.50.

Anglo-American Brass Co.
4146 Mitzi, Box 9792
San Jose, CA 95157
(800) 222-7277
(408) 246-0203 (CA)

Ball and Ball

If you need a set of brass pulls to finish that old chest you just purchased, or finials for a pair of lamps, or cabinet locks or hinges —just about any conceivable brass hardware item—order Ball and Ball's comprehensive catalogue. Chances are you'll find just what you need. The company has been noted for its superb reproduction hardware since 1931; a special attraction is its wide selection of Victorian pieces.

Catalogue, $5.

Ball and Ball
463 W. Lincoln Hwy.
Exton, PA 19341
(215) 363-7330

The Bedpost

As you would expect, The Bedpost specializes in just one thing—beds, and only brass ones at that. If you already have a treasured antique and need replacement parts for it, this is a good place to try. In addition to its selection of antique and reproduction brass beds, the company has a good supply of finials, fasteners, tubing, brackets, caps, balls, and rail fittings—in sizes to fit any standard bed. If you need special sizes, The Bedpost can fabricate them for you.

Catalogue available.

The Bedpost
Box 155, RD 1
Pen Argyl, PA 18072
(215) 588-4667

The Brass Tree

In addition to its stock of cast-brass pulls, knobs, and hinges, The Brass Tree carries a good selection of hard-to-find cupboard locks, including specialty locks and hinges for roll-top desks and old trunks. It also stocks trunk tacks and nails, brass-plated rivets, and other utilitarian items. The Brass Tree's retail outlet is open from 9:30 to 5:00 Monday through Saturday, but a mail-order catalogue makes home shopping convenient at any time.

Catalogue, $2.

The Brass Tree
308 N. Main St.
St. Charles, MO 63301
(314) 723-1041

The Brotman Forge

This New Hampshire company imports wrought-iron hardware from Europe. While its architectural hardware has been described earlier in ths chapter, the firm also offers a good selection of cabinet escutcheons, latches, and hinges in a variety of sizes. Each piece is crafted of solid iron treated with a special process which adds luster and resists oxidation.

Catalogue, $2.

The Brotman Forge
Box 511
Hanover, NH 03755
(802) 295-6393

18th Century Hardware

18th Century Hardware operates its own foundry, making sand castings in yellow brass, bronze, and aluminum. In addition, the firm imports furniture locks and other hardware items that are dif-

ficult to find in the United States. Its name notwithstanding, the company offers furniture hardware in a variety of styles, ranging from William and Mary and Chippendale to late Victorian. Standard materials are brass (satin or polished finish) and iron (painted flat black). A selection of the com-

pany's late 19th-century and early 20th-century bin pulls is illustrated here.

Catalogue, $3.

18th Century Hardware Co., Inc.
131 E. 3rd St.
Derry, PA 15627
(412) 694-2708

Furniture Revival

Late-Victorian brass reproduction hardware is a specialty of this Oregon company. In addition, however, it offers wooden drawer pulls for massive old desks in a choice of oak, walnut, cherry, or mahogany. Furniture Revival also has one of the widest selections of trunk hardware we've seen, including corners, locks, bolts, stays, clamps, and hinges.

Catalogue, $2.

Furniture Revival
Box 994
Corvallis, OR 97339
(503) 754-6323

Brian F. Leo

While Brian Leo's catalogue illustrates a number of furniture pulls and drawer grips such as the two shown here, he emphasizes that the vast majority of his work is done to custom order. He fashions architectural and furniture hardware from any of

several metals and delights in reproducing exact duplicates (or "hybrids," as he calls them) of customer's pieces.

Catalogue available.

Brian F. Leo
7520 Stevens Ave. S.
Richfield, MN 55423
(612) 861-1473

Period Furniture Hardware

If you're in the Boston area, you'll probably want to visit Period Furniture's retail shop, since even its extensive (120 pages) catalogue can't do justice to the thousands of brass hardware items the firm carries. The shop is, in a word, spectacular—one of the best stocked hardware stores in the nation. If you're on the other side of the country, however, the catalogue will just have to do. But be warned: the catalogue's listings are so extensive that you'll have a tough time deciding on just the right drawer pulls (see the samples illustrated here), finials, latches, handles, or whatever else you need. If you don't see exactly what you're looking for in the catalogue, call. Chances are that Period Furniture has it in stock.

Catalogue, $3.50.

Period Furniture Hardware Co., Inc.
Box 314, Charles Street Station
123 Charles St.
Boston, MA 02114
(617) 227-0758

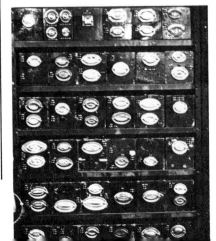

Squaw Alley

Squaw Alley specializes in hardware and furnishings for old-house aficionados. The company boasts of having one of the largest selections of solid-brass reproduction hardware in the Midwest, as well as an ever-changing line of antique hardware. It also has a wide variety of wooden drawer pulls and knobs.

Catalogue, $3.

Squaw Alley, Inc.
401 S. Main St.
Naperville, IL 60540
(312) 357-0200

W. T. Weaver

Weaver, in business since 1889, prides itself on being a good source for hard-to-find hardware items. Its attractive showroom is a good place to begin; failing that, you'd do well to order the catalogue. Among the more unusual furniture hardware items we've found listed there are oriental brass hinges, pulls, and latches. The company's stock covers a wide range of decorative styles— William and Mary, Hepplewhite, early to late Victorian, and more.

Catalogue, $2.50.

W. T. Weaver and Sons, Inc.
1208 Wisconsin Ave., N.W.
Washington, D.C. 20007
(202) 333-4200

M. Wolchonok & Son

Wolchonok stocks a complete line of furniture casters designed for either carpets or bare floors; architectural hardware; and furniture replacement hardware. Among the items listed in the firm's brochure are several decorative brass stair riser bars and brackets available in standard lengths or cut to special order. Wolchonok also carries a large assortment of furniture legs in many sizes and styles.

Send SASE for brochures.

M. Wolchonok & Son, Inc.
155 E. 52nd St.
New York, NY 10022
(212) 755-2168

Tools

Even if you are not a do-it-yourself craftsman in need of tools and special building and cabinetry supplies, you will find the catalogues of the major suppliers an unending delight. These publications range from the very simple offerings of the specialty toolmaker who supplies only one particular type of instrument to the glorious color publications of suppliers of thousands of items from all over the earth. Undoubtedly, even if you are all thumbs, you will discover something that you must have because it is not only handy to have around the house but is, in itself, a work of art.

Frog Tool Co.

Whether you're looking for a professional workbench, a woodcarving set, special veneer tools, scrapers, vises, or saws, you'll have a wide range to choose from in this Illinois firm's catalogue. Frog Tool is both a manufacturer of quality woodworking tools and a dealer in special items made by other manufacturers. It offers, for example, a handsome workbench made from fully cured red beech, which is hand-fitted in Germany and guaranteed, according to the company, to withstand several lifetimes of abuse. The cost of the catalogue entitles you to a two-year subscription, which includes both the annual catalogue and quarterly supplements. In addition, the price is refundable with your first purchase.

Catalogue, $2.50.

Frog Tool Co., Ltd.
700 W. Jackson Blvd.
Chicago, IL 60606
(312) 648-1270

Garrett Wade

Even if your interest in do-it-yourselfmanship is only a passing phase, run, don't walk, to your nearest mailbox with an order for Garrett Wade's colorful catalogue. One look at the superb design, photography, and information contained therein and you'll be hooked. There's no doubt that it's an exceptional catalogue; no wonder it's been called a necessity for every woodworker. Its handsome pages are chock-full of supplies to suit both the home handyman and the professional. You may even be tempted to try your hand at one of draftsman Carlyle Lynch's plans for reproduction antique furniture. Each is an exact representation of a piece in an American museum; all come with complete instructions and lists of materials needed. Garrett Wade will be issuing a second catalogue of reproduction cabinet hardware in the near future; call or write for information.

Woodworking catalogue, $3.

Garrett Wade Company
161 Avenue of the Americas

New York, NY 10013
(800) 221-2942
(212) 807-1155 (NY, AK, HI)

Goldblatt Tool Co.

From brick and masonry hammers to carbon-steel and stainless-steel trowels, Goldblatt carries virtually every tool needed for all kinds of construction work. If you're working with brick, stone, cement, or plaster, you'll probably want to either send for a copy of Goldblatt's catalogue or ask the company for the name of your nearest Goldblatt dealer.

Catalogue available.

Goldblatt Tool Co.
511 Osage, Box 2334
Kansas City, KS 66110
(913) 621-3010

Newton Millham

Artist-blacksmith Newton Millham is best known for his hand-wrought early American architectural and household hardware. In addition, he undertakes commissions of a more specialized nature, such as the crafting of the two boarding axes illustrated here. Millham writes that axes of this type were used by the navy during the first quarter of the 19th century, both to cut lines and rigging torn dur-

ing battle and to effect boarding of an enemy vessel by driving the sharp spike into the side of its hull. These particular axes were commissioned for a reenactment of an historical naval encounter in Boston recently.

Catalogue, $1.

Newton Millham
672 Drift Rd.
Westport, MA 02790
(617) 636-5437

M.R.S. Industries

Restoring and refurbishing an old house can be a lot of fun and can provide a great deal of satisfaction. It can also be dangerous. Knowing when to wear protective clothing, and what type to choose, can forestall costly—and painful—accidents. M.R.S. Industries is in the business of providing safety supplies—from hard hats and goggles to gloves, first-aid kits, boots, masks, and aprons.

Catalogue available.

M.R.S Industries Inc.
115 Fernwood Dr.
Rocky Hill, CT 06067
(203) 563-4082

PRG

We've mentioned PRG's Form-a-Gage before, but it's certainly worth reiterating its practical appeal. Any old-house owner knows how difficult it is to measure intricately molded architectural woodwork so as to be able to duplicate missing pieces. The Form-a-Gage is a profile-measuring device in which every rod is suspended in a uniform magnetic field on its own individual track. Once you have recorded the profile, the contour can be locked into place, giving a very precise measurement. In addition to the Form-a-Gage, PRG offers a number of other unusual tools, including a collection of temperature, humidity, condensation, and moisture instruments.

Catalogue available.

PRG
5619 Southampton Dr.
Springfield, VA 22151
(703) 323-1407

Sculpture Associates

If you have ornamental plaster moldings that need repair or wish to duplicate sections that have disappeared, Sculpture Associates can help. The firm offers casting and mold-making materials, intricate tools for paint removal, and more.

In addition, it can supply stone

adhesives for repairing fireplaces and statuary, along with fine wood-carving tools for reproducing ornamental wood detailing.

Catalogue, $2.
Sculpture Associates Ltd., Inc.
40 E. 19th St.
New York, NY 10003
(212) 777-2400

Williams & Hussey

Williams & Hussey specializes in quality woodworking machinery for the do-it-yourselfer as well as the professional. Illustrated here is one of the company's most recent offerings, a rugged woodworking vise which features cast-iron jaws, a generous 10½″ jaw width, and precision-ground adjusting screws. A special bench attachment permits its use for oversize work; the machine-smoothed jaws won't scratch delicate pieces.

Brochures and price lists available.

Williams & Hussey Machine Co.
Elm St.
Milford, NH 03055
(800) 258-1380
(603) 673-3446 (NH)

The Woodworkers' Store

Another first-rate source for vises and other woodworking tools, The Woodworkers' Store also offers stains, furniture plans, hardware, and anything else you might need to refurbish an old piece or create a new one.

Catalogue, $1.

The Woodworkers' Store
21801 Industrial Blvd.
Rogers, MN 55374
(612) 428-4101

Other Suppliers of Hardware

Consult List of Suppliers for addresses.

Architectural Hardware

Bona Decorative Hardware
Eighteenth Century Hardware Co.
William Hunrath Co., Inc.
H. Pfanstiel Hardware Co.
Renaissance Decorative Hardware Co.
Ritter & Son Hardware
Wallin Forge

Household Hardware

Blaine Window Hardware, Inc.
Bona Decorative Hardware
P. E. Guerin Inc.
R. Hood & Co.
Ritter & Son Hardware
Wallin Forge

Bath and Kitchen Hardware

Bona Decorative Hardware
Broadway Supply Co.
Chicago Faucet Co.
DeWeese Woodworking Co.
Kohler Co.
P & G New and Used Plumbing
  Supply
Walker Industries

Furniture Hardware

Bona Decorative Hardware
Albert Constantine & Son, Inc.
Faneuil Furniture Hardware
Horton Brasses
William Hunrath Co., Inc.
H. Pfanstiel Hardware Co.
Renaissance Decorative Hardware Co.
Woodcraft Supply Corp.

Tools

Albert Constantine & Son, Inc.
Cumberland General Store
Iron Horse Antiques
Marshalltown Trowel Co.
Woodcraft Supply Corp.

7.

Paints and Papers

Nothing provides such instant gratification in home renovation and decoration as newly painted or papered walls. The completion of such a project is the reward for all of the hidden structural work, painstaking repair jobs, and hours of decision-making which precede it. Paint, of course, is the simplest and least costly of wall decorations, and many companies offer color series designed for period decor. Decorating magazines never tire of showing rooms painted in "authentic colors"—colors that have become virtual decorating clichés. But there are no rules stating that Colonial rooms, for example, must be painted faded gray-green or barn red. In fact, new techniques in paint analysis have shown that our forebears chose lively colors and vivid combinations when possible, using available materials to create whatever colors were in vogue. Painting attains the stature of art in the use of decorative finishes such as glazing, stippling, trompe l'oeil, and sponging. While many of these techniques can be tried by the adventurous amateur, we have described in the pages that follow the work of some experts in this field.

Papers provide even more decorating potentiality than paint, and the old-house owner faces a dizzying number of choices—from genuine antique papers to historically accurate reproductions and modern interpretations of period patterns. Papers can also be used in combinations, and many rooms are enhanced by the use of one sidewall paper, a complementary ceiling border, and yet another lower wall (dado) paper.

While the selection of appropriate paints and papers will be dictated to a large extent by personal taste and imagination, the rules of good design should also apply. The size of the room, the availability of natural light, and the primary use to which the room is put will determine, to some extent, how its walls should be finished. Different patterns and colors are thought to produce different emotional responses; they can be used, as well, to make a room look larger or smaller, to diminish the effects of awkward architectural details, or to highlight the effects of others.

Whether your choice is to stay strictly within the confines of an historical period or to interpret it loosely to fit your own ideas, colors and designs are available to suit the simplest or most baroque decor.

Bedroom decorated with reproduction late 19th-century Anglo-Japanese papers, Bradbury & Bradbury Wallpapers, Benicia, California.

Paints

The choice of a paint color or of coordinating colors is as subjective a decision as any to be made when renovating or restoring a house. Despite all that we are told regarding "historic" colors, those hues that most please us are the ones finally selected. It is useful, nevertheless, to consult the various palettes of recommended period colors which are offered for exterior and interior use. Nearly every major paint manufacturer now offers a line of historic colors. These are shades which are considered correct for various types of Colonial or Victorian buildings. Many of the colors are, indeed, true copies of shades popular in the past; other colors are adaptations or interpretations of old-fashioned paint schemes.

Allentown Paint

Allentown is America's oldest ready-mixed paint company. Its small line of Pennsylvania Dutch Breinig exterior oil-based paints has proved itself over and over again in our experience. There are ten basic shades, any one of which is appropriate for a country Colonial or Victorian home. For trim, there are eight complementary colors. Allentown also offers a super oil-based exterior barn paint in, naturally, Bright Red. All of these paints are made up from pure linseed oil and quality pigments.

If you prefer to use latex paints, consider Allentown's line of basic one-coat exterior and accent colors. Of special interest are the Pennsylvania Dutch accent colors—Dutch Yellow, Iris Blue, Medium Green, Cocoa, Pine Green, and Fire Red—that would add a dramatic touch to any interior.

Contact your local Allentown Paint dealer or, for further information, write or telephone:

Allentown Paint Manufacturing Co.
East Allen and Graham Sts.
Allentown, PA 18105
(215) 433-4273

Chromatic Paint

Chromatic Japan colors are concentrated paste colors that will add a dimension of richness to mid- to late-Victorian interiors. Widely used in a variety of decorative painting techniques, such as antiquing, stenciling, tole work, staining, and graining, the colors are dead flat and dry very quickly to the touch. The paint adheres well to wood, metal, and paper and would be wonderful on picture frames, even floors and walls. These paints are also useful for tinting flat paints to control the luster. Chromatic offers a choice of thirty-one superb colors.

Color card available.

Chromatic Paint Corp.
Box 105
Garnerville, NY 10923
(914) 947-3210

Devoe Paint

Devoe's acrylic latex exterior paints, while not a line of historic colors, are nonetheless suitable for various types of old houses. Featuring such interesting shades as Shutter Green, Tiverton Blue, and Sutter's Gold, Devoe's ready-mixed colors, custom-mixed colors, and custom-mixed deep accent colors are "keyed" to make it relatively easy to select harmonious colors for the various elements of a home's facade.

Devoe paints are available nationwide. If you need assistance in contacting a supplier, write or telephone:

Devoe & Raynolds Co.
4000 Dupont Circle
Louisville, KY 40207
502) 897-9861

Fuller-O'Brien

Fuller-O'Brien has recently introduced a line of seventy Victorian colors—the Palette of Cape May—that is well researched and aesthically pleasing. Appropriate for both exterior and interior use, the hues are rich and bold, some of them exuberantly fanciful in fact. Over the next few years, 600 early- and late-Victorian buildings

in the charming New Jersey seaside town of Cape May will be decorated in these bright, handsome colors. Each color is named after the building for which it is being used.

In addition to this unique line, Fuller-O'Brien also offers the Heritage Color Collection of interior and exterior paints. These are soft earthtone shades with such names as Tavern Green, Quaker Green, Newport Brown, Williamsburg Gold, Cape Cod Blue, and Pilgrim Gray meant to suggest a Colonial palette of colors. There are forty-six such shades to choose from.

If there is no Fuller-O'Brien dealer in your area, contact the company for a list of suppliers.

Fuller-O'Brien Paints
450 E. Grand Ave.
South San Francisco, CA 94080
(800) 227-6159

Glidden

For both Colonial and Victorian homes, Glidden offers the American Color Legacy, a line of exterior paints. Available in both oil-based and latex formulas, the line includes twenty-eight hues which are warm and authentic in appearance. Among the most striking are Canton Rose, Spiced Cognac (mustard), and Main Street (blue-green).

Glidden's regular line of exterior latex paints is also suited for use on the older house. There are twelve strong basic colors and thirty-six complementary accent tones.

Glidden paints are distributed nationally; if there is no dealer in your area, contact the firm for further information.

Glidden Coatings & Resins
3rd and Bern Sts., Box 1097
Reading, PA 19603
(215) 373-4111

Martin-Senour

Martin-Senour produces the official Colonial Williamsburg line of exterior and interior paint colors. The product line is the oldest of all historical color collections available today and is based on research accomplished some time ago at the famous Virginia historical site. The exterior colors—thirty-five in all—are as imaginative as the buildings of Colonial Williamsburg, some of which display as many as five different shades. The interior paints, in flat and satin latex, range from very muted pastels such as Russell House Green and Palace Chambers Yellow to such strong hues as Raleigh Tavern Chinese Red and Palace Supper Room Brown.

In addition to this wide assortment of colors, Martin-Senour offers a simulated whitewash for interior walls and ceilings. Used over plaster, wallboard, wood trim, or other surfaces, the whitewash gives a glowing, rough-textured finish with none of the disadvantages of the old-fashioned product.

Colonial Williamsburg paints are available nearly everywhere. If you need assistance in locating a supplier, however, contact:

The Martin-Senour Co.
1370 Ontario Ave., NW
Cleveland, OH 44113
(216) 566-3178

Benjamin Moore

Benjamin Moore's Historical Color Collection of interior paints is most suitable for Colonial and early 19th-century homes. The primary shades are delicate tones such as Monticello Rose, Wedgwood Gray, and Palladian Blue. The full line of forty-eight colors is offered in a flat latex, a latex eggshell finish, a latex satin enamel, and a low-luster enamel.

Benjamin Moore paints are manufactured and distributed throughout the United States and Canada. If there is no dealer close by, contact the company for further information.

Benjamin Moore & Co.
51 Chestnut Ridge Rd.
Montvale, NJ 07645
(201) 573-9600

Old-Fashioned Milk Paint

Milk-based paint was commonly used 200 years ago. Old-Fashioned is one of several firms that have revived its use for furniture and interiors. The paint is packaged in powdered form in pints, quarts, or gallons. There are eight basic colors to choose from—Barn Red, Pumpkin, Mustard, Bayberry, Lexington Green, Soldier Blue, Oyster White, and Pitch Black.

The paint is easy to mix at home. It is best used on raw wood or bare plaster, but can be applied to a previously painted surface if it has been thoroughly sanded. The company warns that its paint is impermeable to paint strippers, so be sure that the shade *is* the one that you can live with. Milk paint will not produce a smooth, glossy appearance, but a flat, grainy look. The effect is not unlike that which would have been achieved years ago when historic homes were new.

Brochure, 50¢. (SASE requested.)

The Old-Fashioned Milk Paint Co.
Box 222
Groton, MA 01450
(617) 448-6336

Pittsburgh Paints

Pittsburgh Paints has a line called Historic Colors for interior and exterior uses that provides a lovely sample of Colonial hues. Some of the deeper colors would be fine for later Victorian homes, too. The collection is available in latex for interiors, enamels for interiors and exteriors, and latex and oil for exteriors. Paint colors range from pastels to deep rustic shades.

Pittsburgh's standard exterior colors are also quite handsome. The firm's current brochure is very helpful, showing coordinating house, trim, and accent colors at a glance. Some of the colors found here are also represented in the Historic Color collection. Pittsburgh's regular line of enamel colors features an alkyd-oil gloss for floors and decks and an interesting selection of high-gloss paints.

For further information and brochures, contact your local Pittsburgh dealer, or:

Pittsburgh Paints
1 Gateway Center
Pittsburgh, PA 15222
(412) 434-3131

Portsmouth Paintworks

A new color line, Portsmouth Paintworks, should prove popular wherever Colonial-style houses predominate. The fifteen custom colors offered are rich, imaginative shades based on examples found in historic homes in the Portsmouth, New Hampshire, area. Fourteen of these are low-sheen, oil-based paints that can be used inside or outside; the fifteenth—New Rye Crimson—is a high-gloss paint. Also included in the line is an off-white "whitewash" shade which is especially useful for interior walls and ceilings.

Portsmouth will custom mix other colors for you if you submit samples.

Color cards, 50¢.

Portsmouth's paints are available at two retail outlets in the Portsmouth area and by mail through either of these outlets.

Portsmouth Paintworks
Partridge Replications
63 Penhallow St.
Portsmouth, NH 03801
(603) 431-8733

Portsmouth Paintworks
Partridge Replications
83 Grove St.
Peterborough, NH 03458
(603) 924-3002

Sherwin-Williams

Sherwin-Williams is to Victorian paint colors what Martin-Senour is to Colonial—the leader. Just as Martin-Senour led the way years ago with its Colonial Williamsburg line, Sherwin-Williams in 1981 was the first to introduce a series of Victorian Heritage Colors and did so in association with the Victorian Society of America. Since that time, of course, several other Victorian "reproduction" paint lines have been introduced. Sherwin-Williams's collection of forty colors is still among the best.

The Heritage Colors are available in exterior latex house and trim paints and in oil-based gloss house and trim paints.

Sherwin-Williams paints are distributed throughout the United States and Canada. If you need assistance in locating a supplier, contact:

Sherwin-Williams Co.
PO Box 6939
Cleveland, OH 44101
(216) 566-2332

Stulb Paint & Chemical

The Old Village Paint Colors are now being manufactured and offered to the public by Stulb. These paints, originally produced by Turco, have been popular with old-house renovators and decorators in the Northeast for many years. The thirteen Old Village Colors (plus Colonial White) are deep, saturated hues that are perfect for accenting architectural features. The paints are oil-base, have a soft sheen, and are recommended for indoor or outdoor use. When used outdoors, they are best mixed with Stulb's own Extra Durable Mixing Oil which gives them added durability and mildew resistance.

For further information and assistance in locating an Old Village supplier, contact:

Stulb Paint & Chemical Co.
PO 297
Norristown, PA 19404
(215) 272-6660

Wolf Paints

New Yorkers have found Wolf a wonderfully resourceful and reliable walk-in retail supplier of paints and papers. Founded in 1869, the firm is still run by the knowledgeable Wolf family. In addition to its own line of custom colors, Wolf carries many other quality brand-name paints. The inventory of papers is also extensive.

Decorators and restorers all over North America have discovered that Wolf is an extraordinary mail-order supplier of hard-to-find decorative tools and materials. Among these are graining, wood-finishing, stenciling, and gilding supplies as well as paperhanging tools and bronzing and glazing materials. There are brushes, combs, and other tools for graining, marbling, stippling, dragging, and other decorative techniques.

For information regarding Wolf's catalogue of supplies for painting, papering, and other decorative techniques, contact:

S. Wolf's Sons
771 Ninth Ave.
New York, NY 10019
(212) 245-7777

Cleaners and Finishers

Old house people often spend more time cleaning and refinishing surfaces and objects than they do in adorning them. Age may take its toll—in tarnish, grime, and material deterioration—but it's a shame to toss something out simply because it looks tacky. In most cases, old hardware, woodwork, plasterwork, ceramic fixtures, and even such especially durable materials as stone and brick can be saved and renewed for many more years of service. But great care and patience must be exercised in the cleaning and refinishing process. It is all too easy, for example to rush a painted wood mantel off to the strippers for a bath of caustic chemicals, agents which may destroy the very grain which one is trying to enhance. Try, instead, any of the products and processes described in the entries that follow.

Bradford Derustit

Locks, hardware, fixtures, and other metal objects that are in bad shape will profit from B-P Metal Cleaner. A similar product, No. 1 Brightener, works even faster and is especially recommended for cleaning brass and copper objects. B-P Metal Cleaner may also come in handy when it is time to clean outdoor iron furniture and accessories such as urns or bases.

Contact the company for information on availability.

Bradford Derustit Corp.
PO Box 151
Clifton Park, NY 12065
(518) 371-5420

Cabot Oils and Stains

Samuel Cabot, Inc., is practically synonymous with wood stains. In business for over 100 years, the firm supplies a larger variety of such finishing materials as solid-color stains, transparent stains, semi-solid stains, bleaching oil, Danish oil, and deck stains than almost any other company. A stain may be more appropriate than a paint for an early American home or a Victorian seaside cottage. If this is the case, one of Cabot's products could be the right choice for you. There are many different colors to select from.

Cabot distributes its products throughout North America. If you need assistance in locating a source, contact:

Samuel Cabot, Inc.
1 Union St.
Boston, MA 02108
(716) 723-7740

Chemique

KRC-7 Cleaner/Restorer is of special use in the bathroom and kitchen. All too often old ceramic tubs, toilets, and basins are thrown out because they have acquired hard water stains over the years; similarly, ceramic tile is often given up for good merely because the grout has become grotty. KRC-7 is a liquid cleaner that will restore these materials to their lily-white original state.

For further information, contact:

Chemique, Inc.
315 N. Washington Ave.
Moorestown, NJ 08057
(609) 235-4161

Daly's Wood Finishing Products

Removing stains and inappropriate finishes can take more time than almost any other old-house task. Few are the homes where the woodwork has not been "touched up" or otherwise ill-treated over the years. Daly's many products—stain removers; paste wood fillers; teak, lemon, and tung oil for finishing—will prove effective for all kinds of wood found throughout the house from moldings and doors to paneling and cabinetwork. The same products are also highly recommended for refinishing furniture.

If these products are not available through your local home center or hardware store, contact:

Daly's Wood Finishing Products
1121 N. 36th St.
Seattle, WA 98103
(206) 633-4200

Diedrich Chemicals

The amazing results achieved on masonry buildings with Diedrich chemical treatments have already been chronicled in chapter 1 in discussing the work of Anderson Building Restoration. Anderson is just one of many contracting firms that makes use of Diedrich's cleaners and paint removers. Use of these solvents in conjunction with high pressure water rinsing has revolutionized facade cleaning and restoration. The two principal Diedrich products are the 101 Masonry Restorer/Cleaner and the 606 Multi Layer Paint Remover. The 606 formula can be used as effectively for wood as for masonry buildings, although the procedure followed is somewhat different.

Diedrich has also formulated a waterproofing preserver which is extremely effective. Preserver 303 is a penetrating preservative resin and volatile thinner-type repel-lent. It deeply penetrates any masonry surface. Unlike other sealers, especially acrylics, which only coat the surface or barely reach beneath it, 303 does not trap moisture. Neither does it give that shiny, glazed look which can ruin the appearance of stone or brick. Polyurethane-like substances are bad enough on wood; they can be extremely damaging to masonry. Use Preserver 303 instead.

For further information regarding Diedrich materials and contractors who make use of them, contact:

Diedrich Chemicals Restoration
Technologies, Inc.
300A E. Oak St.
Milwaukee, WI 53154
(414) 761-2591

Howard Products

Refinishing materials that actually improve a natural wood surface rather than ruin it are not always readily at hand. Stripping with chemicals is often the worst possible solution when furniture, cabinets, paneling, or woodwork have to be cleaned. Howard's Restor-a-Finish is a non-caustic one-step cleaner that will eliminate some of the most noxious surface blemishes and signs of wear and tear. It is available in seven different wood tones—neutral, maple/pine, golden oak, walnut, mahogany, dark walnut, and dark oak.

For information regarding the availability of Restor-a-Finish, contact:

Howard Products, Inc.
411 W. Maple Ave.
Monrovia, CA 91016
(818) 357-9545

McCloskey Varnish

McCloskey offers one of the finest lines of quality varnishes and stains available for both interior and exterior purposes. The very best of these for old wood surfaces are the low-sheen phenolic or alkyd-base varnishes which make use of various combinations of tung oil, drying oils, resins, alcohols, or organic acids.

McCloskey's clear natural flat interior varnish has been a household staple for years and is specially recommended for paneling, cabinets, and doors. For floors, we'd suggest McCloskey's Gymseal; it is much tougher than polyurethane and creates a more pleasing finish.

If you require assistance in locating McCloskey products, contact:

McCloskey Varnish Co.
7600 State Rd.
Philadelphia, PA 19136
(215) 624-4400

North Coast Chemical

Northco is best known for its special non-caustic copper and brass cleaners and stainless-steel polish. The manufacturer also carries a full line of other specialty cleaners such as clear concentrated coconut oil soap and 727 cement truck cleaner which, despite its name, is used for masonry, fireplace brick, and metal objects.

For further information, contact:

North Coast Chemical Co.
PO Box 80366
6300 17th Ave. S.
Seattle, WA 98108
(206) 763-1340

QRB Industries

Removing old paint is never any fun, and, when it is woodwork that requires attention, even more patience is required. QRB stands for Quickly Restores Beauty. We won't guarantee that QRB's paint remover will do just that, but it will certainly make your job easier. Unlike many paint strippers, the QRB product is not caustic but, rather, contains petroleum-based materials. It does not evaporate quickly, and may be applied with an old washcloth. The manufacturer claims that even milk paint—that most penetrating of finishes—will come up with the use of the remover.

Literature available.

150 | *QRB Industries*
3139 US 31 N.
Niles, MI 49120
(616) 683-7908 or 471-3887

TALAS

TALAS, a division of Technical Library Service Inc., is a supplier of specialty tools, equipment, and books for the restoration and repair of fine materials. Many museum conservators regularly use this source for obscure items not carried by hardware or paint stores. TALAS carries cleaners useful for some building materials as well as fabrics.

TALAS will supply a price list of its offerings useful to home restorers.

TALAS
213 W. 35th St.
New York, NY 10001
(212) 736-7744

Decorative Painters

The decorative painter was once an important member of the building and decorating trades. Well into the 1900s, the house painter might be called on to grain or varnish wood-work, to glaze walls, to execute sten-ciled or freehand designs, and to gild or otherwise embellish plaster decora-tion. All of these tasks were under-taken in addition to the routine work of painting walls and ceilings. For-tunately, the special skills once prac-ticed by the house painter have not been totally lost. Today there are prob-ably more practitioners of ornamental painting than at any time in the past fifty years. Some of the best of these artists are presented in the following listings.

Dick Adcock

Wood graining and marbling are two of the special skills mastered by Little Rock decorative painter Dick Adcock. He has worked on several important Arkansas restorations, including the old State House in Little Rock and Old Washington courthouse at Hope, and has practiced his talents in homes in Little Rock's well-known Quapaw Quarter preservation district.

Illustrated are examples of his work at the Old State House—a wood-grained door and a marbleized fireplace mantel.

For further information, contact:

Dick Adcock
5404 Walnut Rd.
North Little Rock, AR 72116
(501) 758-8979

Biltmore, Campbell, Smith Restorations

The English firm of Campbell, Smith & Co. was formed in 1873 and since that time has been responsible for the decoration and restoration of some of the major historic properties in the United Kingdom, including every state room in Buckingham Palace, St. Paul's Cathedral, Westminster Ab-bey, and the Houses of Parlia-ment. In 1982 a branch of this venerable company of craftsmen was established in Asheville, North Carolina, in order to oversee the on-going restoration work at the famed Vanderbilt mansion, and to undertake other American commissions.

It is unlikely that Biltmore, Camp-bell, Smith Restorations will find it feasible to exercise its con-siderable skills on everyday restorations; major projects such as San Francisco Plantation in Louisiana are more its mission. This is the type of restoration which calls for such expert detail work as gold leafing; stenciling, graining, and marbling; cleaning and restoration of murals and paintings; cleaning of stonework; and meticulous paint restoration. If a major restoration project is in the offing, it would be wise to consult this talented group of ar-tisans who will be pleased to prepare detailed job specifications and cost estimates.

Brochure available.

Biltmore, Campbell, Smith Restora-
tions, Inc.
One Biltmore Plaza
Asheville, NC 28803
(704) 274-1776

Larry Boyce & Associates

If you can find Larry Boyce, hold on to him. He is among the most talented decorative painters in America and attracts like-minded artists to assist him. Larry is often in San Francisco where he has ex-ecuted some gloriously ornamen-tal ceilings and cornices. He works with traditional Victorian designs of indisputable historical authenticity, but he interprets them in his own brash, polychromatic manner. The results are always breathtaking.

Larry and his fellow artists have formed an organization which is San Francisco-based. They work, however, throughout the West, and from time to time make forays farther east. Since they make their excursions to a new job site by bicycle, contact is sometimes difficult to make. But once they are on a job, they are really on top of it; Larry and any necessary helpers live-in while work is in progress.

Larry Boyce & Associates
PO Box 421507
San Francisco, CA 94142
(415) 462-2122

If you are unable to reach Larry at this address or number, contact Bradbury & Bradbury's Bruce Bradbury, who is likely to be *au courant* on the latest Boyce project and work site.

Bruce Bradbury
Bradbury & Bradbury Wallpapers
PO Box 155
Benicia, CA 94510
(707) 746-1900

Bob Buckter, Color Consultant

Buckter is one of the painters responsible for creating San Francisco's colorful Painted Ladies—Queen Anne row houses which have been brought to life with imaginative new color schemes. It is quite instructive to compare before and after photograhs of these buildings. A well thought-out, imaginatively applied paint job can dramatically improve almost any building, but many-faceted late-Victorian facades especially profit from the application of base and complementary trim colors.

Buckter's contracting firm performs jobs throughout the Bay area, but his design services are also available through the mail. He will provide specifications for residential and commercial projects as well as information on surface preparation and what to expect in regard to exposure to the elements.

Brochure available.

Bob Buckter, Color Consultant
3877 20th St.
San Francisco, CA 94114
(415) 922-7444

John Canning

John Canning is an artist and a scholar. A Scotsman trained in the old-fashioned techniques of the Victorian decorative painter, he can execute or restore just about any type of ornamentation called for in an old-house project, including painted ceilings, grained woodwork, marbleized mantels and baseboards, stenciled floors and wall panels, and trompe l'oeil effects.

Canning's great love is Victorian decoration, and he has worked on distinguished projects in the United States and the United Kingdom. As he states, "I really think Victorian decoration has not received enough credit. It is well thought-out, full of symmetry and order, with no discordant color schemes."

From time to time Canning has been called on to reproduce so-called Colonial stenciling, the simple designs executed by itinerant artists in the 18th- and early 19th-centuries. As he notes, decoration of this type is very appropriate for Colonial homes but is often mistakenly chosen for later interiors. "A lot of interior decoration in Victorian houses," he writes, "is still being carried out in terms of 18th-century decorations." Canning simply won't do what he doesn't think is right. Would that there were more John Cannings.

For further information, contact:

John Canning
132 Meeker Rd.
Southington, CT 06489
(203) 621-2188

Crown Restorations

This fine group of craftsmen has

achieved an enviable reputation for historically correct restoration work. Crown's specialty is Victorian and early 20th-century decoration. Among the techniques the members of the Crown team have mastered are stenciling, pounce painting, graining, glazing, application of various types of metallic leaf, marbling, and polychrome exterior painting. A member of the Crown group is shown here at work on the restoration of the Roberson Mansion, Binghamton, New York, a part of the Roberson Center for the Arts and Sciences. Other projects have included the restoration of the Grand Foyer of the Landmark Theatre, Syracuse, New York; stenciling restoration at the 1890 House Museum, Cortland, New York, and at the Hudson River Museum, Yonkers, New York; and exterior restoration of Manderfield Manor, Syracuse.

Crown Restoration is also prepared to undertake any historical research and materials analysis necessary to a successful restoration project.

Brochure available.

Crown Restoration
18 Homer Ave.
Cortland, NY 13045
(607) 756-2632

Designed Communications

During the past five or six years, Becky Witsell and Suzanne Kittrell have helped to bring the Victorian decorative past alive again in the Little Rock area, and now, through Designed Communica-

tions, are offering their services more widely. They have documented and restored some wonderful examples of late-Victorian stenciling, in particular cornice and ceiling designs. Illustrated is one recent commission, the re-creation of authentic Craftsman stenciled designs in a 1917 restoration.

Designed Communications is now preparing a sourcebook of late stencil designs—*Authentic Stencil Patterns: 1890-1930*—for publication. This sixty-page compilation of design is selected from the actual catalogues used by painters and decorators to order hand-cut stencils, and sells for $10.95. Over 500 designs will be reproduced in the same scale as the catalogue originals. Most of the designs are for drop borders and friezes, but there are also ceiling patterns as well as designs suggested for walls and dadoes.

In addition to the stenciling services, Designed Communications will also execute Tiffany-glaze finishes, grain painting, bronze-powder gilding, mural painting, and will create silk-screened facsimile papers and borders.

For further information, contact:

Designed Communications
704 Boyle Bldg., 103 W. Capitol
Little Rock, AR 72201
(501) 372-2056

Edward K. Perry Co.

Four generations of the Perry family have directed the operations of this distinguished Boston decorating and design firm since the 1850s. It is perhaps fitting, then, that such august institutions as Boston's Museum of Fine Arts, Faneuil Hall, Houghton Library at Harvard University, The Breakers in Newport, Colonial Williamsburg, and Old Sturbridge Village have been among the company's regular clients.

Routine painting constitutes the bulk of the firm's business, but specialty decorative techniques are often called for. Perry's craftsmen are talented at executing oil and water glazes, graining, gilding, marbling, combing, and stenciling. Trompe l'oeil work, painted floors, and wall murals are yet other specialties.

Pamphlet available.

Edward K. Perry Co.
322 Newbury St.
Boston, MA 02115
(617) 536-7873

Rambusch

This important New York-based restoration and design firm has never forgotten its beginnings in the 1890s as primarily a decorative painting contractor. The Decorative Painting Studio remains an important part of the Rambusch operation. Such skilled techniques as applying metallic leaf, graining, marbling, gilding, glazing, and stenciling are routinely practiced by members of the studio staff. Among the studio's most important recent assign-

ments have been the Helmsley Palace Hotel/Villard Houses restoration, the Newark Museum's Ballantine House, and the New York State Capitol in Albany.

For further information, contact:

The Rambusch Co.
40 W. 13th St.
New York, NY 10011
(212) 675-0400

Valley Craftsmen

The decorating and custom design firm of Valley Craftsmen specializes in dramatic interior effects such as trompe l'oeil work, faux marquetry and marbleized floors, and glazed walls. This type of on-site work is undertaken only in the Baltimore/Washington area. The firm, however, will also execute custom-ordered murals on canvas that can be shipped anywhere desired.

For further information, contact:

The Valley Craftsmen Ltd.
Box 11
Stevenson, MD 21153
(301) 484-3891

Waterman West

Scott Waterman and his associates in Atlanta offer a wide range of decorative services. Trained as fine artists, they have mastered the techniques of marbling, stenciling, trompe l'oeil, glazing, gilding, and the execution of other faux finishes. Among their most ambitious recent projects has been the dramatic lobby of the Ponce Building in Atlanta. This interior had deteriorated badly, and it was necessary to restore nearly every square inch of the lofty space. Shown opposite is a working sketch of the project which required the re-creation of stenciled and marbleized decoration, as well as glazing, gilding, limestone "mottling," bronzing, and hand painting.

For further information, contact:

Waterman West
741 Ponce de Leon Court, Suite 4
Atlanta, GA 30308
(404) 874-9678

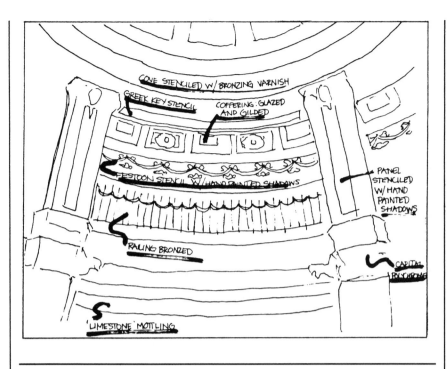

Papers

Ever since wallpaper could be inexpensively produced in continuous rolls by high-speed printing presses in the mid-19th century, papers have found numerous practical and decorative uses in the home. Today's homeowner will find papers similarly useful and ornamental. Available in various finishes and textures, modern papers are generally easier to hang and to keep clean than the old-fashioned variety. There are hundreds of well-documented reproduction designs from the 18th and 19th centuries to choose from, as well as thousands of adaptations and inter-

pretations of traditional florals, stripes, and geometrics. Slowly but steadily, the old practice of using two or three papers in a room is once again gaining favor. Wallpaper borders can be effectively used to create cornice and frieze designs; other papers are appropriate for use on the ceilings or as wall panels. Special embossed and textured Victorian papers such as Lincrusta Walton and Supaglypta are being produced once again and are especially appropriate and attractive substitutes for wainscoting in hallways and dining rooms.

Laura Ashley

Each year the Laura Ashley wallpaper collection becomes more comprehensive. It has expanded far beyond the small-print sprigged country florals for which it first was famous. Ashley papers now include a good selection of stripes, moirés, and geometrics, several in bright, vivid colors. Many of the wallcoverings are suitable for formal rooms, and include 19th-century arborescent prints; Victorian designs in flowers, stripes, and swirls; and adaptations of period designs.

Of special interest is a diamond-

motif pattern by 19th-century designer, Owen Jones, which is aptly named Mr. Jones. Laura Ashley produces it in the original color combination of navy, sand, and burgundy. "Masculine" designs such as this are a far cry from the delicate pastels we had come to expect from this company.

Of course, the Ashely collection still includes many wonderful, traditional designs in a great range of subtle decorator colors. The company also offers a new Decorator Collection, available

only to the design trade. The majority of the firm's papers and fabrics are nonetheless available in Laura Ashley retail outlets and through its home furnishings catalogue.

Home furnishings catalogue, $3.50.

Laura Ashley
Box 5308
Melville, NY 11747
(800) 367-2000

Bassett & Vollum

Using a hand-silkscreen process, Bassett & Vollum reproduces many fine antique wallpapers and borders. The three-part wall treatment illustrated here is from a document taken from a home in Versailles and dates from the Louis Phillippe period of 19th-century decoration. The frieze, Les Peaux Rouges, and the base, Feston et Pompon, each require sixteen screens to produce the intricate detail of the original wood blocks. The sidewall paper, Draperie, is an excellent example of the trompe l'oeil technique. The paper and the frieze and base borders are reproduced in the original colors—amethyst, teal, and gray—as well as in three other colorways.

Bassett & Vollum has a collection of over thirty superb borders suitable for period decoration, borders that can be used alone or in conjunction with sidewall papers. The firm can also custom

154 | color any of their papers and will handle special orders.

Free brochure of borders available.

Bassett & Vollum
217 N. Main St.
Galena, IL 61036
(815) 777-2460

Bentley Brothers

Bentley serves as the American distributor of Crown Decorative Products of England, the principal manufacturer of specially embossed papers. Included among these materials are Supaglypta, Anaglypta, Lincrusta, and pelmet.

Beginning in the 1870s, various types of heavily ornamented papers began coming on the market. These were a great deal less expensive than leather wall-coverings or plaster ornamentation and found practical use in hallways, dining rooms, and other areas of the home where it was important to have a handsome but very durable wallcovering.

Frederick Walton, inventor of linoleum, patented Lincrusta-Walton in 1877, and this linseed oil compound was later manufactured in considerable quantities in North America. For some time, Lincrusta-Walton has been impossible to find, and anyone seeking to restore a room containing this material has had to come up with substitutes. But no longer.

Illustrated is one of the Lincrusta wainscot patterns produced by Crown and available through Bentley. This is RD 1951 and is made in 21¼" by 36" panels.

Supaglypta is much lighter in weight than Lincrusta and can be used to cover ceilings as well as walls. Supaglypta has higher relief than Anaglypta and is a combination of cotton fibers and wood pulp; Anaglypta is simply a pressed paper product, although a vinyl version is also available. The octagonal design shown in is Crown's #148 Supaglypta, which is supplied in rolls.

The last of the designs illustrated is of a material known as pelmet and made up of cotton fibers and pulp. Shown is border #651; two other Crown pelmet border designs are offered.

Illustrated brochure available.

Bentley Brothers
918 Baxter Ave.
Louisville, KY 40204
(502) 589-2939

Louis W. Bowen

From an office lined with authoritative texts on historical decorating (in several languages), Louis Bowen oversees the production of top-quality period wall-coverings, including murals, landscapes, and handmade book papers, as well as fine reproduction wall panels. One feature of the Bowen offices is a wall adorned with Palais Royale, a hand-painted scenic paper from the Directoire period, and a portion of which is illustrated here. The complete set is composed of thirty panels, each 19¼" wide, and would make a magnificent addition to a large formal room

Shown on the opposite page is Cupid and Psyche, discovered in an 1818 Salem house. This handsome series of wall panels reproduces an 1814 design by the French firm Desfosse. Three of the four available panels are shown here; the original design was made up of many more panels. Bowen also offers some of the rare antique originals.

The company carries marbleized flotation squares, all handmade, which may be used in various combinations to form panels or moldings, or to give the illusion of an architectural element. As a less expensive alternative, Bowen has marbleized vinyl papers available in rolls.

The papers described here are clearly meant for houses built on a grand scale. But Bowen has a fine selection of papers suitable for other types of period decoration.

For further information, contact:

Louis W. Bowen, Inc.
979 Third Ave.
New York, NY 10022
(212) 392-5810

Bradbury & Bradbury

Bradbury & Bradbury has become the favorite supplier of every professional restorer of late-Victorian interiors—and for good reason. No other firm has so mastered the design and color vocabulary of the post-Civil War period in papers. The selection of wallpapers, frieze papers, and borders that are representative of the best of English and American designers of the 1870s through the early 1900s is simply without equal.

Illustrated at the beginning of this chapter is a bedroom decorated with Anglo-Japanese papers, including—on the walls—what Bradbury & Bradbury calls its Eastlake frieze paper, Eastlake dado paper, and Claire's Willow wallpaper.

Shown here is a detail of the ceiling ornamentation of that room with Ivy Block Enrichment, a small geometric pattern of gilded ivy, enclosing the Sunflower corner block and Sunburst Ceiling papers.

The company's handprinted frieze papers are very handsome. There are six basic designs, including the Neo-Grec frieze shown here. 12"-wide samples of these are available for $2.50 each by writing to Bradbury.

There are over thirty Victorian-inspired patterns to choose from for use as ceiling, dado, or overall wallpapers. Among them are the designs illustrated here: Lily, designed by P. B. Wight in 1875, and available in russet, orange, and metallic bronze on lacquer green or deep burgundy, metallic gold, and shell on terra cotta; Lattice Dado, an 1875 Christopher Dresser design, available in marigold, chocolate, and turquoise on midnight blue; and William Morris's Bird & Anemone design of 1882, reproduced by

Bradbury & Bradbury in ultramarine on French blue, deep maroon on Pompeiian red, or golden wheat on vanilla.

Catalogue of designs, $1.

Bradbury & Bradbury Wallpapers
Box 155
Benicia, CA 94510

| **Brunschwig & Fils**

Brunschwig is justly known for its historic reproduction papers, many of which are exact copies of museum- or privately-owned antique papers or other decorative designs. The seven papers shown here span many periods and are historically correct as well as beautifully produced.

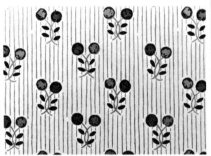

Cerises is a simple design from 1750-60. It is taken from a French block print, as are many Brunschwig papers. The original colors are brick and blue. The paper is also offered in green and coral, rose and mauve, Wedgwood and ginger, or in shades of blue.

Fox and Rooster, also taken from a French block print, dates from 1780-1800. It is reproduced from a document at the Museum of Early Southern Decorative Arts and comes in two colorways—rose and blue on clay, which is the original color scheme, and salmon and gold on beige.

Ashlar, hand-printed for the restoration of Boscobel, is an American block print from

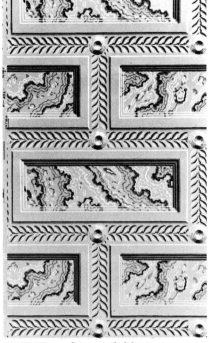

1800-10, and is available in tan.

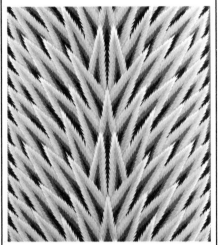

Christaux is a monochromatic French block print available in any one of seven colors: sand, green, coral, apricot, amethyst, and gray, which is the document color. The original is owned by the Musée des Arts Décoratifs in Paris and dates from 1825-35.

Fuchsia Trellis uses the bamboo motif so popular with the Vic-

torians. It dates from 1870-85 and is offered in six different colors, including pistachio (the original), shell, and light blue.

Mignonne is a new Brunschwig paper and is also available in a matching fabric. The paper and its border are superb examples of 19th-century trompe l'oeil. It is adapted from an example in the collection at the Musée des Arts Décoratifs and is offered in the original gray as well as in six other colors—sand, vanilla, blue, gold, celadon, and dusty rose.

Brunschwig papers are available only through interior designers or decorating departments of selected retail outlets. Contact the company for more information.

Brunschwig & Fils
979 Third Ave.
New York, NY 10022
(212) 838-7878

Greeff

Over the years, Greeff has been responsible for a number of historic reproduction papers and fabrics. The Shelburne Museum collection, for example, is taken from various fabrics and decorative items, including quilts and stencil patterns, found at the Shelburne Museum in Vermont. A trip to Salzburg by members of Greeff's design studio led to the discovery of a unique set of 18th- and 19th-century hand-carved wood blocks which inspired the Lindenwood collection. The

wallcovering shown here, Lorraine, is a part of this group of provincial prints. The tiny floral spring pattern would serve as a good background paper for a country bedroom.

Greeff papers are available to the trade through its showrooms and through the design departments of selected retail stores. Contact the company for information.

Greeff Fabrics, Inc.
155 E. 56th St.
New York, NY 10022
(212) 888-5060

Lee Jofa

Many of Lee Jofa's papers are reproductions or adaptations of documents with French, English, or Chinese origins. The two designs shown here are just a sampling of the company's many charming floral prints.

Carnation is a sophisticated print of English garden flowers and foliage that dates back to 1750. The design incorporates eleven different colors and is offered in nine colorways, including one

with a dramatic red background. Matching fabric is available.

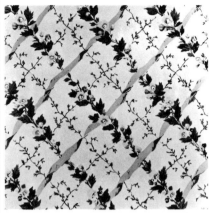

Ribbon and Trail Trellis is a ribbon-and-vine floral paper with a geometric pattern. It is derived from an 18th-century child's dress and is available in nine different colors, including several attractive pastels.

The Lee Jofa Wallcovering Collectin is sold exclusively through its showrooms.

For further information, contact:

Lee Jofa
800 Central Blvd.
Carlstadt, NJ 07072
(201) 438-8444

Katzenbach & Warren

Katzenbach & Warren wallpapers may look familiar to anyone who has pored over the Williamsburg Reproductions catalogue or visited Colonial Williamsburg. These historic papers, licensed by the well-known restoration, are carefully reproduced from documents and are eminently suitable for period decor.

The Tavern Resist pattern, shown here, was reduced in scale from

the original, an 18th-century fabric print, probably made in the Colonies by the "resist" method of waxing in the design and then dipping the waxed cloth in a color vat to obtain the background. The paper comes in a smoky blue on white and in several other colors.

Kennebunkport, Maine, is the source of the 18th-century walllpaper fragment from which "Lafayette Floral," pictured here, is copied. The old English paper, bearing the Georgian tax stamp, was discovered under several layers of more recent papers in a house built about 1757. It is offered in bright floral colors against a pale ground.

Katzenbach & Warren papers are available through designers and in selected retail shops.

Katzenbach & Warren, Inc.
950 Third Avenue
New York, NY 10022
(212) 759-5410

Sanderson

The venerable English design house, Arthur Sanderson & Sons, has recently opened a New York showroom for its traditional fabrics and papers. A particular sepcialty is the superb collection of William Morris papers. These are hand-printed from Morris's own stock of intricately carved and inlaid printing blocks, which Sanderson now owns. Each of the twenty original Victorian designs is available in two to five colors. Several of these papers have proven so perennially popular that Sanderson has made the designs available in silkscreeen reproductions which are some-

158 | what more affordable than the hand-blocked papers.

For further information, contact:

Arthur Sanderson & Sons
979 Third Ave.
New York, NY 10022
(212) 319-7220

San Francisco Victoriana

Best known for its superb reproduction millwork, San Francisco Victoriana also possesses a valuable stock of German turn-of-the-century wallpaper borders. There are eight highly fanciful designs in widths ranging from $2\frac{7}{8}''$ to $14\frac{1}{4}''$; all except one are available in 3' lengths, the eighth being half that size. Samples of these antique papers have been authenticated by the Smithsonian Institution.

San Francisco Victoriana is also a prime supplier of Crown Decorative Products' Anaglypta and Supaglypta embossed papers.

Sample packet of eight border patterns, $15.

San Francisco Victoriana
2245 Palou Ave.
San Francisco, CA 94124

Scalamandré

As anyone with an interest in period design knows, Scalamandré is a leader in the field of historic papers and fabrics. Its studio and mill can handle the most complex documentary designs as a matter of course. The firm also takes on many private restoration projects, for which it authentically reproduces specific fabrics and wallcoverings. The four custom papers shown here were produced for such projects and have not, as yet, been released to the public. These papers are representative of the type of well-documented materials which Scalamandré offers as part of its standard repertoire.

#81329 dates from 1846 and has been reproduced for the Second Parlor/Dining Room of the Elizabeth Cady Stanton House in Seneca Falls, New York. It is

hand-printed in three colors.

Also from the Stanton House, #81328 is reproduced from the paper in the stair hallway. It is

#81318 is a reproduction of wallpaper in the Chintz Room of

done in oyster and green on polar white and was originally produced in 1850.

One of the papers that will soon be added to the regular Scalamandré line is #81264, based on wallcovering in the Grant Kohrs Ranch in Deer Lodge, Montana. This delicate design dates from 1890 and gives us a good idea of how Victorian patterns were modified as they moved away from the two coasts. It is produced in oatmeal and metallic silver on smoke.

Franklin D. Roosevelt's home in Hyde Park, New York.

Scalamandré papers are available only through designers and the decorating departments of selected retail stores. Contact the company for more information.

Scalamandré, Inc.
950 Third Ave.
New York, NY 10022
(212) 361-8500

Schumacher

The Loire Valley collection of wallcoverings, newly available from Schumacher, is interpreted from French design motifs. They are especially appropriate in country settings, as the three room settings pictured here illustrate.

Fleurs de Beauvais and Beauvais border are adapted from a fabric document found at the Mulhouse Museum in Alsace, a renowned printing and textile museum. The sprigged paper and ribbon frieze are offered in the original red.

La Faye Vine is an airy floral pattern available in five color combinations, including French blue and mauve. The companion border is shown in ash.,

Courson, with its subtle striped undertones is offered in five color combinations, including the parchment and blue shown in this hallway.

Schumacher carries many collections of papers suitable for period homes.

F. Schumacher & Co.
939 Third Ave.
New York, NY 10022
(212) 644-5900

160 | Richard Thibaut

Thibaut's American Colonial Collection was produced in conjunction with the Historical Society of Early American Decoration. The company's design team worked closely with the society to reproduce faithfully the beauty of the original techniques, including stenciling, painting, and gold leaf.

Hanbury Tulip, shown here, is an example of Pontypool painting, sometimes called "lace-edged" or "pierced-edged." The process originated in Wales in the 17600s, when John Hanbury and his foreman invented a rolling mill to produce smooth, thin sheets of iron and a method of lacquering which gave craftsmen a perfect surface to decorate. This floral paper is available in five color combinations, including reds on dark green, blue and rust on white, and peach and gold on black.

Neville Rose is adapted from a design of George Neville, a master of the art of Victorian painting. About 1831, he established a trend of realistic flower painting, as seen in this paper. It is offered in some lovely color combinatinons, including mauve, blue, and beige on tan; peach and light blue on teal; creams and off-whites on metallic gold; and red and blue on yellow.

For further information, contact:

Richard E. Thibaut, Inc.
706 S. 21st St.
Irvington, NJ 07111
(201) 399-7888

Victorian Collectibles

Several years ago, Florence Schroeder and her associates discovered a cache of 3,000 rolls of pristine, unused Victorian wallpaper in a storeroom in Wisconsin. Samples of these papers are now a part of the Cooper-Hewitt Museum's decorative arts collections, but the actual papers are for sale through Ms. Schroeder's company, Victorian Collectibles. The 3,000 rolls include 1,400 different designs ranging from Renaissance Revival to Arts and Crafts to Art Nouveau patterns. They date from the late 19th century through World War I. Some of the papers come with companion borders. In addition, the company has produced some reproductions from this treasure trove of Victoriana.

The room setting photograph shows 19th-century papers used in a modern low-ceilinged room. Both the sidewall and ceiling are covered in antique papers. The lower wall is covered in an antique border that would have been used as ceiling trim in fifteen-foot-high Victorian rooms.

The Regal Medallion paper is a baroque Victorian design from an antique paper which Victorian Collectibles has reproduced as a sidewall paper and matching fabric.

Information packet available upon request.

Victorian Collectibles Ltd.
845 E. Glenbrook Rd.
Milwaukee, WI 53217
(414) 352-6910

The Wallpaper Works

This company has become an important supplier of early 20th-century wallpapers for film production companies bent on recreating just the right residential interior. Although some would be reluctant to call these papers "antique," most of the rolls are more than fifty years old and certainly suitable for post-Victorian interiors. Quantities, of course, are limited. The selection is quite broad, and, if possible, the firm suggests that prospective buyers should arrange to examine the various patterns.

For further information regarding the current stock and samples, contact:

Lawrie Weiser
The Wallpaper Works
749 Queen St. W.
Toronto, Ontario, Canada
* M6J 1G1*
(416) 366-1790

Zina Studios

This design studio specializes in hand-printed wallcoverings and fabrics, custom made for the design trade. Besides its own collection of approximately 150 designs, the firm is often commissioned to reproduce documents for historic buildings and restorations. The papers shown here were reproduced for Chateau-sur-Mer, the extraordinary mansion in Newport, Rhode Island, which was built in 1852 by William Wetmore.

The Griffon paper for the Butternut Room, pictured here, is a reproduction of a tooled leather original, encrusted with gold and silver threads. Zina Studios recreated the effect of the stitches and used a subtle metallic paint to print it. The Griffon border, in aqua and lavender, accompanies the paper.

The paper for the Turkish Sitting Room, also illustrated, was reproduced line-for-line from slides and photcopies of the original wallcovering. Again the stitch effect was reproduced with gold, silver, and black paint aginst a blue background.

Curiously, Zina Studios had a descendant of the Wetmore family as a client for many years, without knowing who she was or where the papers ordered by her were being used. It wasn't until the firm was commissioned for the reproductions and visted Chateau-sur-Mer that Zina Studios discovered its work, roped-off as a museum exhibit!

Zina Studios, Inc.
85 Purdy Ave.
Port Chester, NY 10573
(914) 937-5661

Other Suppliers of Paints and Papers

Consult List of Suppliers for addresses.

Paints

Cohasett Colonials
Cook & Dunn Paint Corp.
Dutch Boy Paints
Hydrozo Coatings Co.
Janovic/Plaza
Munsell Color
Pratt & Lambert

Papers

Charles Barone, Inc.
Cole & Son
Colefax & Fowler
S. M. Hexter
Jones & Erwin, Inc.
Manuscreens, Inc.
Old Stone Mill
Thomas Strahan Co.
The Twigs, Inc.
Albert Van Luit & Co.

Decorative Painters

Adele Bishop, Inc.
The Ceiling Lady
Form & Texture
A. Greenhalgh & Sons
Hudson-Shatz Painting Co.
Megan Parry
John L. Seekamp
The Toby House
D. B. Wiggins

8.

Fabrics

As with wallpaper, the use of decorative fabrics was at one time restricted only to the very rich. Before the 19th century, textiles were handwoven and used sparingly for decoration. And especially in North America, most fabrics had to be imported from Europe, except for the basic homespuns, cottons, and muslins. As fabrics became easier to mass produce, they began to be used all over the house. The Victorian age witnessed the peak of fabric used as decoration. Windows were festooned, lined, and draped, often with several different materials. Sofas were overstuffed and fringed, and every conceivable piece of furniture was covered. As if all this weren't enough, almost any surface could sport doilies or silk table squares.

Today, most topnotch fabric companies offer a multitude of materials suitable for many period decors. In fact, reproduction fabrics are big business, with new collections coming out each season. The higher-priced collections are often produced from what the design trade calls documents, which are actual remnants of period fabrics or other items, such as belts, coverlets, or clothing. These are often produced in several colors, including the original, or document, color. Many historical collections also contain interpretations, loosely based on an earlier style or pattern. These are often more appealing to contemporary tastes and budgets, while still offering the flavor of an historical period.

As in all elements of decoration, certain rules of good sense apply. Lightweight cotton prints which would be perfect for curtains simply can't hold up as upholstery, for example. And rich damasks and velvets would probably overpower a simple Colonial-period living room. But, within the limits of reason and taste, a home renovator should have no problem selecting appropriate materials, given the wide range of price, style, and quality available.

Fishing Lady, 100% cotton print,
Greeff Fabrics, New York, New York.

164 | Laura Ashley

As we have described in chapter 7, Paints and Papers, the Laura Ashley Company has added innovative new designs to its collection, as well as expanded its fine line of small-print cottons. Now offered are several "drawing room" fabrics in a heavyweight cotton sateen, suitable for draperies and light upholstery. Many of these are large-scale designs, including florals and flamestitch-type patterns which are appropriate for formal rooms. In addition, Ashley has expanded its collection of chintzes, upholstery fabrics, and quilted materials. Another Laura Ashley first is the new Decorator Collection, which is available only to the design trade. The fabrics shown here are from this group and are similar in style to the designs offered through its retail outlets.

The sofa and armchair are covered in a Decorator Collection chintz, #F356, which is currently offered in one colorway—smoke, stone, and sage. The draperies are made from #F253 and are also offered in chintz in the same colors.

Except for the Decorator Collection, Ashley papers and fabrics are available in the firm's retail

outlets around the country and by mail through its annual home furnishings catalogue. For information about store locations and sources for the Decorator Collection fabrics, contact the company.

Home furnishings catalogue, $3.50.

Laura Ashley
Box 5308
Melville, NY 11747
(800) 367-2000

Brunschwig & Fils

While especially known for its delightful cotton prints, Brunschwig & Fils is equally expert at producing historical reproductions of heavier fabrics, such as the 100% wool damask shown here. The seven fabrics illustrated are from several periods and many of them were created for restoration projects and museum collections.

Verplanck Damask is seen here on a chair in the American Wing of the Metropolitan Museum of Art in New York. The design dates from the late 18th century and is English or Flemish in origin. In addition to the original gold color, it is offered in red or green.

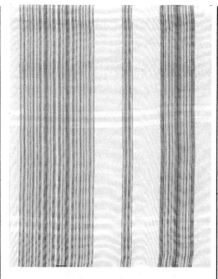

Sherwood is a fine example of a late 18th-century block print. It is 100% cotton and available in spice and slate or in dark brown and gray.

Reproduced from a late 18th-century copperplate, New Zinnia Toile is printed on 100% cotton. The simple floral and stripe design is either French or English in origin and comes in four color choices on a white ground—red, blue, melon, or black.

Baltimore Stripe is reproduced from a European woven silk stripe from 1790-1830. It is a documentary design of a drawing-room fabric and is part of the Winterthur collection at the Henry Francis du Pont Winterthur Museum in Delaware. The fabric is made of viscose rayon in five colors, including the document colors which are pink and green.

Glazed chintz was a hallmark of the 19th century and is still a favorite as a decorative element. Coraux, which dates from 1835, is an intricately-patterned chintz from the Musée des Arts Décoratifs in Paris. It is offered in its original blue and in red, green, coral, plum, or brown.

The design for Napolean Trois is Victorian in origin, the original dating from 1870-90. It is a 100% cotton French roller print, an example of a more advanced technology in textiles. The design is available in three colors—red, blue, and green, which is the document color.

Savannah Glazed Chintz is a fine example of the delicate floral chintzes of the 19th century. The design is offered with several ground colors, including white, cream, red, aubergine, brown, and black.

Brunschwig fabrics are only available through interior designers and decorator departments of selected retail outlets. Contact the company for further information.

Brunschwig & Fils
979 Third Ave.
New York, NY 10022
(212) 838-7878

Colefax & Fowler

This English company continues to produce the chintzes so dear to the hearts of decorators and Anglophiles everywhere. Its Brook Collection is composed of new designs that have the look and feel of earlier times. Two outstanding examples from this collection are illustrated here.

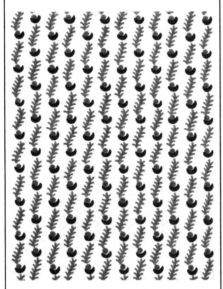

Bibury is a geometric floral print that is easily adaptable to 18th- and early 19th-century decor. It is produced in yellow and brown, pink and green, brown and blue, mauve and green, and other color combinations, and is designed to be used in conjunction with other Brook Collection materials.

Lymington is a more formal floral print, but we have seen it used

handsomely with simple stripes and with Bibury, described above. It is offered in the same color range.

Colefax & Fowler showrooms are located in London, but the firm's fabrics are distributed in the United States through Clarence House, New York.

For further information, contact:

Clarence House
40 E. 57th St.
New York, NY 10022
(212) 752-2890

Cowan & Tout

To many designers, the name Cowtan & Tout is synonymous with sumptuous English glazed chintzes. A walk through the company's showroom, where hundreds of beautifully-executed materials are arrayed, is enough to make an Anglophile's head swim. And one can be sure that this firm's 19th-century designs and colors will be absolutely authentic, although some patterns are also reproduced in additional contemporary colors.

The Hollyhoock & Swag fabric shown here is based on a hand-blocked pattern from the mid-19th century. The intricately shaded rose and green colors follow the original closely. Also available in other colorways, this design is printed on 100% cotton glazed chintz.

For further information, contact:

Cowtan & Tout, Inc.
979 Third Ave.
New York, NY 10022
(212) 753-4488

Greeff Fabrics

For over fifty years, Greeff has been producing high-quality prints and woven fabrics, many of which are historical reproductions or adapations. One of the firm's more recent collections is taken from documents found in the houses of The Street in Deerfield, Massachusetts. Through the efforts of Historic Deerfield, many of these houses now operate as museums open to the public. Two typical patterns are ilustrated in these pages.

Indian Palace Rug, shown here, is taken from a small fragment of a late 17th- or early 18th-century Indian Mughal rug. It is printed on 100% cotton in four colorways— blue on old rose, chamois and olive on terra cotta, rose on lapis, and turquoise on ruby.

Fishing Lady is one of our favorites. The design, illustrated at the beginning of this chapter, is taken from a needlework fire-screen depicting a young girl fishing while her beau looks on. It is printed in England on 100% cotton and is offered in turquoise on natural, fern on oak, or blue on taupe.

Flowering Centerpiece is from Greeff's Shelburne Museum Collection, which includes authen-

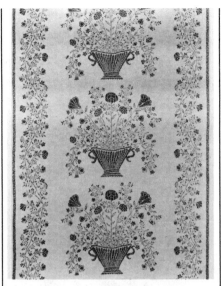

tically reproduced prints and weaves from the Shelburne Museum in Vermont. The designs are taken from quilts, hooked rugs, clothing, and other decorative items. Flowering Centerpiece is reproduced from a delicate reverse appliqué flower basket sewn on a cotton bed cover. It is offered in four colorways, among which are red and aqua on parchment and terra cotta and willow on forest, and is printed on 100% cotton.

Greeff fabrics are available to the design trade in the firm's showrooms, and through the decorating departments of selected retail stores. Contact the company for further information.

Greeff Fabrics, Inc.
155 E. 56th St.
New York, NY 10022
(212) 888-5060

Lee Jofa

Like its papers, discussed in chapter 7, many of Lee Jofa's fabrics are reproductions from French, Chinese, and English documents. Two particularly handsome fabrics are illustrated here.

Chinese Water Lilies is an adaptation of a design found on an antique Chinese robe. The medallion-and-butterfly design, an ancient symbol of power and wealth, is printed on 100% cotton. Available in several colors, in-

cluding deep violet, jade green, yellow, and light pink, it is offered with a companion border.

The Marbles fabrics are new designs which are interpreted from 19th-century marbleized book papers. These voiles and cottons are suitable for drapery and light upholstery and are adaptable to various period design schemes.

All Lee Jofa fabrics are available through interior decorators at Lee Jofa showrooms around the country. Contact the company for further information.

Lee Jofa, Inc.
800 Central Blvd.
Carlstadt, NJ 07072
(201) 438-8444

Arthur Sanderson & Sons

The British have flocked to Sanderson in London for years. The firm's line of traditional chintzes, linens, and cottons is deservedly famous. Now Sanderson is coming to New York, and

all of the excellent designs are available through the company's showroom. Sanderson possesses the exclusive stock of William Morris's hand blocks first used in creating some of the most handsome and noteworthy late-Victorian fabric designs. The firm is equally well known for its hundreds of flowery prints, most with that diffuse, genteely faded appearance of the traditional English middle-class sitting room.

For further information, contact:

Arthur Sanderson & Sons
979 Third Ave.
New York, NY 10022
(212) 319-7220

Scalamandré

Recently, Scalamandré designers traveled to Ireland and discovered a virtual treasure trove of decorative documents in various stately homes and castles. From these sources they have created the Irish Georgian collection, which is the newest in a long line of extraordinary historic reproductions from this company. The fabrics illustrated here are a sampling of this collection.

Leixlip Castle is an adaptation of a drapery found in, where else, Leixlip Castle, in County Kildare. The 19th-century formal floral pattern copies the original faithfully. The 100% glazed cotton fabric is available in a multicolored design against five background colors: oatmeal, cream, canary, mint, and Prussian blue.

William Kilburn's works, now in the Victoria & Albert Museum, are the inspiration for Mayo Grasses. His drawings, executed in the 1790s, are outstanding for their realism and clarity of color. This flower and leaf pattern is printed in Europe on either cotton chintz or glazed silk, which makes it adaptable to both formal and informal settings. It is available in gold and rose on white, pumpkin and lilac on ash, and magenta and blue on yellow.

Tarbert Roses is a reproduction of a 20th-century English glazed chintz drapery panel found in Kerry. It is a good example of the expertise with which Scalamandré designers and mill craftsmen reproduce intricate design detail.

Although relatively modern in origin, this fabric would be equally at home in a Victorian parlor. Like Mayo Grasses, it has been printed on silk as well as on cotton. The colorways range from aqua and rose on cream to coral and gold on ivory and gray and peach on teal.

Of course, all of Scalamandré's other historical collections, including Historic Charleston and the firm's William Morris designs, are still available and are more than suitable for period interiors.

Scalamandré fabrics are only available through designers or the decorating departments of select stores. Contact the company for information.

Scalamandré, Inc.
950 Third Ave.
New York, NY 10022
(212) 361-8500

F. Schumacher & Co.

The Abby Aldrich Rockefeller Folk Art Collection at Colonial Williamsburg contains over 2000 paintings, carvings, and decorative items created from Colonial times to the present. Schumacher has now created a group of fabrics, each reproduced, adapted, or interpreted from the Folk Art Collection. The fabrics shown here offer a lively alternative to the more grandiose and elaborate designs of many historical textile collections.

Theorem painting, which involves stenciling on velvet, was a popular folk art of the 19th century. Bradley Theorem is an adaptation from one such piece done in 1825 by Mary Bradley. It is distin-

guished by its unpretentious, homey design and realistic shading. The 100% cotton print is offered in plum and sage, green, aubergine, and a multicolor on cream, which is the document color.

Stencil Repeat is taken from a velvet belt design in which the designer used decorative brushwork as a substitute for embroidery. It was probably made in New England in 1835. Of 100% cotton, the fabric is available in the document color, vermillion, as well as in ivory, mallard green, teal, or powder blue.

Summer Stripe is a 100% glazed cotton fabric and comes in various

colorways, including French blue and pink, beige on white, and rose and maple. It is adapted from a whitework bed cover, composed of white cotton embroidery on a white ground. Dating from 1818, it was made by Sarah B. Wisdom, probably in celebration of her wedding.

This collection and others are available through designers and in selected retail stores.

For further information, contact:

F. Schumacher & Co.
939 Third Ave.
New York, NY 10022
(212) 644-5900

Stroheim & Romann

The Winterthur Museum has selected the 120-year-old firm of Stroheim & Romann to reproduce documentary fabrics from the museum's textile archives. The choice is in keeping with Stroheim's reputation for high-quality fabrics, ranging from original designs to historical adaptations.

The photograph illustrates two of the fabrics reproduced for Winterthur. The sofa is upholstered in Orne, an arborescent design printed on glazed cotton chintz, based on a set of window hangings in the Winterthur collection made in France in 1775-90. The chairs are covered in Rutland, which is derived from an English striped silk of the late 18th cen-

tury, and is now manufactured in a synthetic blend. Fabrics such as Orne and Rutland were considered the proper upholstery material for the delicate room furnishings of the Federal period.

The collection also includes damasks, velvets, and cotton taffetas. All are available to the design trade in Stroheim & Romann showrooms and are also offered in selected retail stores.

For further information, contact:

Stroheim & Romann, Inc.
155 E. 56th St.
New York, NY 10022
(212) 691-0700

Richard E. Thibaut

Like the Thibaut papers described in chapter 7, these fabrics are part of the American Colonial collection, created in conjunction with the Historical Society of Early American Decoration.

The floral print Esther may be used with the matching or complementary papers that are part of the collection. It comes in six colorways, including blue and pink on yellow, mauve and jade on tan, and rust and peach on slate, and is printed on glazed cotton; the design has its origins in early gold-leaf decoration

Scripture Hospitality bears the 18th-century symbol of welcome, the pineapple. The cotton print is offered in peach and beige, yellow and green, rust and forest, mauve and beige, and gold and teal, and is also available in a matching paper.

For further information, contact:

Richard E. Thibaut, Inc.
706 S. 21st St.
Irvington, NJ 07111
(201) 399-7888

Waverly Fabrics

Some period fabrics can be over-whelming in their seriousness (and high cost). Waverly has, for years, been producing an exten-sive range of medium-priced fabrics, many in traditional American designs. The fabrics shown here are from two recent collections.

The sofa shown here is covered in Stonington, one of the many fabrics in the Waverly Place collec-tion. The trellis pattern has always been popular in American decora-ting, and is here loosely inter-preted from an 1810 design from Alexandria, Virgina.

These and other Waverly fabrics are available in many retail stores around the country.

For further information, contact:

Waverly Fabrics
58 W. 40th St.
New York, NY 10018
(212) 644-5900

The cushions and pillows in this photograph are covered in Port-folio Prints, a collection of small-scale, casual patterns. They are printed on 100% cotton sailcloth which is particularly durable. These designs would be appropri-ate in any traditional, informal setting.

Rue de France

We were delighted to learn about this new importer of French lace. Although most of the fabric used is synthetic, it has the snap of 100% cotton material and washes very well. Rue de France sells five different patterns as yard goods or as ready-made curtains, valences,

Old World Weavers
Restorations
Studio One
Shaker Workshops
Standard Trimming Corp.
Sunflower Studio
The Twigs, Inc.
Albert Van Luit Co.

and tiebacks. Illustrated are two of the imaginative patterns—Belle Fleur and Old Calais—that would flatter any Victorian window or door. Rue de France also offers hard-to-find lace trim—petit point, petit galon, grand galon, and point de Paris—by the yard.

Brochure, $1; samples catalogue, $2.

*Rue de France
77 Thames St.
Newport, RI 02840
(401) 846-0317*

Other Suppliers of Fabrics

Consult List of Suppliers for addresses.

Amazon Vinegar and Pickling Works
  Dry Goods
The Astrup Company
Bailey and Griffin
Samuel Beckenstein
Nancy Borden
Braid-Aid
Cane & Basket Supply
Charterhouse Designs Ltd.
Clarence House
Cohasset Colonials
Diane Jackson Cole

Country Bed Shop
Country Curtains
Rose Cummings Chintzes
Decorator's Walk
Dentelle De France
A. L. Diament & Co.
Fonthill
Gill Imports
Grand Silk House
Guild of Shaker Crafts
Gurian's
S. M. Hexter Co.
S. & C. Huber, Accoutrements
Liberty & Co.

9.

Furniture

While furniture is usually a last, and often peripheral, step in renovation, there are few purchases more pleasurable. In the quest for an appropriate period room, however, there are pitfalls. Antique furniture, for example, is often over-priced and not sturdy enough to the rigors of modern life. Before you spend the year's grocery money on that wonderful French Empire armoire, make sure it is suitable for your needs and is genuinely what it's supposed to be. An alternative to costly items are the wares of flea markets, garage sales, and the like. With a little work, many such pieces can be quite lovely and comfortable to live with.

Another danger is the easy availability of shoddily-made mass-produced reproduction furniture "ensembles." Since a living house usually reflects several styles and periods, an overlaminated "pine" living room suite in ye-olde Colonial style would appear lifeless and jarring—like a bowl of plastic fruit. Conversely, a house furnished within strict period limitations can feel like a museum instead of a home.

A beautifully crafted piece of furniture can add interest and vitality to a room. The focus, in these pages, is primarily on individual craftsmen who use traditional methods and expertise to produce handsome reproductions and original furniture designs. Most of the wood-workers use traditional joinery and finishing techniques that, while sometimes raising the cost, provide pieces of enduring beauty.

If reproductions are not to your taste, there is nothing wrong with furnishing a room in a mixture of antique styles. In fact, some of the loveliest rooms we've seen are furnished in a comfortable jumble of thrift shop finds, superb handcrafted one-of-a-kind pieces, and articles saved from grandmother's house.

A last note: When choosing a piece of furniture, examine the materials and workmanship carefully. Turn it upside down, jiggle it to see if it's sturdy, check for comfort. Remember that hand-formed joints will last longer than glue, and solid wood will hold up better than veneer. And if it isn't sturdy and well made, don't buy it—it will not get better with use.

Library cabinet, Edward Ludlow, Cabinetmaker, Pluckemin, New Jersey.

Alexandria Wood Joinery

New England has been renowned as a center of furniture manufacturing for over 200 years. George and Judy Whittaker are among the craftsmen who keep this tradition alive and add to it. All of their work is custom order and includes cabinets and other furniture forms. The Whittakers also repair, restore, and reproduce antique pieces.

Mail inquiries invited.

Alexandria Wood Joinery
Plumer Hill Rd.
Alexandria, NH 03222
(603) 744-8243

Artisan Woodworkers

Both modern and traditional cabinets are handsomely executed by the craftsmen working with John Ward of Artisan. Kitchens, designed for today's needs but retaining the look of yesterday, are a specialty of the firm. The woodworkers will also execute a wide variety of pieces for home or office use, including exact reproductions of classic antiques. If you are a do-it-yourself cabinetmaker or have aspirations in this direction, you might find a new book, *Commercial Cabinetmaking Procedures* by John Ward and Kevin Fristad, especially helpful. It is available from Artisan Woodworkers for $10 postpaid, $10.60 in California, and $12.50 (U.S. $) in Canada.

For further information, contact:

Artisan Woodworkers
21415 Broadway
Sonoma, CA 95476
(707) 938-4796

Robert Barrow

Robert Barrow's fine Windsor chairs put to shame the assembly-line products found in most commercial outlets. Chairs such as the braced Newport continuous-arm model shown here are produced with old-fashioned tools and fine woods. The chair seat, for exam-

ple, is cut to shape, beveled, and then scooped out to produce the comfortable sculpted form. Pine, oak or ash, and maple are used for the various parts. In form, most of the chairs and other pieces follow 18th-century Rhode Island examples, but designs developed in Pennsylvania, Massachusetts, and Connecticut are also available. Chairs are either left natural with the addition of a stain and varnish, or finished with a milk paint in black or in one of four traditional colors.

Catalogue, $2.

Robert Barrow, Furnituremaker
412 Thames St.
Bristol, RI 02809
(401) 253-4434

Berkeley Upholstering

Traditional furniture is by no means a requirement for a tradi-

tional home, but, for those who wish to have both the comfort and style of an earlier period, Berkeley is a good place to shop. In business for many years, Berkeley eschews assembly-line techniques. Each piece of furniture is assembled largely by hand and is custom made for the buyer. The style is almost invariably Chippendale, Hepplewhite, or Queen Anne. The wing chair illustrated here is the Adam Stephen model, 43" high, 31" deep, and 29" wide. The firm stocks a wide assortment of natural upholstery fabrics.

Literature available.

Berkeley Upholstering Co.
PO Box 1147
Martinsburg, WV 25401
(304) 267-2975

The Caning Shop

Do-it-yourself enthusiasts will find all the supplies they need for chair caning in the Caning Shop catalogue. Cane is just one of the materials available for repairing furniture. The shop also supplies rush, splint, Danish cord, rattan, rawhide, binder cane, wicker, and Shaker fabric tapes. Complete pressed-fiber seats for late-Victorian chairs are also kept in stock along with the various tools required in doing upholstery work.

Catalogue, $1 (refundable with order).

The Caning Shop
926 Gilman St.
Berkeley, CA 94710
(415) 527-5010

Carolina Caning Supply

A good supply of chair caning materials is also available from this North Carolina firm, as are materials other than cane, such as rush, reed, and seagrass. Carolina's offerings are a bit less extensive than the Caning Shop's, but East Coast craftsmen may find this a more convenient source of supply.

Brochure available (SASE required).

Carolina Caning Supply
PO Box 2179
Smithfield, NC 27577
(919) 934-0291

The Country Bed Shop

We have confidently presented the wares of Charles Thibeau and his craftsmen for many years now, and our enthusiasm remains undiminished. One of the few American members of the English Guild of Master Craftsmen, he has developed one of the best collections of reproduction beds available in North America. Anyone who has tried to sleep on a diminutive antique bed will appreciate the comfort and style achieved by Thibeau's staff. There are many different styles and forms to choose from—pencil post, turned pencil, half-headed, plain post, tester, field, and trundle beds as well as cribs and cradles. All are made from quality woods stocked in the firm's own lumberyard. Maple, curly maple, walnut, cherry, ash, and mahogany are among the hardwoods employed. There are ten standard headboard styles to choose from, but other designs can be made.

steads may be fitted for rope springs, box springs, or plywood platform.

In addition to beds, Thibeau also makes other types of traditional furniture. The Shaker trestle dining table shown here is made of maple but can be fabricated of cherry. As shown, it is 30" high, 34" wide, and 96" long. Other

Many of the beds are available in sizes ranging from twin to king. The 18th-century half-headed bed illustrated here can be made up in twin, queen, or king sizes. A folding version with rope springs only is also offered. Other bed-

sizes are available.

Catalogue, $4.

The Country Bed Shop
Box 222
Groton, MA 01450
(617) 448-6336

Cornucopia

Cornucopia is a direct-mail supplier of a select collection of traditional New England-style furni-

ture of the late 18th and early 19th centuries. Among the most handsome of the pieces is the Windsor triple bow settee. It measures 38" tall and 72" wide. Oak is used for

the bows, birch and maple for the turnings, and white pine for the seat. As with any fine piece of furniture, the woods are given a hand-rubbed oil and wax finish and not cheapened with a polyurethane coating.

Literature available.

Cornucopia
Wayland Rd., Box 44
Harvard, MA 01451
(617) 456-3201

from fine-grained walnut. The carving of the crest rail, splat, cabriole legs, and seat frame is as accomplished as any to be found today. Curry undertakes only commission work in his Maine studio and executes various types of furniture from an impressive walnut highboy to a lowly walnut New England footstool.

Catalogue, $2.

Gerald Curry, Cabinetmaker
Pound Hill Rd.
Union, ME 04862
(207) 785-4633

Crowfoot's

Norman Crowfoot is an Arizona artisan who specializes in Mexican-style furniture, including reproduction pieces. The heavy pine chest illustrated here is representative of his work. It can be made in just about any size desired, and is cedar-lined. In ad-

dition to the construction of new pieces, Crowfoot will undertake the restoration of antiques.

For further information, contact:

Crowfoot's Inc.
PO Box 1297
Pinetop, AZ 85935
(602) 367-5336

Cohasset Colonials

Furniture kits are the specialty of this well-known Massachusetts manufacturer and supplier. Everything in the bedroom illustrated was assembled from Cohasset kits. You can believe the words of the manufacturer: "We have done everything humanly possible to make assembly of these kits simple—and we know from thousands of letters from satisfied customers that we have succeeded." Yes, they have. The instructions, parts list, and information about finishing which come with every kit make it possible for even the most klutzy of home craftsmen to suc-

Gerald Curry

The one-of-a-kind pieces that come from Gerald Curry's workshop may someday command prices almost as high as the antiques which serve as their mod-

els. Curry is an acknowledged expert at reproducing high-style furniture of the 18th century. The Philadelphia Queen Anne chair shown here is superbly formed

in museums and restorations, including Thomas Jefferson's Monticello.

For further information, contact:

Michael Dunbar
Box 805
Portsmouth, NH 03801
(603) 431-8852

The Ground Floor

This Charleston firm, a division of John Ragsdale Interiors, specializes in fine hand-painted reproductions of antique chairs, mirrors, trunks, cabinets, tables, pedestals, and clocks. The pieces are not covered with folksy stenciled designs, but rather with expertly executed Oriental or neoclassical motifs. Hand-painted classic chinoiserie designs of the 18th century appear on trunks which can be used as coffee or end tables, stands useful for plants or sculpture, a magnificent desk-bookcase, and shieldback and Queen Anne arm and side chairs. Neoclassical decoration such as swags and urns is reserved for such Federal-period reproductions as a mahogany demi-lune table and a pedestal suitable for sculpture.

Brochure available.

The Ground Floor
95½ Broad St.
Charleston, SC 29401
(803) 722-3576

ceed. Maple and pine are the primary woods used. And each piece of furniture has a story of its own, as Cohasset has copied museum examples. The low bed shown in the illustration, for example, is copied from one at the Metropolitan Museum of Art. The headboard is of pine and the posts and foot rail are of maple. The foot rail contains holes for what would have been a support of roping, but the roping has been eliminated and the frame is

equipped, instead, with brackets to hold a modern box spring.

Cohasset Colonials also supplies a wide variety of country-style furnishings such as curtains; brass, pewter, and glass accessories; and lighting fixtures.

Catalogue, $1.

Cohasset Colonials by Hagerty
Cohasset, MS 02025
(617) 383-0110

Michael Dunbar

The fascination with Windsor chairs seems to have no end. The basic design is so simple and effective that it is no wonder that chairs of this design are used in both traditional and contemporary settings. Michael Dunbar is one of the most accomplished of modern Windsor chair craftsmen. He works alone in his New Hampshire studio and follows the procedures which were first perfected in the 18th century. The bow-back armchair illustrated here was made by hand with the use of antique tools. His chairs are found

Christopher Hayes

Hayes brings to his work an extraordinary sensitivity to line and form. He possesses all the technical skills required of a cabinetmaker attempting to recapture the grace and style of the past. There is something more to his work, however, which sets it apart from that of other copyists—and that is his imagination. The Queen Anne candlestand and Chippendale wing chair illustrated here are properly termed by him "interpretations" of classic forms. Although each piece is one-of-a-kind, he has been working for ten years and has on hand numerous

examples of tea tables, stands, dining tables, bedsteads, cupboards, and chair and sofa frames.

Portfolio available, $5.

Christopher Morris Hayes
Box 212
Pine Meadow, CT 06061
(203) 379-3956

The acknowledged leader of quality brass bed manufacturers is Isabel. Probably not since beds of this type were first introduced in the 1800s has such a well-wrought product been available. It is no longer necessary, as in the past, to wrap thin sheets of brass around steel. The beds made today by Isabel are assembled with seamless solid tubing. Isabel has a number of standard designs such as the fanciful Bourbon model illustrated here, but will also work up a custom design. You can buy a complete unit—headboard, footboard, and brass frame system—or select just one of the components which can then be attached to a standard steel frame. But practice caution in this regard as fitting one element to another may require special planning and care. Isabel can advise you on this. One of the features that we like best about this firm's beds is the natural finish; the bedsteads are not lacquered and thus have a welcome warmth. Highly lacquered brass beds and accessories often remind us of a gleaming gold tooth in a rotten mouth, an unfortunate advertisement in bad taste.

Full-color catalogue, $4.

Isabel Brass Furniture, Inc.
120 E. 32nd St.
New York, NY 10016
(212) 689-3307

David Hicks

Sturdy and handsome country pieces are available from David Hicks, a Missouri craftsman. He often works with antique lumber and also has a supply of old glass on hand for case furniture with glass doors such as the walnut wall cupboard pictured here. Hicks follows traditional methods of joinery and takes considerable care to endow each piece with just the right finishing touches. This is not your run-of-the-mill "ye olde" type of cheap reproduction work, but carefully thought-out and executed cabinetwork.

Isabel Brass Furniture

Brochures available.

David Hicks, Cabinetmaker
Rte. 1, Box 7
Labadie, MO 63055
(314) 742-2232

Jos. Kilbridge, Antiques of Early America

Proper restoration work can measurably increase the worth of an antique piece, both aesthetically and financially. Kilbridge, a well-known Massachusetts dealer in fine antiques, is becoming equally noted for his restoration

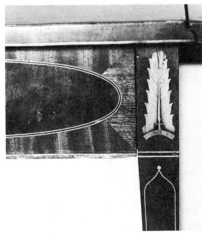

work. Illustrated are two examples: the replacement of fruitwood inlay on a drop-leaf table leg and the construction of a bracketed-foot base for a Federal tiger maple slant-front desk.

Kilbridge keeps a good stock of aged wood on hand for matching antique materials.

For further information, contact:

Jos. Kilbridge, Antiques of Early
America
Main St.
Groton, MA 01450
(617) 448-3330

James Lea, Cabinetmaker

Well-wrought furniture from the time of the great cabinetmakers in the mid- to late-18th century is now beyond the pocketbooks of all but the very wealthy. James Lea recognized the need for quality reproductions and was fortunate enough to inherit from his father and grandfather the skills and dedication required to fashion authentic work. In his own words, "I build furniture that will increase in value over the years, since each piece is individually handcrafted in every detail." Included in his standard repertoire are Windsor chairs and settees, highboys, and lowboys; he will undertake commissions for other types of period furniture.

Catalogue, $3.

James Lea, Cabinetmaker
9 West St.
Rockport, ME 04856
(207) 236-3632

Gerald LePage

LePage has made his reputation reproducing early Colonial furniture and continues to excel in this genre. There are few craftsmen who can turn spindles and carve rails with greater skill than he. Illustrated is an early bannister-back side chair of maple which is typical of his work. He is now producing later and lighter Colonial pieces as well. Also illustrated is a simple Queen Anne table suitable for use in a living room or bedroom. Among the other late Colonial and early 19th-century pieces which have been added to his offerings are Windsor chairs and Shaker chairs and tables.

Catalogue, $2.

Gerald LePage
Rte. 66
Hebron, CT 06231
(203) 228-9958

C. Alan Lightcap

It is always sad to discover that the spinet, harpsichord, or player piano in an old house can emit nothing more than squeaks or groans. Various types of keyboard instruments are difficult to repair and even more difficult to restore. Yet the cost of replacing many of these instruments with new or reproduction models of the same quality is practically prohibitive. Fortunately, there are craftsmen such as Alan Lightcap who are intrigued by old instruments and who have developed the special skills needed to bring them back to useful life. Lightcap's specialty is automatic musical instruments, and illustrated is one of his most difficult challenges—a seven-foot Steinway grand with a Welte-Mignon player mechanism. Restoration required a year's time. More typical of the instruments brought to his Delaware Valley workshop are nickleodeons, smaller-scale reproducing player pianos, and table-top roll-played "organettes." Lightcap is also available to work on residential

pipe organs of the type installed in many mansions during the early 1900s.

For further information, contact:

C. Alan Lightcap
PO Box 173
Lambertville, NJ 08530
(609) 397-1758

Edward Ludlow

Many cabinetmakers are good copy artists, and are deservedly praised for their ability to follow the dictates of the past. A few cabinetmakers combine traditional skills with imagination. Ludlow is one of them. His work has the quality of the old craftsman, but is very much his own. The bookcase shown at the beginning of this chapter and the linen cabinet illustrated here are two examples of his work. Ludlow will restore pieces and, indeed, does a great deal of this work for antique dealers. He does reproduction work, including pieces for the Morristown National Historical Park, but, in his own words, "I usually don't like to do a straight reproduction, and I don't build furniture for shock value. If you're not quite sure if one of my pieces is traditional or modern, that pleases me." All of his work is custom ordered.

For further information, contact:

Edward Ludlow, Cabinetmaker
PO Box 646
Pluckemin, NJ 07978
(201) 658-9091

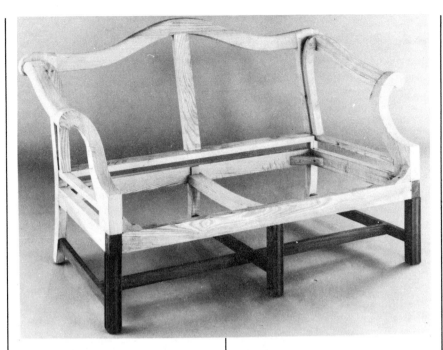

North Woods Chair Shop

The simple Shaker aesthetic informs all of the pieces produced by Lenore Howe and Brian Braskie at North Woods. Their shop is located close to the old

Canterbury, New Hampshire, Shaker settlement. Almost all of the chairs are of cherry or maple; those illustrated here are of cherry in a natural finish. Seats may be made of cane, as at left in the photo, or 100%-cotton Shaker tapes. Ten different solid colors or combinations are available in the seating fabric. The ladder-back design originated at the Enfield, New Hampshire, Shaker community about 1830.

North Woods has recently added the Canterbury Collection to its offerings. Included are a rocker, an ironing stool, and a side chair. The originals of the reproductions are on display at the nearby Canterbury Shaker Village museum.

Catalogue available with tape and stain samples, $2.

The North Woods Chair Shop
RFD 1, Old Tilton Rd.
Canterbury, NH 03224
(603) 783-4595

Mazza Frame & Furniture

For those wishing to upholster their own seating furniture, there is no better supplier of basic frames than Mazza. Traditional English, American, French, and Italian designs are available in various woods, including mahogany, walnut, maple, and ash.

There are many different models of chairs and sofas to choose from. Illustrated is one model known as the 1748 love seat.

Catalogue available.

Mazza Frame & Furniture Co.
35-10 10th St.
Long Island City, NY 11106
(212) 721-9287

Newell Workshop

Midwesterners will find Newell a good source for cane and other seating materials. Illustrated is a typical caned seat for which Newell has provided the material. Flat weaving, rush seating, and cane webbing materials are available, as well as chair caning kits that are of special use for beginners. The kits include natural cane sufficient to cover one average chair, the tools needed, wooden pegs used in assembly, and an instruction booklet. The kits cost $6.50; enough additional cane for a second chair costs $3.50.

Literature available.

Newell Workshop
19 Blaine Ave.
Hinsdale, IL 60521
(312) 323-7467

Craig Nutt Fine Wood Works

Craig Nutt began his career as a furniture restorer, and, as he gained more and more knowledge about the methods of the past, he became increasingly venturesome in his own work. While he works with traditional forms, he does not call his pieces reproductions, but "interpretations" of classic designs. As the illustration of the huntboard shows, he is perfectly capable of executing furniture that would be at home in almost any kind of setting. This piece is primarily walnut, with recycled heart pine used as a secondary wood; the jonquil-design inlay is of satinwood. The small Southern country table—29½" high, 25" wide, and 19½" deep—also displays his craftsmanship. It is constructed solely of heart pine

and, as is the case with all of Nutt's furniture, has pinned mortise and tenon joinery and hand-dovetailed drawers. The walnut rocking chair departs the furthest from traditional form, the curving of the back providing much more support than the classic rocker.

Brochure, 50¢.

Craig Nutt Fine Wood Works
2014 Fifth St.
Northport, AL 35476
(205) 752-6535

Shaker Workshops

The leading supplier of Shaker reproduction furnishings and furniture, Shaker Workshops provides kits or ready-assembled pieces. The types of objects the firm has offered over the years have become more and more popular, and deservedly so. Each piece is, in the words of a 19th-century Shaker, "good and substantial quality." The bed illustrated here is probably the only Shaker bed now being offered commercially and is available in kit or assembled and finished form. It is made with either a rope foundation or with metal brackets to hold a box spring and mattress. There are two sizes: twin, 39" x 76", and full, 54" x 76". The headboard is of pine and the posts and frame are of rock maple.

Among the workshops' other offerings—available in kit form or assembled and finished—are chairs, tables, settees, rockers, stools, and sewing stands.

Catalogue, 50¢.

Shaker Workshops
PO Box 1028
Concord, MA 01742
(617) 646-8985

Calvin Shewmaker

Shewmaker is the type of craftsman who works because he loves what he is doing and does it well. Trained at Colonial Williamsburg,

he now spends some time at Shakertown at Pleasant Hill, Kentucky. But, principally, he is busy turning out millwork for Georgian Colonial and Federal-style houses and furniture that would be at home in such period interiors. The wine cabinet show here is typical of his fine work.

For further information, contact:

Calvin M. Shewmaker III,
  Cabinetmaker
606 Cane Run
Harrodsburg, KY 40330
(606) 734-9926

Smith Woodworks & Design

Todd Smith and his associates are especially taken with early country antiques and reproduce a variety of chairs, tables, hutches, cupboards, sideboards, rockers, and settees which will fit in any simple setting, traditional or contemporary. Shown here is a Shaker rocker of maple with a tape seat and a pine night stand. Most Smith furniture is made of pine, maple, or cherry, but oak

and mahogany and other more rare woods can be specified. All of the pieces produced are custom ordered.

Brochure, $1.

Smith Woodworks & Design
Box 42, RR 1
Califon, NJ 07830
(201) 832-2723

Valley Craftsmen

This group of Baltimore-area artists and craftsmen undertakes everything from painting murals and marbelizing and glazing floors, walls, and ceilings, to reproducing antique furniture. Illustrated is a drawing of a wall

cabinet recently completed for one client. As both decorative artists and cabinetmakers, the firm's principals undertake many different kinds of custom design and restoration work. They have completed projects involving furniture

184

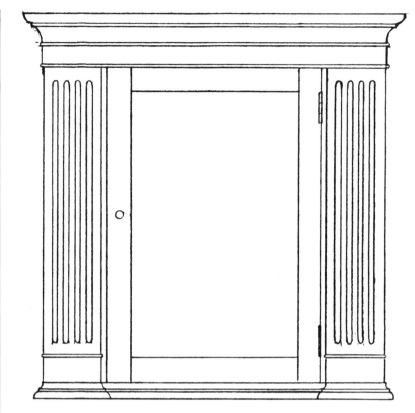

restoration and reproduction in homes and commercial establishments from New Orleans to New York.

Literature available (SASE required).

The Valley Craftsmen, Ltd.
Box 11
Stevenson, MD 21153
(301) 484-3891

Norman Vandal

Readers of previous *Old House Catalogues* will recognize Norman Vandal's work as being among the very best available in North America. And readers of *Fine Woodworking Magazine,* for whom Vandal has written extensively, appreciate his exceptional command of the cabinetmaker's skills. All of his work is custom ordered and includes both high-style and country pieces in cherry, maple, pine, mahogany, or walnut. A Federal-period corner cupboard, a five-drawer country chest, and a swinging cradle are among his most interesting designs.

Recently added to his repertoire is the bonnet-top Queen Anne highboy illustrated here. Tiger maple is the primary wood, with pine used secondarily for drawer bottoms and backboards. An antique

original would cost at least ten times more than the reproduction.

Brochure and price list, $3.

Norman Vandal, Cabinetmaker
Box 67
Roxbury, VT 05669
(802) 485-8380

Robert Whitley

Robert Whitley's beautifully formed contemporary rocker of American walnut is found in many homes. He is equally famous for the important reproductions of classic antiques commissioned by Independence National Historical Park, the White House, and the Kennedy Library.

If Whitley did not sign his pieces, it would be extremely difficult to tell them apart from the antique. He is often called upon to fill out a set of antique chairs, such as the example illustrated here, or to produce extras. Whitley will also execute custom reproductions of such high-style forms as highboys, lowboys, and chests of drawers.

Brochure on the Whitley rocker, $4. For further information on reproductions, contact:

The Robert Whitley Studio
Laurel Rd.
Solebury, PA 18963
(215) 297-8452

E. Stanford Young

Young continues to produce a very handsome 18th-century writing desk (first offered in *The Third Old House Catalogue*) and now has added a handcarved desk stool that can be used with it or for other purposes. The two

pieces are shown here. The stool, like the desk, is made of cherry. It measures 17" high, 20" wide, and 15" deep, dimensions which allow it to be used as extra seating in a hall or living room as well as before a desk. Young will upholster it in any material you supply (needlepoint, damask, or brocatelle recommended) or will ship it padded and covered in muslin for you to have completed.

Brochure, $2.

E. Stanford Young
PO Box 368, 1107 Cypress Point
Placentia, CA 92670
(714) 993-4248

Other Suppliers of Furniture

Consult List of Suppliers for addresses.

Bedlam Brass Beds
The Bedpost
Berea College Student Craft
   Industries
Brass Bed Company of America
Marion H. Campbell
Davis Cabinet Co.
Guild of Shaker Crafts
Heritage Design
Historic Charleston Reproductions
The Hitchcock Chair Co.
The Hope Co.
Magnolia Hall
Thos. Moser
Simon Newby
Old Colony Crafts
J. F. Orr & Sons
Renovation Products
Robinson Iron Corp.
The Rocker Shop
Santa Cruz Foundry
The Seraph
Up Country Enterprises Corp.

10.

Outdoor and Garden Areas

Chances are that as you plan and sweat to restore your period home or to complete a new one in an early style, the last thing on your mind will be the grounds and gardens surrounding it. But eventually, when the last wall is painted and the last piece of furniture put in place, you'll be able to turn your attention to what is, after all, the setting for the house that has demanded and received so many hours of pleasurable toil.

When your eyes do turn outdoors, the last thing you'll want to do is to plunk down some modern aluminum furniture on your patio or to erect an ugly concrete birdbath under the nearest tree. And if a gazebo or other outbuilding is part of your plans, make sure that it complements the main house, rather than distracting attention from it.

There are a number of suppliers who can help you to achieve just the right effect, whether you want a pair of urns to flank your front entrance or a fountain to accent a formal garden. Some of them offer original pieces of statuary; others have antique molds from which to create fine reproductions. And there's no need to settle for an ugly prepackaged metal or wood shed in which to store garden equipment; a number of companies listed in this chapter can supply plans for period outbuildings to harmonize with the style of your home.

If you're fortunate enough to have purchased an old house with its original wrought-iron fencing still in place, you'll probably need some restoration work done. If the fence is long gone, you may want to replace it. A number of craftsmen listed in this chapter will duplicate an old pattern to your specifications, whether you need several hundred feet or just a few yards.

When it comes to illuminating the exterior of your home, you can choose from a number of excellent period reproductions, whether you need a lantern to set atop a cedar post or a set of oil lamps to accent a garden path. Chapter 4 contains a special section on outdoor fixtures suitable for just about any architectural style, from Colonial to Queen Anne.

In any event, because the grounds around your home are so immediately visible, it would be senseless to ignore their part in the overall impression you have striven to create, whether you have many acres to ramble in or just a front lawn and a cozy back yard.

Wrought-iron gate, D. A. Rinedollar, Blacksmith, Augusta, Missouri.

Fencing, Gates, and Window Grilles

Fences don't always make good neighbors, especially when the material and design are downright ugly. Chain-link or cyclone fencing is not particularly recommended for enclosing the yard of an old house. Split-rail or stockade fencing may do just fine, and this type of fencing is available from lumber dealers everywhere. But if you have your heart set on a picket fence or an old-fashioned iron model, you will have to do some searching. Salvage yards (see chapter 1) often inventory materials of this type. If they can't be located, there are individual craftsmen and companies that still produce both wood and iron fencing and gates. Some of the best are included in the following listings.

Marmion Plantation

David Newhall III and Larry Tomayko are escapees from the pressure cooker of Washington politics; seven years ago they joined forces to purchase and restore Marmion, a late-17th-century plantation house which

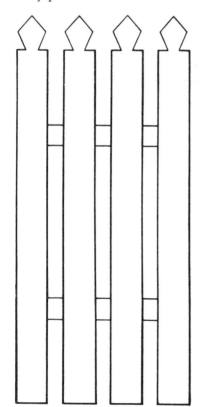

has been designated a Virginia Historic Landmark. During restoration they discovered four fence pickets with unusual diamond-shaped tops which had, in the thrifty Colonial way, been recycled for use as shoring in an interior archway. Now the two have established a company to manufacture accurate pine reproductions of their discovery, designated as the oldest surviving wooden fence pickets in the country by the Association for the Preservation of Virginia Anti-

quities. The diamond-top pickets are 4½" wide and ¾" thick; they are available in two lengths: 57", which makes a standard five-foot fence when set 3" above the ground, and 72", certainly a welcome alternative to stockade fencing when total privacy is required.

Brochure available.

Marmion Plantation Co.
RD 2, Box 458
Fredericksburg, VA 22405
(703) 775-3480

D. A. Rinedollar

For more than two decades Missouri blacksmith D. A. Rinedollar has been working the leather bellows at his forge to create beautiful wrought-iron work reminiscent of 17th- and 18th-century pieces. Illustrated here and at the beginning of this chapter are two of his intricately fashioned gates. All of his work is done to special order; he can copy a fence from one of the rare books in his extensive library, or can

work from your photos, drawings, and suggestions. Rinedollar has completed a great deal of restoration work as well, so if your extant iron fence is missing some of its components, he may be able to fill in the gaps for you.

Brochures available.

D. A. Rinedollar, Blacksmith
Box 14
Augusta, MO 63332
(314) 228-4583

Schwartz's Forge and Metalworks

Official recognition of an artist does not come quickly or easily. That makes the beautiful wrought-iron pieces created by blacksmith Joel Schwartz, which have been exhibited at many fine museums, even more impressive. All of his work is designed to meet the customer's specific requirements; the results, while certainly practical, are beautiful as well. Witness, for instance, the entrance doors he completed for the Gainsborough Studios in New York City. Schwartz welcomes inquiries; his work includes gates, window grilles, staircases, and smaller pieces such as fire screens and weather vanes.

Brochures available.

Schwartz's Forge and Metalworks
Box 205, Forge Hollow Rd.
Deansboro, NY 13328
(315) 841-4477

Stewart Iron Works

Stewart has been in business for nearly a century; in this age of mass production and short cuts, it is unusual to find a company that still handcrafts iron fences, gates, window grilles, railings, and posts. A number of the stock fencing designs are based on mid-Victorian models and all are fabricated of heavy wall tubing and solid-steel pickets. There are also fifteen different malleable iron picket-top designs to choose from. If it is a custom design or restoration of old work that you require, Stewart will be glad to work with you. Illustrated are one of the company's ornate window grilles, an ornamental newel post, the No. 43-R/44-R fence and No. 2 gate, and an assortment of picket-top designs.

Catalogue available.

Stewart Iron Works Co.
511 Enterprise Dr.
Covington, KY 41017
(606) 331-9000

Outdoor Furniture

Until recently, about the only type of old-style outdoor furniture commercially available was the standard wood and iron park bench. While suitable in many locations where vandalism is a major problem, the look of this urban classic is rather forbidding. Now there are a number of suppliers of graceful lawn and terrace furniture with an old-fashioned appeal. Rustic wood chairs and tables are again being made of such materials as willow and ash, and there are craftsmen ready to supply carefully crafted iron benches, stands, chairs, tables, and settees.

Ken Heitz

Using simple tools, socket and tenon joinery, and kiln-dried select native hardwoods, Ken Heitz fashions a line of rustic furniture in the Adirondack tradition, which he calls Backwoods Furnishings. Each frame is handcrafted of ironwood, ash, yellow birch, or peeled poplar; cherry and birch are employed for the twig work. Both of the pieces shown, a simple armchair and a four-legged table, would be perfect choices for an informal garden patio or wrap-around porch.

Brochure available.

Ken Heitz
Box 161, Rte. 28
Indian Lake, NY 12842
(518) 251-3327

Carroll Milligan

Milligan fashions a number of unusual pieces from black willow, such as the armchair shown here. Some of his designs stem from his own imagination; others are copies of antiques he has seen and admired. Baskets, planters,

fern stands, side tables, coffee tables, dining tables, chairs (including rockers), and love seats are among the items he has crafted. He will undertake custom work as well.

For further information, contact:

Carroll Milligan
Box 62
Cave in Rock, IL 62919
(618) 289-3935

Putnam Rolling Ladder

Good solid-oak furniture suitable for outdoor use is difficult to find, especially at a time when aluminum and plastic are seemingly ubiquitous. Putnam, familiar to readers of *The Old House Catalogue* for its excellent line of ladders, is now offering solid-oak patio furniture with black metal supports. The pieces include a table 42" by 31" and 26" high, which will accommodate an umbrella; armchairs 21" wide; and a 60"-long armless bench.

Brochure available.

Putnam Rolling Ladder Co., Inc.
32 Howard St.
New York, NY 10013
(212) 226-5147

Robinson Iron

Many of the patterns still used by Robinson in the creation of cast-iron patio and garden furniture had their origins before the Civil War. Among the pieces the company manufactures are delicate filigreed tables and chairs, settees, and stools, whose lacy appearance belies their strength and durability. Each is available in a choice of finishes: verde gris, white, black, and terra cotta. All will withstand years and years of use. The company also undertakes expert restoration work.

Brochures $3.

Robinson Iron
Box 785, Robinson Rd.
Alexander City, AL 35010
(205) 329-8486

Schwartz's Forge and Metalworks

Joel Schwartz is probably best known for his intricate wrought-iron fences, doors, and window grilles discussed earlier in this chapter. In addition, however, he fashions exceptionally handsome oak benches with graceful wrought-iron supports. One example is illustrated here. Schwartz welcomes inquiries and creates most of his unique work on a commission basis.

Brochures available.

Schwartz's Forge and Metalworks
Box 205, Forge Hollow Rd.
Deansboro, NY 13328
(315) 841-4477

Lawn and Garden Ornaments

Fountains and sculpture add a roman-
tic and pleasing dimension to any
outdoor scene. Sometimes we become
so obsessed with the perfect lawn that
we forget how commonly ornaments
of various types were used in the
past. The available amount of outdoor
space will determine to some extent

just how extensively durable objects of
stone and iron such as urns, sculp-
tural figures, birdbaths, sundials, and
fountains may be employed. But even
in the small outdoor area found
around the typical town house, or-
namental objects can be effectively
used.

Nostalgia

In addition to its line of cast-iron
reproduction firebacks (see chapter 5), Nostalgia offers a wide
range of iron and stone sculpture,
statuary, and table bases for outdoor use. Among the many items
available—most copied from Sa-
vannah-area originals—are cast-
stone whippets, iron gargoyles
and griffins, and five different
styles of fountains.

Catalogue, $2.50.

Nostalgia, Inc.
307 Stiles Ave.
Savannah, GA 31401
(912) 232-2324

S. Chris Rheinschild

What better way to stem foot traf-
fic through the kitchen in the
summer months than with this
decorative cast-iron drinking
fountain? Rheinschild, best
known for his superb reproductions of bathroom and kitchen
hardware (see chapter 6), offers
the pedestal base in a wide range
of colors; it is fitted with a
stainless-steel bowl and polished-
brass fittings. Height to the rim is
32".

Brochures, $1.35.

S. Chris Rheinschild
2220 Carlton Way
Santa Barbara, CA 93109
(805) 962-8598

Robinson Iron

Outdoor sculpture in the form of
fountains, urns, and animal
figures has been part of the
American scene since before the
Civil War. It is possible, of course,

that plastic pink flamingos and plaster-of-Paris deer will someday achieve historical status, but, for now, we would be more than satisfied in displaying any one of Robinson Iron's wonderful animal statues. The whippet or greyhound was one of Queen Victoria's favorites, and is our favorite, too. You won't have to worry too much about losing this noble beast to a predatory iron thief as the creature weighs 150 lbs. and is made of 1″ to 3″-thick welded cast-iron plates. If you insist on a deer—and why not?—Robinson has a graceful creature so life-like that even the real species will be fooled. And then there is the king of the jungle—the lion—who, at 205 cast-iron lbs., would reign supreme at any entranceway. A pair of these noble fellows, smaller but not unlike those guarding the New York Public Library, deserve a prominent place.

Less dramatic, but no less pleasing is Robinson's fine line of reproduction cast-iron fountains, one of which—the Mediterranean—is illustrated here. The two-tiered model features three griffins and three dolphins among its ornamentation. Another of the firm's handsome designs is the three-tier Janney Crane fountain, first introduced by Janney & Co. of Birmingham, Alabama, before the Civil War.

Urns and planters also have their place on a graceful property, and

Robinson makes a number of models, including the French Medallion urn shown. There are, as well, several different types of neoclassical designs, the Venetian Fluted urn being the most famous.

Catalogue, $3.

Robinson Iron Corp.
Box 785, Robinson Rd.
Alexander City, AL 35010
(205) 329-8484

Winterthur Museum

Most cement birdbaths leave a lot to be desired in design and ornamentation, even though the sight of a group of birds splashing away in one of them can warm even the coldest heart. Why settle for the ordinary, however, when you can have one or two of these graceful scallop shells? Cast in cement by sculptor Leon Russell, the design was taken from a mid-18th-century iron plaque. The shell measures 20″ by 24″; it is 14″ tall.

Catalogue available.

Direct Mail Marketing Office
Winterthur Museum and Gardens
Winterthur, DE 19735
(800) 441-8229
(302) 656-8591 (DE)

Outdoor Structures

Outbuildings such as the gazebo, pavilion, carriage house, and barn have attracted more and more attention in the past few years. Back in the early 1900s, a prosperous country property might have contained a number of outbuildings, possibly including a summer kitchen, icehouse, carriage shed, privy, smokehouse, gazebo, springhouse, and a barn or two. There is very little practical need for many of these auxilliary structures today, but they do form a part of an historical record. Lack of utility notwithstanding, a gazebo or pavilion can provide a welcome shady nook on a hot summer day; the old-fashioned carriage shed is easily adapted for use as a garage and is a great deal more attractive than its usual modern counterpart. Barns, of course, are very fashionable today and are used for residential purposes as well as for animals and feed by country gentlemen and real farmers alike.

Catalogue, $1.

*Cape Cod Cupola Co., Inc.
78 State Rd.
N. Dartmouth, MA 02747
(617) 994-2119*

Building Conservation

The plans and patterns offered by Building Conservation vary in complexity and size to match the skills and interests of both the amateur and professional carpenter. The company has plans for cottages, cabins, studios, garages, sheds, gazebos, and more. Illustrated are designs for an open pavilion and a carriage shed, inspired by the Eastlake style. The shed measures 12' by 20' and includes a canopied porch 6' wide and 14' long. The pavilion is a simpler version of the company's plans for a Stick-style gazebo. Each set of plans contains elevations, construction details, and a list of materials needed.

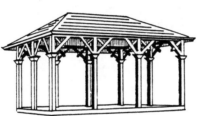

Brochures available.

*Building Conservation
6326 W. Wisconsin
Wauwatosa, WI 53213
(414) 475-1896*

Cape Cod Cupolas

This Massachusetts company has long been a pioneer in the manufacture and sale of fully-assembled cupolas for garages and other outbuildings. Cape Cod offers several styles and many sizes of cupolas: most are available with a choice of aluminum or copper-clad roofs. Some are six-sided, some square; and all are constructed of pine and painted with two coats of quality white paint (unless you specify that you wish them left unprimed for staining). The largest models are made to order; the company suggests that these allow room for electric lights or ventilating fans to be installed if desired.

New Jersey Barn

If you've driven by an old barn recently and wished that it could be relocated to your property to serve as an outbuilding, guest house, or even a primary residence, you're not alone. The New Jersey Barn Company was established to fulfill such wishes. It deals exclusively in barn frames, and has a limited number of antique frames in storage (in a barn, naturally) which can be reassembled on your site. All of the company's frames were originally built in New Jersey; the major timbers are hand-hewn, joined by mortise and tenon, and secured with wooden pegs. Most are of oak, a wood known for its strength and resilience. Each frame is photographed, measured, labeled, blueprinted, and reproduced in a scale model before disassembly. It is then cleaned and reconditioned. Foundations, flooring, sheathing, and roofing are left to the discretion of the new owners and their local contractor or architect; New Jersey Barn, however, will be happy to offer assistance and suggestions. Illustrated are two of the barns now in storage—the Everitt barn and the broad Isaac Dumont Dutch barn.

Brochure available.

The New Jersey Barn Co.
Box 702
Princeton, NJ 08542
(609) 924-8480

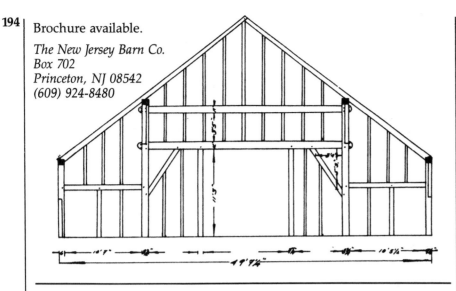

Sun Designs

If you're handy with a hammer or have a good carpenter to call upon, you'll want to study the offerings of Sun Designs before purchasing lumber for that new garden structure. We recommend that your first step be to order each of the company's books of designs. There are currently three available (at $7.95 each): *Gazebos and Other Garden Structures; Bridges and Cupolas;* and *The Classic Outhouse Book.* Each is crammed with history and lore, lots of sketches (of both exteriors and interiors), and selected plans. Complete plans for each structure—from bridges to privies, cupolas to arbors—are available separately. Pictured here are just two of the many different designs offered. The octagonal Stratford, one of Sun's more appealing gazebo models, measures 13' from point to point and is 16' 4" high. The Potomac bridge certainly wouldn't

span the river which inspired its name, but, at 20' long, it will probably do quite nicely as a crossing for the creek in your back yard.

Brochures available.

Sun Designs
Rextrom, Inc.
Box 206
Delafield, WI 53018
(414) 567-4255

Outdoor Pests and Friends

There are indoor pests, too, but the critters outside the house are the ones that concern us—before they get in. Your local exterminator is probably the one to turn to after you've released 10,000 lovely lady bugs (guaranteed to take care of Japanese beetles) into the air, only to see them fly away from the yard two minutes later. If the problem is pigeons or starlings, you may need some more permanent protection such as the device presented in the following listing. As for the other side of the coin, there are the friendly birds who mean neither you nor your house any harm. Provide them with a stylish home so that they will stay around and devour grubs and leaf-eating insects.

Nixalite of America

Sometimes you just can't win. You can spend lots of time and effort installing bird feeders, marten houses, and birdbaths to attract the more desirable of the feathered species, only to discover that you've lured the less desirable ones as well. If you're a city dweller, the problem is likely to be pigeons—flocks of them. In the country, it's more apt to be starlings. No matter. What to do to keep hordes of the creatures away from your beautifully renovated house and grounds (short of bringing out the shotgun, that is)? Nixalite may have the answer for you. The company offers several different models of stainless-steel needle strips, such as the one illustrated, which can be applied to dormers, gutters, roof ridges, and any other areas where you wish to repel birds. Nixalite's bird control system will not harm the birds, only deter them from landing. It is relatively inobtrusive, easy to install, and permanent. It can also be used to keep squirrels and the family cat away from the bird feeders, or even to keep human intruders from climbing where they're not wanted.

Brochures available.

Nixalite of America
417 25th St.
Moline, IL 61265
(309) 797-8771

Sun Designs

In addition to its wide array of designs for garden structures, Sun offers a number of suggestions for birdhouses and feeders of various sizes and complexity. Pictured here are just two: the Oriole, a 14"-square feeder with glass inserts, and the Warbler, a 42"-high bird house certain to attract the smaller varieties at nesting time. Plans are available for a nominal charge; first you may wish to order the book which pictures them—*Gazebos and other Garden Structures*—available for $7.95 postpaid.

Brochures available.

Sun Designs
Rextrom, Inc.
Box 206
Delafield, WI 53018
(414) 567-4255

Other Suppliers for Outdoor and Garden Areas

Consult List of Suppliers for addresses.

Fencing, Gates, and Window Grilles

Colonial Charm
Image, Inc.
G. Krug & Son
Moultrie Manufacturing Co.

Outdoor Furniture

Adirondack Chair Co.
Chilstone Garden Ornament
Gazebo & Porchworks
Sculpture Design Imports, Inc.
Southern Heritage
Welsbach Lighting
Wood Classics, Inc.

Lawn and Garden Ornaments

Chilstone Garden Ornament
Columbia Cascade Timber Co.
International Terra Cotta, Inc.
Kenneth Lynch & Sons

Outdoor Structures

Gazebo & Porchworks
Lord & Burnham
Native Wood Products, Inc.
Sun Systems

Outdoor Pests and Friends

King's Natural Pest Control
Necessary Trading Co.

11.

Decorative Accessories

As any dictionary will tell you, an accessory is a supplement; an adjunct, rather than a primary object. Decorative accessories—mirrors, pillows, baskets, weather vanes, wall hangings, quilts, vases, etc.—can provide just the right finishing touch in a period decor. Unfortunately, they tend to be the last thing we think about when decorating a home, and we may have a tendency to buy such objects on impulse—from a flea market or garage sale, perhaps. Items bought in that way, however, frequently find their way back to the same type of sale a year or two later. But that doesn't have to be the case. There are many beautifully designed, well-made objects to enhance a period setting while serving a useful function as well. Some are illustrated in this chapter; many others are available from craftsmen and established firms listed in previous chapters. A beautifully wrought fire set, for instance, is as much a decoration for the hearth as it is a useful tool (see chapter 5). A handsome solid copper hurricane lamp will enhance the look of a wrought-iron patio table and provide illumination at the same time (see chapter 4).

What counts with any decorative accessory is its design, its quality, and the use to which it will be put. Dust catchers are just that, so unless you have a treasured collection of Chinese export porcelain to display, you'll probably find that the kitsch you've amassed over the years has no place in your design scheme.

One of the best sources for handsome decorative objects is a fine museum. Delaware's Winterthur, for instance, lists many handsome and useful objects in its catalogue, each a fine reproduction of a treasured antique from the museum collection. The Metropolitan Museum of Art in New York is another excellent source. And there are many others spread across the country.

A final word of caution is in order. One or two superb pieces can make just as good an impression as a whole gallery of lesser ones. In choosing accessories, as in choosing much else for your home, less is usually more.

Cherry bride's boxes, Orleans
Carpenters, Orleans, Massachusetts.

John Morgan Baker, Framer

John Morgan Baker became a framer to frame the work of his father, Jim Baker, a painter. The younger Baker's work is still all custom designed to complement individual pieces of art. He sells mostly to artists and galleries, but his frames can beautifully grace old portraits and watercolors, folk art, and samplers.

Baker's frames are handcrafted from curly or bird's-eye maple. Standard widths are 1½″, 2¼″, and 3″, but other widths are available. Frames can be flat or beveled, and many options, such as decorative carvings or a gold-leaf strip around the inside of the frame, can be requested.

Brochure and color photos of stains available upon receipt of a stamped business-sized envelope.

John Morgan Baker, Framer
Box 149
Worthington, OH 43085
(614) 885-7040

Burdoch Silk Lampshades

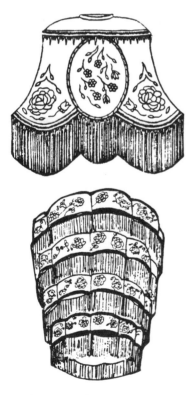

Handsewn and embroidered Victorian lampshades in old-fashioned hues—usually called "silk lampshades"—are now made of satinized polyester to better withstand the heat of electric bulbs.

Shown are "Victorian Joy," which has a lower width of 18″ and a height of 15½″, and the three-tier "Victorian Chandelier." The chandelier is 2′ x 3′ and can also be made even more dramatic with four or five tiers, with a 6′ maximum diameter of the upper tier.

For a color brochure, send $2 and SASE to:

Burdoch Silk Lampshade Co.
11120 Roselle St., Suite G
San Diego, CA 92121
(619) 458-1005

The Candle Cellar & Emporium

Handmade wooden boxes that held candles or tapers were essential in Colonial homes. Now these boxes can serve as decorative catchalls. Pictured here are a wall box that is a copy of an 18th-century knife box; a candle box which can be hung or set on a table; and an upright taper holder which can fit into a small space. The wall box measures 13½″ x 7″ x 4½″; the candle box 11″ x 12″ x 4″; and the taper holder, 13″ x 5″ x 5″.

Other items available through the

Candle Cellar & Emporium include folk-art animals and handcrafted candles.

Catalogue, $1.

The Candle Cellar & Emporium
Box 135, South Station
Fall River, MA 02724
(401) 624-9529

Cedar Swamp Stoneware

Traditional New England pottery of the late 1800s is being faithfully recreated by Cedar Swamp. All items are formed of lead-free clay and glazes (using native clays and following authentic clay formulas)

and fired to a temperature of 2,300° F. Pieces are oven- and burner-proof and can also be used for storing and pickling. The hand-painted motifs—all done by artist Jack Boyko—capture the designs of the period.

Shown here are a brown kitchen crock, a small pitcher, and three examples of spongeware.

Catalogue, $1 (refundable with first purchase).

Cedar Swamp Stoneware Co.
30 Perseverance Way
Hyannis, MA 02601
(617) 771-6633

The Country Loft

Country Loft has a large variety of country-style items available by mail-order. Prices are quite reasonable and there is something for every room in your house, from Shaker reproductions to farm bells.

Shown here is a copy of a turn-of-the-century wall shelf. Made of solid oak, it has two deeply slotted grooves that make it the perfect display for plates. It measures 24½″ long, 7¾″ deep, and 12″ high, and the back of the shelf rises 4¾″ above the shelf surface.

Catalogue available.

The Country Loft
South Shore Park
Hingham, MA 02043
(800) 225-5408
(617) 749-7766 (in MA)

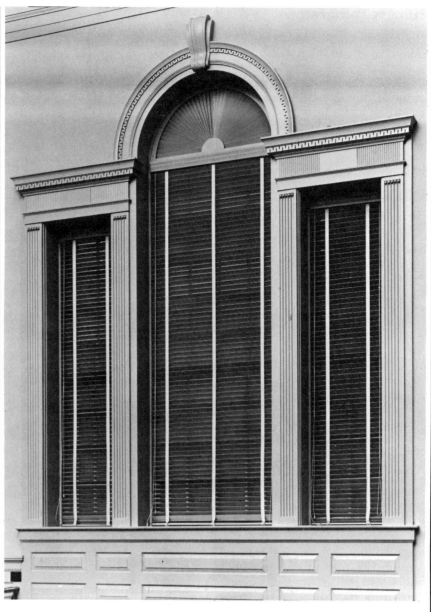

Hudson Venetian Blind Service

Some of the most prominent homes in the country, including governors' mansions and historic landmarks, are adorned with Hudson's handsome, custom-crafted wood blinds. Illustrated here is a Palladian window in one of these homes, finished with Hudson blinds.

Hudson's blinds are constructed of kiln-dried Ponderosa pine and come in 1″, 1¾″, 2″, and 2⅜″ sizes. Stains are available in a wide range of wood tones from natural to black. High gloss and mat varnish finishes are offered. Blinds can be equipped with either tradi-tional cotton tapes or with braided cable ladder.

Brochure and price list available.

Hudson Venetian Blind Service, Inc.
2000 Twilight Ln.
Richmond, VA 23235
(804) 276-5700

Hungry Point Farm

Holly Wesley, a Minnesota framemaker and folk painter, specializes in making new frames that look authentically like those of the 19th century. A talented artisan, she hand-decorates basswood to simulate woods of the period, such as mahogany and cherry, and offers a choice of ten moldings, which she will decorate to taste. She also cuts down and repairs old frames and uses acid-free materials for museum-quality mounting and hand-made old-fashioned matting.

For further information, contact:

Holly Wesley
Hungry Point Farm
6 Old Deerfield Rd.
Welsh, MN 55089
(612) 388-3997

Alice Moulton-Ely

Using pen and ink, Alice Moulton-Ely produces finely detailed drawings that will truly capture the individuality of your home within its setting. Illustrated here is the Shields house in Lake Forest, Illinois. This drawing was made into a Christmas card.

Sizes of Moulton-Ely drawings range from miniature (3½″ x 5½″) to large (15″ x 24″). She prefers to work on location or from her own photographs, but customer-supplied photographs will do if necessary.

Samples available.

Alice Moulton-Ely
144 E. Westminster Rd.
Lake Forest, IL 60045
(312) 295-3152

Orleans Carpenters

These Massachusetts craftspeople have been busy adding new products to their line of reproductions of Colonial and Shaker furniture, tools, and toys.

The cherry bride's boxes illustrated here are recent additions. Crafted in the tradition of Pennsylvania-German folk art, they are finely sanded, ready to be painted. They come tacked or laced in three sizes: 19¼″ x 12½″ x

7″, 17¼″ x 10″ x 6″, and 15¼″ x 7½″ x 5″.

Also available are cherry and maple carriers and boxes, all made in the Shaker tradition using the lightest materials available for maximum strength.

Catalogue, 50¢.

Orleans Carpenters
Box 107-C, Rock Harbor Rd.
Orleans, MA 02653
(617) 255-2646

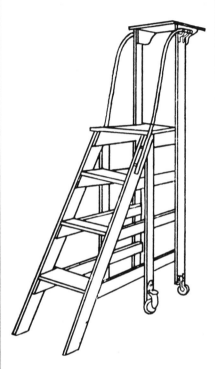

Putnam Rolling Ladder

The Putnam Rolling Ladder Co. makes handsome and functional solid-oak ladders to order.

Shown here is the aptly named Pulpit Ladder that is particularly suited to work in narrow places and around short corners. It comes with brakes, which prevent it from moving when you are using it, and with swivel casters, which make it easy to turn. The shelf is ideal for sorting papers or resting books. Standard sizes are 3′, 4′, 5′, and 6′.

Putnam, well known for its wooden rolling ladders, also makes folding ladders, stools, stepstools, and industrial ladders.

Catalogue available.

Putnam Rolling Ladder Co., Inc.
32 Howard St.
New York, NY 10013
(212) 226-5147

Don Richmond

San Francisco craftsman Don Richmond is a designer and manufacturer of stenciled window shades suitable for Victorian interiors. Richmond uses Johanna Mills cloth for spring roller shades. Six border designs are available to be stenciled in one of six colors—red, blue, yellow, violet, green, or apricot—on an off-white, off-black, or colored ground. Cloth can be translucent, blackout, or Kashmir linen. Shade widths range from 18″ to 12′ with a maximum length of 12′.

Literature available.

Don Richmond
1036 Florida St.
San Francisco, CA 94110
(415) 931-1000

Erwin Rowland

Patchwork quilts are a joyous part of our American heritage. Since 1973 Erwin Rowland has been capturing patterns that have been handed down for generations and redesigning them for contemporary colors and fabrics. All of her quilts are completely handmade by Amish and Mennonite women, many of them fifth- or sixth-generation quilters.

One of the most graceful quilt patterns is the "Double Wedding Ring," shown here in a contemporary setting. It can be made in shades of one color or by combining two or more colors. A star-

flower design is quilted in the center of the rings. The very dramatic "Lone Star" quilt, also illustrated, is composed of hundreds of small diamond-shaped pieces. Graceful circles of feather quilting add dimension to the background.

All quilts are available in single, double, queen, and king sizes. They are made of high-quality cotton and cotton-blend fabrics and are filled with polyester batting. They can be machine-washed. Sixteen patterns are available.

Catalogue, $3.

Erwin Rowland
181 East 73rd St.
New York, NY 10021
(212) 249-1246

Shaker Workshops

The craftsmen of Shaker Workshops are committed to reproducing precisely the functional and simplistically beautiful furniture that was commonplace in Shaker homes. Two towel racks are typical of Shaker Workshops' functional design:

The hanging towel rack is an exact copy of one that hung in the ironing room of the Mt. Lebanon, New York, communal wash house. Made of clear pine, its height is 16″, width 24″, and depth 4″. The freestanding towel rack might have been found in a Shaker wash house, kitchen, or retiring room. The unusual octagonal rails make it ideal for airing quilts and blankets or for drying woolens. It, too, is made of clear pine with a height of 33½″,

202

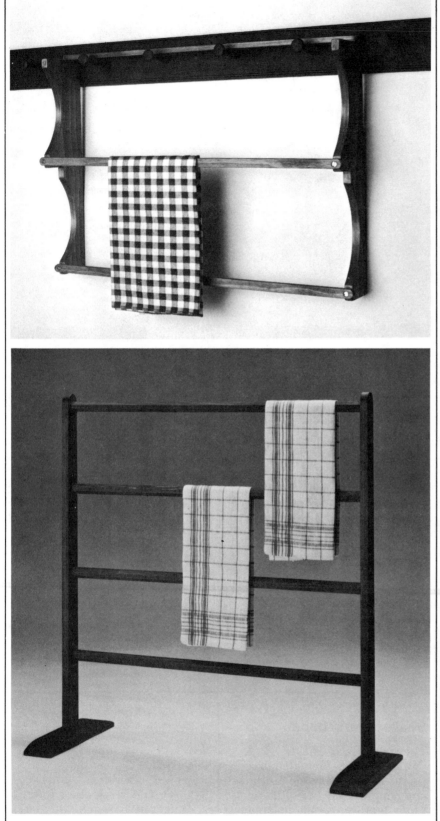

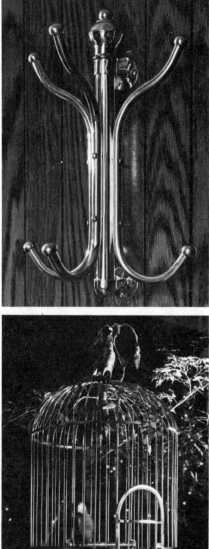

Ship 'n Out

Ship 'n Out fabricates an array of accessories from solid heavy-wall, hard-drawn brass tubing. None of the firm's items is plated. Some standard products, including a variety of standing and mounted coat racks, are available, but Ship 'n Out will make to order any project of your own.

width 33⅞", and length of foot 13". Both racks, and many other Shaker Workshop items, can be purchased fully assembled or in do-it-yourself kits.

Catalogue, 50¢.

Shaker Workshops
Box 1028
Concord, MA 01742
(617) 646-8985

The coat rack shown here is just 15" high and 10" wide, but can hold at least six coats and hats. The very ornate 9' high birdcage is thus far one of a kind, custom-made for a tavern in southern New Jersey.

Other standard pieces include pot racks and bar items, such as wine and glass racks.

Color brochure available.

Ship 'n Out
8 Charles St.
Pawling, NY 12564
(800) 431-8242
(914) 855-5947 (in NY)

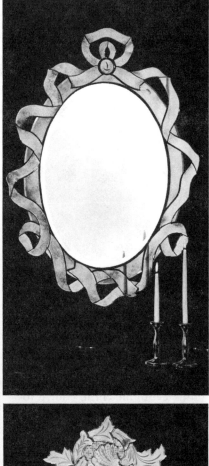

Smith-Cornell

Buildings of historic interest are deserving of special recognition and can be marked with one of Smith-Cornell's solid-bronze plaques. Plaques are 10" x 15", ⅜" thick, can be mounted anywhere, and will last for centuries. These plaques already mark over 12,000 historic properties in all fifty states.

Smith-Cornell also makes plaques and markers from solid aluminum and from marble. Photographs, lithographs, and lettering can be placed on permanently iodized aluminum plaques.

Brochure and price list available.

Smith-Cornell, Inc.
Box 686
Auburn, IN 46706
(219) 925-1172

I. Schwartz Glass & Mirror

The mirrors handcrafted by I. Schwartz are based on the decorative designs of 16th- and 17th-century Venetian artisans. They are ornate, intricately detailed, and are made from as many as ninety pieces of glass, ranging in size from several feet across to delicately carved glass no bigger than the head of a nail.

Shown here are an irregularly shaped mirror, measuring 33" x 44", with an exquisite border, and a 34" x 47" oval mirror with a smoked antique frame.

Schwartz also supplies other types of traditional handmade wall mirrors as well as glass for table tops.

Catalogue available.

I. Schwartz Glass & Mirror Company, Inc.
412-418 E. 59th St.
New York, NY 10022
(212) 759-7866

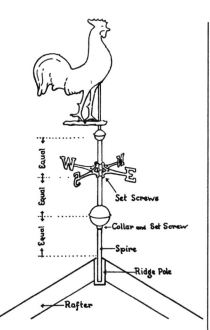

Stoneham Pewter

Ted and Cheryl White of Stoneham Pewter produce original pewter pieces that are both functional and beautiful, using antique techniques little known today. Ted White studied with master pewterers in a London company that has been in business since 1700. His methods follow those of pewterers who worked from 1700 to 1870.

The Whites use 92 percent pure tin, hardened and strengthened with copper and antimony. Each piece is individually gravity cast, turned freehand into a final design, and buffed or polished to a fine finish. All pieces are signed and dated.

Shown here are 5¼" goblets, 3" cordials, 5½" candle holders, and a snuffer with finial.

Brochure, 50¢.

Stoneham Pewter
RFD #1, Box 656
Brookfield, NH 03872
(603) 522-3425

E. G. Washburne

Handmade copper weather vanes in traditional early American styles are still being made by the craftsmen of E. G. Washburne & Co. This firm, established in 1853, uses original cast-iron molds, many of which are based on even earlier wooden molds of primitive weather vanes.

Each vane is full- or swell-bodied, which appears to add a third dimension to the piece. Some of the forms available are roosters, cows, horses, eagles, and fish.

Shown here is a mounted full-bodied rooster, which measures 21" high and 18" long.

All vanes come ready for mounting, and custom vanes can be made to order.

Brochure available.

E. G. Washburne & Co.
85 Andover St., Rt. 114
Danvers, MA 01923
(617) 774-3645

W. T. Weaver & Sons

W. T. Weaver & Sons makes traditional American weather vanes out of copper. Vanes come in a natural copper finish, which darkens naturally over time, or a verde green finish, which holds its appearance longer. Offered are four sizes of eagles, two roosters,

Daniel Strawser

Daniel Strawser, a Pennsylvania folk artist, makes traditional wood carvings by hand. Using only a pocket knife, he whittles country creatures like roosters, eagles, dogs, cats, and birds. Illustrated here is Strawser's "bird tree" incorporating fourteen multihued, humorously posed birds. The birds are on real branches, which are "growing" out of a hand-crafted pedestal.

For further information, contact:

Daniel G. Strawser
126 Main St.
Stouchsburg, PA 19567
(215) 589-4651

a running horse, a goose, and a fish.

Catalogue, $2.50.

W. T. Weaver & Sons, Inc.
1208 Wisconsin Ave.
Washington, D.C. 20007
(202) 333-4200

Martha Wetherbee

Martha Wetherbee is producing baskets that truly capture the spirit of Shaker craftsmanship. These are absolutely authentic replicas of basket designs that were created originally for their function but are now also recognized for their beauty and distinction.

Pictured here is Wetherbee's fruit basket, based on one of the Mt. Lebanon Shaker colony's most celebrated designs. The basket's arched bottom allows air to pass through, so fruit will stay fresh. The basket's diameter is 9½", its height 5½", with handle, 10".

Handbook, $3.50.

Martha Wetherbee
Star Route, Box 35
Sanbornton, NH 03269
(603) 286-8927

Other Suppliers of Decorative Accessories

Consult List of Suppliers for addresses.

Arrowhead Forge
Laura Ashley, Inc.
Berea College Student Craft
  Industries
Lester and Barbara Breininger
Cape Cod Cupola Co.
The Colonial Casting Co.
The Copper House
Custom House
Historic Charleston Reproductions
S. C. Huber, Accoutrements
Hunter Ceiling Fans
Hurley Patentee Lighting
J. J. Jaxon Co., Inc.
Kenneth Lynch & Sons, Inc.
Metropolitan Museum of Art
Newton Millham
R. Jessee Morley, Cabinetmaker
R. Wayne Reynolds
Matthew Richardson, Coppersmith
Robinson Iron Corp.
Travis Tuck, Metal Sculptor and
  Blacksmith

Directory of State Preservation Agencies, Preservation Organizations, and American Institute of Architects Preservation Coordinators

Whether you need guidance in submitting a property for State or National Register certification or are merely seeking technical advice on how to proceed with preservation work on your own old house, the following agencies, organizations, and individuals are available to help. Presented state by state are public historic preservation offices and officers (the initials "SHPO" in the listings stand for state historic preservation officer); private state preservation organizations; and American Institute of Architects state preservation coordinators. All the officials listed work with both private and public groups and with private individuals.

In addition to these sources, the following National Park Service regional offices for cultural programs and National Trust for Historic Preservation regional offices can provide useful information and advice:

NATIONAL PARK SERVICE

Alaska Area Office
1011 E. Tudor, Suite 297
Anchorage, AK 99503
(907) 277-1666

Mid-Atlantic Regional Office
143 S. Third St.
Philadelphia, PA 19106
(215) 597-2283

CT, DE, DC, IN, ME, MD, MA, MI, NH, NJ, NY, OH, PA, RI, VT, VA, WV

Rocky Mountain Regional Office
Denver Federal Center
PO Box 25287
Denver, CO 80225
(303) 234-2560

CO, IL, IA, KS, MN, MO, MT, NB, ND, NM, OK, SD, TX, VT, WI, WY

Southeast Region
R. B. Russell Federal Building
75 Spring St.
Atlanta, GA 30303
(404) 221-5180

AL, AR, FL, GA, KY, LA, MS, NC, SC, TN, PR, VI

Western Regional Office
450 Golden Gate Ave.
San Francisco, CA 94102
(415) 556-7741

AZ, CA, HI, ID, NV, OR, WA, AM. SAMOA, GU

NATIONAL TRUST FOR HISTORIC PRESERVATION:

Mid-Atlantic Regional Office
1600 H St., NW
Washington, DC 20006
(202) 673-4203

DE, DC, MD, NJ, PA, PR, VA, VI, WV

Midwest Regional Office
407 S. Dearborn St., Suite 710
Chicago, IL 60605
(312) 353-3419

IL, IN, IA, MI, MN, MO, OH, WI

Mountains/Plains Regional Office
1407 Larimer St., Suite 200
Denver, CO 80202
(303) 837-2245

CO, KS, MT, NE, NM, ND, OK, SD, TX, WY

Northeast Regional Office
Old City Hall
45 School St.
Boston, MA 02110
(617) 223-7754

CT, ME, MA, NH, NY, RI, VT

Southern Regional Office
456 King St.
Charleston, SC 29403
(803) 724-4711

AL, AR, FL, GA, KY, LA, MS, NC, SC, TN

Western Regional Office
681 Market St., Suite 859
San Francisco, CA 94105
(415) 974-8420

AK, AZ, CA, GU, HI, ID, Micronesia, NV, OR, UT, WA

State Historic Preservation Offices

ALABAMA

Alabama Historical Commission
725 Monroe St.
Montgomery, AL 36130
(205) 261-3184

F. Lawrence Oaks, Executive Director
Timothy A. Smith, Deputy
David Hughes, Grants Mgr.
Ann Hutchins, Fiscal Off.

ALASKA

Office of History and Archaeology
Division of Parks
Alaska Department of Natural Resources
225 A Cordova St.
Anchorage, AK 99501
(907) 274-4676

Ty L. Dilliplane, Chief
Tim Smith, Deputy
Katherine Torzy, Grants Mgr.
Larry Gordon, Fiscal Off.

AMERICAN SAMOA

Department of Parks & Recreation
Government of American Samoa
Pago Pago, American Samoa 96799

Raymond E. Dole, HPO

ARIZONA

Office of Historic Preservation
Arizona State Parks
1688 W. Adams
Phoenix, AZ 85007
(602) 255-4174

Donna Schober, Chief
Frank B. Fryman, Deputy
Neal Weiner, Grants Mgr.
Virginia Stone, Fiscal Off.

ARKANSAS

Arkansas Historic Preservation Program
The Heritage Center, Suite 200
225 E. Markham
Little Rock, AR 72201
(501) 371-2763

Wilson Stiles, Director
Jackie Carfagno, Grants Mgr.
Pat Bray/Veda Story, Fiscal Offs.

CALIFORNIA

Office of Historic Preservation
Department of Parks & Recreation
PO Box 2390
Sacramento, CA 95811
(916) 445-8006

William S. Briner, SHPO
Connie Finster, Grants Mgr.
Russ Greenlee, Fiscal Off.

COLORADO

Colorado Heritage Center
1300 Broadway
Denver, CO 80203
(303) 866-2136

Barbara Sudler, SHPO
Jim Hartmann, Deputy
Irv Jackson, Grants Mgr.
Kathy Tolliver, Fiscal Off.

CONNECTICUT

Connecticut Historical Commission
59 S. Prospect St.
Hartford, CT 06106
(203) 566-3005

John W. Shannahan, Director
Dawn Maddox, Deputy
Duarte Alves, Grants Mgr. & Fiscal Off.

DELAWARE

Division of Historical & Cultural Affairs
Hall of Records
Dover, DE 19901
(302) 736-5314

Daniel R. Griffith, Director
Gerron Hite, Grants Mgr.
Mae Hiscox, Fiscal Off.

DISTRICT OF COLUMBIA

Department of Consumer and Regulatory
  Affairs
614 H St., NW
Washington, DC 20001
(202) 727-7120

Carol B. Thompson, Director
Jeanette Johnson, Grants Mgr.
Derek Wheeler, Fiscal Off.

FLORIDA

Division of Archives, History & Records
  Management
Department of State
The Capitol
Tallahassee, FL 32301
(904) 487-2333

George W. Percy, Director
Bill Thurston, Grants Mgr.
Troy Reeves, Fiscal Off.

GEORGIA

Historic Preservation Section
Dept. of Natural Resources
270 Washington St., SW, Room 703C
Atlanta, GA 30334
(404) 656-2840

Elizabeth A. Lyon, Chief
Carol Griffith, Deputy
Karen Luehrs, Grants Mgr. & Fiscal Off.

GUAM

Department of Parks & Recreation
P.O. Box 2950
Agana, Guam 96910
(overseas oper.) 477-9620/21, ext. 4

Joseph E. Paulino, Director
Laura Caso, Grants Mgr.

HAWAII

Department of Land & Natural Resources
P.O. Box 621
Honolulu, HI 96809
(808) 548-7460

Susumu Ono, SHPO
Don Hibbard, Deputy & Grants Mgr.
Alvin Tomashiro, Fiscal Off.

IDAHO

Idaho Historical Society
610 N. Julia Davis Dr.
Boise, ID 83706
(208) 334-2120

Merle W. Wells, HP Coordinator
Arthur A. Hart, Deputy
Bill Dougal, Grants Mgr.
Lisa Berriochoa, Fiscal Off.

ILLINOIS

Dept. of Conservation
State Office Building
400 S. Spring St.
Springfield, IL 62706
(217) 782-6302

David Kenney, Director
William Farrar, Deputy
Steve Gonzales, Grants Mgr. & Fiscal Off.

INDIANA

Dept. of Natural Resources
608 State Office Building
Indianapolis, IN 46204
(317) 232-4020

Jams M. Ridenour, Director
John T. Costello, Deputy
Richard A. Gantz, Grants Mgr.
Allen Goebes, Fiscal Off.

IOWA

Iowa State Historical Dept.
Office of Historic Preservation
Historical Building
E. 12th St. & Grand Ave.
Des Moines, IA 50319
(515) 281-5113 or 6949

Adrian D. Anderson, Director
R. Stanley Riggle, Deputy
Jack Lufkin, Grants Mgr. & Fiscal Off.

KANSAS

Kansas State Historical Society
120 W. 10th St.
Topeka, KS 66612
(913) 296-3251

Joseph W. Snell, Exec. Director
Richard Pankratz, Deputy & Grants Mgr.
Mike Kidwell, Fiscal Off.

KENTUCKY

Kentucky Heritage Council
Capitol Plaza Tower, 12th Fl.
Frankfort, KY 40601
(502) 564-7005

Mary Cronan Oppel, SHPO
Brian Cowherd, Grants Mgr. & Fiscal Off.

LOUISIANA

Office of Cultural Development
P.O. Box 44247
Baton Rouge, LA 70804
(504) 925-3884

Robert B. DeBlieux, Assistant Secretary
Ann Jones, Deputy
Barbara Bacot, Grants Mgr.
Ruth McDonner, Fiscal Off.

MAINE

Maine Historic Preservation Commission
55 Capitol, Station 65
Augusta, ME 04333
(207) 289-2133

Earle G. Shettleworth, Jr., Director
Robert Bradley, Deputy
Rex Reed, Grants Mgr.
Rita Obie, Fiscal Off.

MARYLAND

Maryland Historical Trust
John Shaw House
21 State Circle
Annapolis, MD 21401
(301) 269-2851

J. Rodney Little, SHPO
Mark R. Edwards, Deputy
Bill Pencek, Grants Mgr.
Rita Brunner, Fiscal Off.

MASSACHUSETTS

Massachusetts Historical Commission
294 Washington St.
Boston, MA 02108
(617) 727-8470

Patricia L. Weslowski, Exec. Director
Valerie Talmage, Deputy
Elsa Fitzgerald, Grants Mgr.

MICHIGAN

Michigan History Division
Department of State
208 N. Capitol
Lansing, MI 48918
(517) 373-6362

Martha Bigelow, Director
Kathryn Eckert, Deputy
Ann Webster, Grants Mgr. & Fiscal Off.

MINNESOTA

Minnesota Historical Society
690 Cedar St.
St. Paul, MN 55101
(612) 296-2747

Russell W. Fridley, Director
Nina M. Archabal, Deputy
Henry Harren, Grants Mgr.
John Wood, Fiscal Off.

MISSISSIPPI

State of Mississippi Dept. of Archives &
    History
PO Box 571
Jackson, MS 39205
(601) 359-1424

Elbert Hilliard, Director
Robert J. Bailey, Deputy
Mary Louise Middleton, Grants Mgr.
Joe Rutledge, Fiscal Off.

MISSOURI

State Dept. of Natural Resources
P.O. Box 176
Jefferson City, MO 65102
(314) 751-4422

Fred Lafser, Director
Orval L. Henderson, Jr., Deputy
Jerald Stepenoff, Grants Mgr.

MONTANA

Montana Historical Society
225 N. Roberts St.
Veterans Memorial Building
Helena, MT 59620
(406) 444-2694

Marcella Sherfy, SHPO
Linda Gamble-Depew, Fiscal Off.

NEBRASKA

The Nebraska State Historical Society
1500 R St., P.O. Box 82554
Lincoln, NE 68508
(402) 471-3850

Marvin F. Kivett, Director
Richard Jensen, Deputy
L. Robert Puschendorf, Grants Mgr.
John Caleca, Fiscal Off.

NEVADA

Dept. of Conservation & Natural Resources
Nye Building, Room 213
201 S. Fall St.
Carson City, NV 89710
(702) 885-4360

Roland D. Westergard, Director
Ronald M. James, Deputy
Patricia A. Greenwald, Grants Mgr. &
    Fiscal Off.

NEW HAMPSHIRE

Dept. of Resources & Economic
    Development
P.O. Box 856
Concord, NH 03301
(603) 271-2411

George Gilman, Commissioner
Ronald Poltak, Deputy
Linda Wilson, Grants Mgr.
Albert J. Nolin, Fiscal Off.

NEW JERSEY

Dept. of Environmental Protection
CN 402
Trenton, NJ 08625
(609) 292-2885

Robert E. Hughey, Commissioner
Hellen Fenske, Deputy
Skkp Forewood, Grants Mgr.
Jack Lawson, Fiscal Off.

NEW MEXICO

Historic Preservation Div., Office of
    Cultural Affairs
Villa Rivera, Room 101
228 E. Palace Ave.
Santa Fe., NM 87503
(505) 827-8320

Thomas W. Merlan, SHPO
Kathleen Brooker, Deputy
Tom McCalmont, Grants Mgr.
Julian Ortiz, Fiscal Off.

NEW YORK

Office of Parks, Recreation & Historic
    Preservation
Agency Building #1
Empire State Plaza
Albany, NY 12238

Orin Lehman, Commissioner
Julia S. Stokes, Deputy
Kevin Burns, Grants Mgr. & Fiscal Off.

NORTH CAROLINA

Division of Archives & History
Department of Cultural Resources
109 E. Jones St.
Raleigh, NC 27611
(919) 733-7305

William S. Price, Jr., Director
John Little, Deputy
Lloyd Childers, Grants Mgr.
Bill Harris, Fiscal Off.

NORTH DAKOTA

State Historical Society of North Dakota
Liberty Memorial Building
Bismarck, ND 58501
(701) 224-2667

James E. Sperry, Superintendent
Lou Hafermehl, Deputy & Grants Mgr.
Bob Schlobohm, Fiscal Off.

NORTH MARIANA ISLANDS

Department of Community & Cultural
    Affairs
Commonwealth of Northern Mariana
    Islands
Saipan, Mariana Islands 96950
(overseas oper.) Saipan 9772 or 9411

Jesus B. Pangelinan, HPO

OHIO

Ohio Historical Society
Interstate 71 at 17th Ave.
Columbus, OH 43211
(614) 466-1500

W. Ray Luce, SHPO
Gretchen Klimoski, Deputy & Fiscal Off.
Mary Beth Hirsch, Grants Mgr.

OKLAHOMA

Oklahoma Historical Society
Historical Building, 2100 N. Lincoln
Oklahoma City, OK 73105
(405) 521-2491

Earle Metcalf, SHPO
Melvena Thurmond, Deputy & Grants
   Mgr.
Armie Armstrong, Fiscal Off.

OREGON

Oregon State Parks & Recreation Division
525 Trade St., SE
Salem, OR 97310
(503) 378-5019

David G. Talbot, Superintendent
David Powers, Deputy
Kim Lakin, Grants Mgr.
Rich Evans, Fiscal Off.

PENNSYLVANIA

Pennsylvania Historical & Museum
   Commission
P.O. Box 1026
Harrisburg, PA 17108
(717) 787-2891

Larry Tise, SHPO
Brenda Barrett, Deputy
Barbara Greenlee, Grants Mgr.
Toby Gilson, Fiscal Off.

COMMONWEALTH OF PUERTO RICO

State Historic Preservation Office
Box 82, La Fortaleza
San Juan, PR 00901
(809) 721-4389

Arleen Pabon de Rocafort, HPO
Jose Rivera, Fiscal Off.

RHODE ISLAND

Rhode Island Dept. of Community
   Affairs
150 Washington St.
Providence, RI 02903
(401) 277-2850

Frederick C. Williamson, Director
Edward F. Sanderson, Deputy
Tricia Kenyon, Grnts Mgr.
Gloria Mollis, Fiscal Off.

SOUTH CAROLINA

Department of Archives & History
1430 Senate St.
Columbia, SC 29211
(803) 758-5816

Charles Lee, Director
Christie Fant, Deputy
Ms. Langdon Edmunds, Grants Mgr.
Rodney Jenkins, Fiscal Off.

SOUTH DAKOTA

Historical Preservation Center
University of South Dakota
Alumni House
Vermillion, SD 57069
(605) 773-3458

Junius R. Fishburne, SHPO
Paul Putz, Deputy, Grants Mgr., & Fiscal
   Off.

TENNESSEE

Tennessee Historical Commission
Department of Conservation
701 Broadway
Nashville, TN 37219
(615) 741-2301

Charles A. Howell, III, SHPO
Herbert Harper, Deputy
Dick Tune, Grants Mgr.
Linda Wynn, Fiscal Off.

TEXAS

Texas State Historical Commission
P.O. Box 12276, Capitol Station
Austin, TX 78711
(512) 475-3092

Curtis Tunnell, Exec. Director
LaVerne Herrington, Deputy
Joe Opperman, Grants Mgr.
Ann Sauser, Fiscal Off.

TRUST TERRITORY OF THE PACIFIC ISLANDS

Land Resources Branch
Department of Resources & Development
Trust Territory of the Pacific Islands
Saipan, Mariana Islands 96950

Scott Russell, Acting HPO

UTAH

Utah State Historical Society
300 Rio Grande
Salt Lake City, UT 84101
(801) 533-7039

Melvin T. Smith, SHPO
Wilson G. Martin, Deputy & Grants Mgr.
A. Kent Powell, Deputy
Lee Byrd, Fiscal Off.

VERMONT

Agency of Development & Community
   Affairs
Pavillion Office Building
Montpelier, VT 05602
(802) 828-3211

Milton A. Eaton, Secretary
Eric Gilbertson, Deputy
Richard Stickney, Jr., Grants Mgr.
Jane Lendway, Fiscal Off.

VIRGINIA

Virginia Historic Landmarks Commission
221 Governor St.
Richmond, VA 23219
(804) 786-3143

H. Bryan Mitchell, Exec. Director
Lynn Bechtle, Grants Mgr.
Anne Miller, Fiscal Off.

VIRGIN ISLANDS

State Historic Preservation Office
PO Box 3088
St. Croix, Virgin Islands 00820
(809) 773-1082 or 774-1730

Roy Adams, HPO
Claudette Lewis, Grants Mgr.
Eddie Quetal, Fiscal Off.

WASHINGTON

Office of Archaeology & Historic
   Preservation
111 W. 21st Ave., KL-11
Olympia, WA 98504
(206) 753-4011

Jacob E. Thomas, SHPO
David Hansen, Deputy, Grants Mgr., &
   Fiscal Off.

WEST VIRGINIA

Department of Culture & History
State Capitol Complex
Charleston, WV 25304
(304) 348-0244

Norman L. Fagan, Commissioner
Rod Collins, Deputy
Mike Gioulis, Grants Mgr. & Fiscal Off.

WISCONSIN

Historic Preservation Division
State Historical Society of Wisconsin
816 State St.
Madison, WI 53706
(608) 262-3266

Jeff Dean, Director
Jim Sewell, Grants Mgr.
Jack Lohrentz, Fiscal Off.

WYOMING

Wyoming Recreation Commission
1920 Thomes St.
Cheyenne, WY 82002
(307) 777-7695

Alvin F. Bastron, Director
Mark G. Junge, Deputy
Wilbur Madrid, Grants Mgr.

Private State Preservation Organizations

ALABAMA

Live-in-a-Landmark Council
C/o Alabama Historical Commission
725 Monroe St.
Montgomery, AL 36130
(205) 832-6621

Douglas C. Purcell, Chairman

ALASKA

Alaska Trust for Historic
   Preservation
524 W. Fourth Ave., Suite 203
Anchorage, AK 99501

Robert Goldberg, Chairman
Thomas G. Beck, Executive
   Director

ARIZONA

Heritage Foundation of Arizona
P.O. Box 25616
Tempe, AZ 85282
(602) 627-2773

Patricia Callahan, President

ARKANSAS

Historic Preservation Alliance of
Arkansas
P.O. Box 305
Little Rock, AR 72203
(501) 372-4757

John Mott, President
Sandra Hanson, Director

CALIFORNIA

California Preservation Foundation
55 Sutter St., Suite 593
San Francisco, CA 94109
(415) 527-7808

James Stickels, President
John Merritt, Executive Director

CONNECTICUT

Connecticut Trust for Historic
Preservation
152 Temple St.
New Haven, CT 06510
(203) 562-6312

Nancy Campbell, Chairman
Wayne Linker, Executive Director

DELAWARE

Historical Society of Delaware
505 Market Street Mall
Wilmingon, DE 19801
(302) 655-7161

Charles Lyle, Director

DISTRICT OF COLUMBIA

D. C. Preservation League
930 F St., N.W., Suite 612
Washington, DC 20004
(202) 737-1519

Robert Peck, President
Vicki Sherman, Administrator

FLORIDA

Florida Trust for Historic
Preservation
P.O. Box 11206
Tallahassee, FL 32302
(904) 224-8128

Roy Hunt, President
Tavia McCuean, Executive Director

GEORGIA

Georgia Trust for Historic
Preservation
1516 Peachtree St., N.W.
Atlanta, GA 30309
(404) 881-9980

John C. Hagler III, President
Gregory B. Paxton, Executive
Director

HAWAII

Historic Hawaii Foundation
P.O. Box 1658
119 Merchant St.
Honolulu, HI 96806
(808) 537-9564

Nathaniel R. Potter, Jr., President
Phyllis Fox, Executive Director

IDAHO

Idaho Historic Preservation
Council
P.O. Box 1495
Boise, ID 83701
(208) 334-2120

William G. Dougall, President

ILLINOIS

Landmarks Preservation Council
of Illinois
407 S. Dearborn, Suite 970
Chicago, IL 60605
(312) 922-1742

Gregory L. Gleason, President
Amy R. Hecker, Executive Director

INDIANA

Historic Landmarks Foundation of
Indiana
4302 Boulevard Pl.
Indianapolis, IN 46208
(317) 926-2301

H. Earl Capehart, Chairman
J. Reid Williamson, Jr., President

KANSAS

Kansas Preservation Alliance
C/o The Wichita-Sedgewick County
Historical Museum Association
204 S. Main
Wichita, KS 67202
(316) 265-9314

Robert A. Puckett, President

KENTUCKY

Commonwealth Preservation
Council of Kentucky
P.O. Box 1122
Campbellsville, KY 42718
(502) 789-2643

Richard Pfefferkorn, President
Joe DeSpain, Executive Director

LOUISIANA

Louisiana Preservation Alliance
P.O. Box 1587
Baton Rouge, LA 70821
(504) 342-7393

Rae Swent, President

MAINE

Citizens for Historic Preservation
P.O. Box 197
Bath, ME 04530
(207) 729-3686

Brooks Stoddard, President
Nancy Thompson, Administrative
Coordinator

MARYLAND

Society for the Preservation of
Maryland Antiquities
2335 Marriottsville Rd.
Marriottsville, MD 21104
(301) 442-1772

W. Boulton Kelly, Jr., President
Nancy Miller Schamu, Executive
Director

MASSACHUSETTS

Architectural Conservation Trust
for Massachusetts
45 School St.
Boston, MA 01208
(617) 523-8678

Ann Beha, President
Martin Adler, Executive Director

MINNESOTA

Preservation Alliance of Minnesota
820 Holly Ave.
St. Paul, MN 55104
(612) 291-7699

Christopher Owens, President

MISSOURI

Missouri Heritage Trust
P.O. Box 895
Jefferson City, MO 65102
(314) 635-6877

Robert Miller, President
Patrick Steele, Executive Vice
President

NEW HAMPSHIRE

New Hampshire Task Force on
Historic Preservation
4 Bicentennial Sq.
Concord, NH 03301
(603) 224-6714

Ms. P. Kenison Smith, Coordinator

NEW JERSEY

Preservation New Jersey
R.D. 4, Box 864
Mapleton Rd.
Princeton, NJ 08540
(609) 452-1754

Constance Grieff, President
Jim Harveson, Executive Director

NEW YORK

Preservation League of New York
State
307 Hamilton St.
Albany, NY 12210
(518) 462-5658

John L. Mesick, President
Diana Waite, Executive Director

NORTH CAROLINA

Historic Preservation Foundation
of North Carolina
P.O. Box 27632
11 S. Blount St.
Raleigh, NC 27611
(919) 832-3652

Robert Stallings, President
Myrick Howard, Executive Director

OHIO

Ohio Preservation Alliance
22 N. Front St.
Columbus, OH 43215
(216) 861-7688

John Simperman, President

OREGON

Historic Preservation League of
Oregon
P.O. Box 40053
Portland, OR 97240
(503) 243-1923

Sharr Prohaska, President
Eric Eisemann, Executive Director

PENNSYLVANIA

Pennsylvania Trust for Historic
Preservation
800 Mill Creek Rd.
Gladwyne, PA 19035
(216) 642-6175

Jane Davidson, Chairman
Michael Harlan, Executive Director

Preservation Fund of Pennsylvania
240 Kissell Hill Rd.
Lancaster, PA 17601
(717) 569-2243

John C. Tuten, President
F. Bogue Wallin, Executive Director

SOUTH CAROLINA

Confederation of South Carolina
Local Historical Societies
Box 11669
Columbia, SC 29211
(803) 758-5816

Mrs. Malcolm Marion, President

SOUTH DAKOTA

Historic South Dakota Foundation
P.O. Box 2998
Rapid City, SD 57709
(605) 341-5820

Jane Day, President
Mark Thomas, Executive Director

TENNESSEE

Association for the Preservation of
Tennessee Antiquities
110 Leake Ave.
Nashville, TN 37205
(615) 352-8247

Tom Shelburne, President

Tennessee Heritage Alliance
C/o Historic Nashville
100 Second Ave. N.
Nashville, TN 37201
(615) 898-2544

Jim Huhta, President

TEXAS

Texas Historical Foundation
P.O. Box 12243
Austin, TX 78711
(512) 472-6784

J. J. Ballard, Jr., President

UTAH

Utah Heritage Foundation
355 Quince St.
Salt Lake City, UT 84103
(801) 533-0858

Stephen B. Smith, President
Stephanie D. Churchill, Director

VERMONT

Preservation Trust of Vermont
104 Church St.
Burlington, VT 05401
(802) 658-6647

Georgianna Brush, President
Paul Bruhn, Executive Director

VIRGINIA

Association for the Preservation
of Virginia Antiquities
2705 Park Ave.
Richmond, VA 23220
(804) 359-0239

Mrs. Robert W. Cabaniss, President
Angus Murdock, Executive Director

Preservation Alliance of Virginia,
Inc.
P.O. Box 142
Waterford, VA 22190
(703) 882-3018

Constance K. Chamberlin,
President

WASHINGTON

Washington Trust for Historic
Preservation
111 W. 21st Ave.
Olympia, WA 89501
(206) 573-0099

Brent Lambert, President
Garry Schalliol, Executive Director

WEST VIRGINIA

Preservation Alliance of West
Virginia
P.O. Box 1135
Clarksburg, WV 26302-1135
(304) 624-9298

Barbara Howe, President
Ralph Pederson, Executive Director

WISCONSIN

Wisconsin Heritages, Inc.
2000 W. Wisconsin Ave.
Milwaukee, WI 53233
(414) 931-0808

H. Nicholas Pabst, President
Bruce Lynch, Executive Director

WYOMING

Wyoming Historic Preservation
Association
P.O. Box 1041
Cheyenne, WY 82003
(307) 635-5044

Betty Ann Beirle, President

AIA State Preservation
Coordinators

ALABAMA

Nicholas H. Holmes Jr., FAIA
Holmes & Holmes
257 N. Conception St.
Mobile, AL 36603
(205) 432-8871

ALASKA

Robert A. Mitchell, AIA
Alaska Office of History and Archeology
619 Warehouse Ave., Ste. 210
Anchorage, AK 99501

ARIZONA

Ellery Green, AIA
College of Architecture
University of Arizona
Tucson, AZ 85712

ARKANSAS

John K. Mott, FAIA
Mott, Mobley, McGowan & Griffin, P.A.
302 N. 6th St.
Ft. Smith, AR 72901
(501) 782-1051

CALIFORNIA

Raymond Girvigian, FAIA
1401 Fair Oaks Ave.
PO Box 220
South Pasadena, CA 91030
(213) 682-3848

COLORADO

Daniel J. Havekost, AIA
HWH Associates
1121 Grant St.
Denver, CO 80203
(303) 861-1121

CONNECTICUT

Henry F. Miller, FAIA
30 Derby Ave.
Orange, CT 06477
(203) 436-8228

DELAWARE

John F. McCune III, AIA
Diamond/McCune
201 Possum Park Rd.
Newark, DE 19711
(302) 737-1600

DISTRICT OF COLUMBIA

Hamilton Morton, AIA
4813 Fallstone Ave.
Chevy Chase, MD 20815
(202) 628-1397

FLORIDA

F. Blair Reeves, FAIA
College of Architecture
University of Florida
Gainesville, FL 32611
(904) 392-0205

GEORGIA

John R. Reiter, AIA
39 Washington Ave.
Savannah, GA 31405
(912) 232-4403

HAWAII

Spencer Leineweber, AIA
Spencer Limited
1050 Smith St.
Honolulu, HI 96817
(808) 536-3636

IDAHO

Ernest J. Lombard, AIA
1221 Shoreline Ln.
Boise, ID 83706
(208) 345-6677

ILLINOIS

Walker C. Johnson, AIA
Holabird & Root
300 W. Adams St.
Chicago, IL 60606
(312) 726-5960

INDIANA

H. Roll McLaughlin, FAIA
James Associates
PO Box 55809
Indianapolis, IN 46205
(317) 547-9441

IOWA

William Wagner, FAIA
RR #1, PO Box 228A
Dallas Center, IA 50063
(515) 283-2315

KANSAS

Bernd Foerster, FAIA
College of Architecture & Design
Kansas State University
Manhattan, KS 66506
(913) 532-5951

KENTUCKY

Robert L. Lape, AIA
1026 Russell Ave.
Covington, KY 41011
(606) 491-4950

LOUISIANA

Phares Frantz, AIA
1100 Jackson Ave.
New Orleans, LA 70130
(504) 581-7023

MAINE

Gridley Barrows, FAIA
35 Ware St.
Lewiston, ME 04240
(207) 783-0803

MARYLAND

Hamilton Morton, AIA
4813 Fallstone Ave.
Chevy Chase, MD 20815
(202) 628-1397

Michael F. Trostel, AIA
1307 Bolton St.
Baltimore, MD 21217
(301) 669-3964

MASSACHUSETTS

Robert G. Neiley, AIA
Bastille-Neiley
286 Congress St.
Boston, MA 02210
(617) 426-9720

MICHIGAN

Louis Goldstein, AIA
630 Merrick #308
Detroit, MI 48202
(313) 494-1776

MINNESOTA

William W. Scott, FAIA
Setter/Leach/Lindstrom
1011 Nicollet Mall
Minneapolis, MN 55403
(612) 338-8741

MISSISSIPPI

Samuel H. Kaye, AIA
PO Box 48
Columbus, MS 39701
(601) 327-6241

MISSOURI

W. Philip Cotton, AIA
806 Chestnut St.
St. Louis, MO 63101
(314) 421-1667

MONTANA

John De Haas, FAIA
1021 S. Tracy
Bozeman, MT 59715
(406) 586-2276

NEBRASKA

Ted A. Ertl, AIA
2435 Sewell
Lincoln, NE 68502
(402) 472-3592

NEVADA

Edward S. Parsons, FAIA
1 E. First St., #901
Reno, NV 89501
(702) 323-1833

NEW HAMPSHIRE

Richard M. Monahon, Jr., AIA
The Granite Block
Peterborough, NH 03458
(603) 924-7581

NEW JERSEY

William H. Short, FAIA
Short & Ford
RD 4, Box 864-Mapleton Rd.
Princeton, NJ 08540
(609) 452-1777

NEW MEXICO

Edith Cherry, AIA
Cherry/See Architects
220A Gold St., NW
Albuquerque, NM 87102
(505) 842-1278

NEW YORK

Giorgio Cavaglieri, FAIA
250 W. 57th St.
New York, NY 10107
(212) 245-4207

NORTH CAROLINA

Jack O. Boyte, AIA
Boyte-Williams Architects
1626 East Blvd.
Charlotte, NC 28202
(704) 332-5901

NORTH DAKOTA

Meredith Larson, AIA
Tvenge-Larson
105 E. Broadway
Bismark, ND 58501
(701) 258-1600

OHIO

Bruce E. Goetzman, AIA
2606 Vine St.
Cincinnati, OH 45219
(513) 281-7244

OKLAHOMA

Bill Peavler, AIA
Oklahoma Historical Society
2100 Lincoln Blvd.
Oklahoma City, OK 73105
(405) 521-2491

OREGON

Sheila Finch-Tepper, AIA
Finch-Tepper & Associates
919 SW Taylor, Ste. 215
Portland, OR 97205
(503) 227-0786

PENNSYLVANIA

Theodore T. Bartley, FAIA
Bartley Long Mirenda
1104 Architects Bldg.
Philadelphia, PA 19103
(215) 567-6980

PUERTO RICO

Jose M. Garcia-Gomez, AIA
G.P.O. Box 1174
San Juan, PR 00936
(809) 725-6762

RHODE ISLAND

Irving Haynes, FAIA
Irving B. Haynes & Associates
128 N. Main St.
Providence, RI 02903
(401) 274-1555

SOUTH CAROLINA

William O. Fulmer, AIA
1520 Richland St.
Columbia, SC 20201
(803) 796-0973

SOUTH DAKOTA

Gary Stanley, AIA
1112 West Ave. N.
Sioux Falls, SD 57104
(605) 336-6891

TENNESSEE

William H. Gaskill, AIA
Yeates Gaskill Rhodes
2080 Peabody Ave.
Memphis, TN 38104
(901) 274-0633

TEXAS

James G. Rome, AIA
Turner, Rome & Boultinghouse
PO Box 3130
Corpus Christi, TX 78404
(512) 882-4251

VERMONT

Martin Tierney, AIA
82 Church St.
Burlington, VT 05401
(802) 863-6852

VIRGINIA

Thomas B. Muths, FAIA
1900 S. Eads, Apt. 228
Arlington, VA 22202
(703) 892-8580

Nathaniel P. Neblett, AIA
PO Box 11244
Alexandria, VA 22312
(703) 750-0135

WASHINGTON

Larry J. Mortimer, AIA
Kahn/Mortimer/Assocs.
4906 Rainier Ave. S.
Seattle, WA 98118
(206) 723-0456

WEST VIRGINIA

Paul D. Marshall, AIA
1033 Quarrier St., Rm 406
Charleston, WV 25301
(304) 343-5310

WISCONSIN

Gordon D. Orr Jr., FAIA
Dept. of Planning & Construction
610 N. Walnut St.
Madison, WI 53706
(608) 263-3000

List of Suppliers

AA-Abingdon Ceiling Co.
2149 Utica Ave.
Brooklyn, NY 11234

A. A. Used Boiler Supply Co.
8720 Ditmas Ave.
Brooklyn, NY 11236

A-Ball Plumbing Supply
1703 W. Burnside St.
Portland, OR 97209

Accurate Metal Weatherstrip Co., Inc.
725 S. Fulton Ave.
Mount Vernon, NY 10550

Acme Stove Company
1011 7th St. N. W.
Washington, DC 20001

Acquisition & Restoration Corp.
423 Massachusetts Ave.
Indianapolis, IN 46204

The Adams Company
100 E. Fourth St.
Dubuque, IA 52001

Adams & Sweet
380 Dorchester Ave.
Boston, MA 02127

Dick Adcock
5404 Walnut Rd.
N. Little Rock, AR 72116

Adirondak Chair Co.
Box 1257
Schuylerville, NY 12871

Advance Lumber and Wrecking Co.
137 Union St.
Toronto, Ontario, Canada
M6N 3N1

A. E. S. Firebacks
334 Grindstone Hill Rd.
North Stonington, CT 06359

Aetna Stove Company, Inc.
S. E. Corner 2nd & Arch Sts.
Philadelphia, PA 19106

Agape Antiques
Box 225
Saxtons River, VT 05154

A. J. P. Coppersmith
34 Broadway
Wakefield, MA 01880

Alcon Lightcraft Co.
1424 W. Alabama
Houston, TX 77006

Alexandria Wood Joinery
Plumer Hill Rd.
Alexandria, NH 03222

Allen Charles Hill Historic Preservation & Architecture
25 Englewood Rd.
Winchester, MA 01890

Allentown Paint Manufacturing Co.
East Allen and Graham Sts.
Allentown, PA 18105

Jeff Alte Roofing, Inc.
Box 639
Somerville, NJ 08876

Amazon Vinegar & Pickling Works Drygoods
2218 E. 11th St.
Davenport, IA 52803

American General Products
1735 Holmes Rd.
Ypsilanti, MI 48197

American Olean Tile Company
1000 Cannon Ave., Box 271
Lansdale, PA 19446

American Wood Column Corp.
913 Grand St.
Brooklyn, NY 11211

Amherst Woodworking & Supply, Inc.
Box 575, Hubbard Ave.
Northampton, MA 01061

Amsterdam Corp.
950 Third Ave.
New York, NY 10022

A & M Wood Specialty, Inc.
358 Eagle St., Box 3204
Cambridge, Ontario, Canada
N3H 4S6

Anderson Building Restoration
923 Marion Ave.
Cincinnati, OH 45229

Anderson & McQuaid Co., Inc.
170 Fawcett St.
Cambridge, MA 02138

Anglo-American Brass Co.
4146 Mitzi Dr., Box 9792
San Jose, CA 95157

Antique Street Lamps
8412 S. Congress
Austin, TX 78745

Arch Associates
824 Prospect Ave.
Winnetka, IL 60093

Architectural Antiques
410 St. Pierre St.
Montreal, Quebec, Canada
H2Y 2M2

Architectural Antiques, Ltd.
1321 E. 2nd St.
Little Rock, AR 72202

Architectural Antiques Exchange
709-15 N. 2nd St.
Philadelphia, PA 19123

Architectural Antique Warehouse
Box 3065, Station D
Ottawa, Ontario, Canada
K1P 6H6

Architectural Components
Box 246
Leverett, MA 01054

Architectural Emphasis, Inc.
2743 9th St.
Berkeley, CA 94710

Architectural Emporium
1011 S. 9th St.
Lafayette, IN 47905

Architectural Iron Co.
Box 126
Milford, PA 18337

Architectural Paneling
979 Third Ave.
New York, NY 10022

Architectural Reclamation, Inc.
312 S. River St.
Franklin, OH 45005

Architectural Resources Group
Pier 9, The Embarcadero
San Francisco, CA 94111

Architectural Salvage of Santa Barbara
726 Anacapa St.
Santa Barbara, CA 93101

Architectural Terra Cotta & Tile, Ltd.
727 S. Dearborn, Suite 1012
Chicago, IL 60605

The Arden Forge Co.
301 Brintons Bridge Rd.
West Chester, PA 19380

Arrowhead Forge
RFD #2, U. S. Rte. 1
Lincolnville, ME 04849

Art, Inc.
315 N. Washington Ave.
Moorestown, NJ 08057

Art Directions
6120 Delmar
St. Louis, MO 63112

Artifacts, Inc.
Box 1787, Federal St.
Middleburg, VA 22117

Artisan Woodworkers
21415 Broadway
Sonoma, CA 95476

Artistry in Veneers
450 Oak Tree Ave.
S. Plainfield, NJ 07080

Laura Ashley
Box 5308
Melville, NY 11747

Astrup Company
2937 W. 25th St.
Cleveland, OH 44113

Authentic Designs, Inc.
The Mill Rd.
W. Rupert, VT 05776

Authentic Lighting
558 Grand Ave.
Englewood, NJ 07631

Babcock Barn Homes
Box 484
Williamstown, MA 01267

Bailey and Griffin
1406 E. Mermaid Lane
Philadelphia, PA 19118

A. W. Baker Restorations, Inc.
670 Drift Road
Westport, MA 02790

John Morgan Baker, Framer
Box 149
Worthington, OH 43085

Baldwin Hardware Mfg. Corp.
841 Wyomissing Blvd., Box 82
Reading, PA 19603

Ball & Ball
463 W. Lincoln Hwy.
Exton, PA 19341

Balmer Architectural Art Limited
69 Pape Ave.
Toronto, Ontario, Canada
M4M 2V5

Bangkok Industries, Inc.
Gillingham & Worth Sts.
Philadelphia, PA 19124

The Bank
1824 Felicity St.
New Orleans, LA 70113

Barclay Products Co.
424 N. Oakley Blvd.
Chicago, IL 60612

The Barn People
Box 4
South Woodstock, VT 05071

Charles Barone, Inc.
9505 W. Jefferson Blvd.
Culver City, CA 90230

Robert Barrow
412 Thames St.
Bristol, RI 02809

Bassett & Vollum Wallpapers
217 N. Main St.
Galena, IL 61036

Samuel Beckenstein, Inc.
130 Orchard St.
New York, NY 10002

Bedlam Brass Beds
19-21 Fair Lawn Ave.
Fair Lawn, NJ 07410

The Bedpost
Box 155, RD 1
Pen Argyl, PA 18072

Bel-Air Door Co.
Box 829
Alhambra, CA 91802

Bernardini Ironworks, Inc.
418 Bryant Ave.
The Bronx, NY 10474

Bendix Mouldings, Inc.
235 Pegasus Ave.
Northvale, NJ 07647

Bentley Brothers
918 Baxter Ave.
Louisville, KY 40204

Berea College Student Craft Industries
CPO No. 2347
Berea, KY 40404

Bergen Bluestone Co., Inc.
404 Rte. 17, Box 67
Paramus, NJ 07652

The Berkeley Upholstering Co.
Box 1147
Martinsburg, WV 25401

Berkshire Porcelain Studios
Deerfield Ave.
Shelburne Falls, MA 01370

L. J. Bernard & Son Woodshop
Rte. 3, Box 92A
Nixa, MO 65714

Berridge Manufacturing Co.
170 Maury
Houston, TX 77026

The Beveled Edge Art Glass Studio
865 Hillcrest Blvd.
Hoffman Estates, IL 60195

Beveling Studio
15507 NE 90th
Redmond, WA 98052

L. Biagiotti
229 Seventh Ave.
New York, NY 10011

Biltmore, Campbell, Smith Restorations, Inc.
One Biltmore Plaza
Asheville, NC 28803

Adele Bishop, Inc.
Box 557
Manchester, VT 05254

The Blacksmith Shop
RR 2, 26 Bridge Rd.
Orleans, MA 02653

Blaine Window Hardware, Inc.
1919 Blaine Dr.
Hagerstown, MD 21740

Morgan Bockius Studios, Inc.
1412 Old York Rd.
Warminster, PA 18974

Bona Decorative Hardware
2227 Beechmont Ave.
Cincinnati, OH 45230

B & P Lamp Supply, Inc.
Rte. 3
McMinnville, TN 37110

Nancy Borden
63 Penhallow St., Box 4381
Portsmouth, NH 03801

Boston Turning Works
42 Plympton St.
Boston, MA 02118

Robert Bourdon
The Smithy
Wolcott, VT 05680

Louis W. Bown, Inc.
979 Third Ave.
New York, NY 10022

Larry Boyce & Associates
Box 421507
San Francisco, CA 94142

Bragunier Masonry Contractors, Inc.
Rte. 2
Clear Spring, MD 21722

Sandra Brauer, Stained Glass
235 Dean St.
Brooklyn, NY 11217

Bradbury & Bradbury Wallpapers
Box 155
Benicia, CA 94510

Bradford Consultants
16 E. Homestead Ave.
Collingswood, NJ 08108

Bradford Derustit Corp.
Box 151
Clifton Park, NY 12065

Braid-Aid
466 Washington St.
Pembroke, MA 02359

Brass Bed Company of America
2801 E. 11th St.
Los Angeles, CA 90023

Brasslight, Inc.
90 Main St.
Nyack, NY 10960

Brass Light of Historic Walker's Point
719 S. 5th St.
Milwaukee, WI 53204

The Brass Tree
308 N. Main St.
St. Charles, MO 63301

Breakfast Woodworks, Inc.
50 Maple St.
Branford, CT 06405

Lester & Barbara Breininger
476 S. Church St.
Robesonia, PA 19551

Broadway Supply Co.
601 W. 103rd
Kansas City, MO 64114

Brotman Forge
Box 511
Hanover, NH 03755

Bruce Hardwood Floors
16803 Dallas Pkwy.
Dallas, TX 75248

Brunschwig & Fils
979 Third Ave.
New York, NY 10022

Bryant Steel Works
RFD #2, Box 2048
Thorndike, ME 04986

Bucher & Cope
The Washington Design
Center, Suite 300
1536 16th St. NW
Washington, DC 20036

Bob Buckter
3877 20th St.
San Francisco, CA 94114

Building Conservation
6326 W. Wisconsin
Wauwatosa, WI 53213

Burdoch Silk Lampshade Co.
11120 Roselle St., Suite G
San Diego, CA 92121

Cabot Stains
1 Union St.
Boston, MA 02108

Campbell Center for Historic Preservation Studies
Box 66
Mount Carroll, IL 61053

Campbell Lamps
1108 Pottstown Pike, Dept. 26,
West Chester, PA 19380

Marion Campbell
39 Wall St.
Bethlehem, PA 18018

Campbellsville Industries, Inc.
Box 278, Taylor Blvd.
Campbellsville, KY 42718

Canal Co.
1612 14th St. NW
Washington, DC 20009

The Candle Cellar & Emporium
Box 135, South Station
Fall River, MA 02724

Cane & Basket Supply Company
1283 South Cochran Ave.
Los Angeles, CA 90019

Caning Shop
926 Gilman St.
Berkeley, CA 94710

John Canning
132 Meeker Rd.
Southington, CT 06489

Canvas Carpets
Box 181
S. Egremont, MA 01258

Cape Cod Cupola Co., Inc.
78 State Rd.
North Dartmouth, MA 02747

Dale Carlisle
Rte. 123
Stoddard, NH 03464

Carolina Caning Supply
Box 2179
Smithfield, NC 27577

Carson, Dunlop & Associates, Ltd.
Home Inspection and
Evaluation
597 Parliament St., Suite B-5
Toronto, Ontario, Canada
M4X 1W3

Cascade Mill & Glass Works
Box 316
Ouray, CO 81427

Vernon M. Cassell & Sons
Box 317
Braddock Heights, MD 21714

Castle Burlingame
RD 1, Box 352
Basking Ridge, NJ 07920

Cathedral Stone Co.
2505 Reed St., NE
Washington, DC 20018

Cedar Swamp Stoneware Co.
30 Perseverance Way
Hyannis, MA 02601

The Ceiling Lady
1408 Main St.
Evanston, IL 60202

Ceilings, Walls & More, Inc.
Box 494, 124 Walnut St.
Jefferson, TX 75657

Celestial Roofing Co.
1710 Thousand Oaks Blvd.
Berkeley, CA 94707

Center City Stained Glass Supply, Inc.
926 Pine St.
Philadelphia, PA 19106

Century Glass Inc. of Dallas
1417 N. Washington
Dallas, TX 75204

C & H Roofing
1713 South Cliff Ave.
Sioux Fall, SD 57105

Charterhouse Designs, Ltd.
979 Third Ave.
New York, NY 10022

Chelsea Decorative Metal Co.
6115 Cheena Dr.
Houston, TX 77096

Chemique, Inc.
315 N. Washington Ave.
Moorestown, NJ 08057

Cherry Creek Enterprises, Inc.
937 Sante Fe Dr.
Denver, CO 80204

Chester Granite Co.
Algerie Rd.
Blandford, MA 01008

Chicago Faucet Company
2100 S. Nuclear Dr.
Des Plaines, IL 60018

Chilstone Garden Ornament
Sprivers Estate
Horsmonden, Kent,
England, UK

Chimney Relining International, Inc.
105 W. Merrimack St., Box 4035
Manchester, NH 03108

Chromatic Paint Corp.
Box 105
Garnerville, NY 10923

Churchill Forest Products, Inc.
91 Franklin St.
Hanson, MA 02341

Cirecast, Inc.
380 Seventh St.
San Francisco, CA 94103

Citybarn Antiques
362 Atlantic Ave.
Brooklyn, NY 11217

City Knickerbocker, Inc.
781 Eighth Ave.
New York, NY 10036

City Lights
2226 Massachusetts Ave.
Cambridge, MA 02140

C. K. Constructions
2565 3rd St., Suite 203
San Francisco, CA 94107

Clarence House
40 E. 57th St.
New York, NY 10022

Jamie C. Clark
Jackson Pike
Harrodsburg, KY 40330

Classic Architectural
Specialties
5302 Junius
Dallas, TX 75214

The Classic Illumination
431 Grove St.
Oakland, CA 94607

Classic Mouldings, Inc.
155 Toryork Dr., Unit 1
Weston, Ontario, Canada
M9L 1X6

Clio Group, Inc.
3961 Baltimore Ave.
Philadelphia, PA 19104

Cohasset Colonials by Hagerty
38 Parker Ave.
Cohasset, MA 02025

E. Cohen's Architectural
Heritage
1804 Merivale Rd.
Nepean, Ontario, Canada
K2G 1E6

Diane Jackson Cole
9 Grove St.
Kennebunk, ME 04043

Cole & Son Wallpapers
P O Box 4 BU
18 Mortimer St.
London, England, UK
W1A 4BU

Colefax & Fowler Designs Ltd.
39 Brook St.
Mayfair, London, England,
UK W1Y 1AU

Colonial Brick Co.
3344 W. Cermak Rd.
Chicago, IL 60623

Colonial Casting Co., Inc.
443 South Colony St.
Meriden, CT 06450

Colonial Charm
Box A-111
Findlay, OH 45840

Colonial Williamsburg
Craft House, Box CH
Williamsburg, VA 23185

Columbia Cascade Timber Co.
1975 S. W. Fifth Ave.
Portland, OR 97201

Conklin Tin Plate & Metal Co.
Box 2662
Atlanta, GA 30301

Conran's
145 Huguenot St.
New Rochelle, NY 10801

The Conservatory
209 W. Michigan Ave.
Marshall, MI 49068

Constantine
2050 Eastchester Rd.
Bronx, NY 10461

John Conti
Box 189, Martins Corner Rd.
Wagontown, PA 19376

The Copper House
Rte. 4
Epsom, NH 03234

Cook & Dunn Paint Corp.
Box 117
Newark, NJ 07101

Cooper Stair Co., Inc.
1331 Leithton Rd.
Mundelein, IL 60060

Coran-Sholes Industries
509 East 2nd St.
South Boston, MA 02127

Dermit X. Corcoran, Antique
Services
Box 568 Montauk Hwy.
East Moriches, NY 11940

Cornerstones
54 Cumberland St.
Brunswick, ME 04011

Cornucopia, Inc.
Wescott Rd., Box 44
Harvard, MA 02451

The Country Bed Shop
Box 222H
Groton, MA 01450

Country Braid House
RFD #2, Box 29, Clark Rd.
Tilton, NH 03276

Country Curtains
Stockbridge, MA 01262

Country Floors
300 E. 61st St.
New York, NY 10021

Country Iron Foundry
Box 600
Paoli, PA 19301

The Country Loft
South Shore Park
Hingham, MA 02043

Cowtan & Tout, Inc.
979 Third Ave.
New York, NY 10022

Craftsman Lumber Co.
Box 222
Groton, MA 01450

Crawford's Old House Store
301 McCall
Waukesha, WI 53186

Crowfoot's Inc.
Box 1297
Pinetop, AZ 85935

Crown Restoration
18 Homer Ave.
Cortland, NY 13045

Cumberland General Store
Rte. 3
Crossville, TN 38555

Cumberland Woodcraft Co.
PO Drawer 609
Carlisle, PA 17013

Rose Cumming Chintzes
232 East 59th St.
New York, NY 10022

Gerald Curry, Cabinetmaker
Pound Hill Rd.
Union, ME 04862

Victor Cushwa & Sons Brick
Co.
MD Rt. 68
Williamsport, MD 21795

Custom Carpentry
263 Union St.
Springfield, MA 01105

Custom House
South Shore Dr., Box 38
Owl's Head, ME 04854

Customwood Mfg. Co.
Box 26208
Alburquerque, NM 87125

Daly's Wood Finishing
Products
1121 N. 36th St.
Seattle, WA 98103

Peter David
8057 28th Ave., NW
Seattle, WA 98117

Davis Cabinet Co.
Box 60444
Nashville, TN 37206

James R. Dean
15 Delaware St.
Cooperstown, NY 13326

Decorators Supply
Corporation
3610-12 S. Morgan St., rear
bldg.
Chicago, IL 60609

Decorators Walk
125 Newtown Rd.
Plainview, NY 11803

Delaware Quarries, Inc.
River Rd.
Lumberville, PA 18933

Bell Corporation
Box 1462
Rockville, MD 20850

Dentelle de France
Box 255476
Sacramento, CA 95865

Depot Woodworking
683 Pine St.
Burlington, VT 05401

Designed Communications
704 Boyle Bldg, 103 W.
Capitol
Little Rock, AR 72201

Designer Resource
5160 Melrose Ave.
Hollywood, CA 90038

Devoe & Raynolds Co.
4000 Dupont Circle
Louisville, KY 40207

DeWeese Woodworking Co.
Box 576
Philadelphia, MS 39350

A. L. Diament & Co.
755 S. Fourth St.
Philadelphia, PA 19147

Diamond K. Co., Inc.
130 Buckland Rd.
South Windsor, CT 06074

Diedrich Chemicals Restoration Technologies, Inc.
300A E. Oak St.
Milwaukee, WI 53154

Dildarian, Inc.
595 Madison Ave.
New York, NY 10022

D'Light
533 W. Windsor Rd.
Glendale, CA 91204

Dobson & Thomas, Ltd.
828 9th
Santa Monica, CA 90403

Dodge, Adams & Roy, Ltd.
Stoodleys Tavern, Hancock
St.
Portsmouth, NH 03801

The Door Store Ltd.
118 Sherbourne St.
Toronto, Ontario, Canada
M5A 2R2

Downstate Restorations
Box 276
Macomb, IL 61455

Dovetail
Box 1569
Lowell, MA 01853

Driwood Moulding Company
Box 1729
Florence, SC 29503

Michael Dunbar
Box 805
Portsmouth, NH 03801

Dutch Products & Supply Co.
166 Lincoln Ave.
Yardley, PA 19067

Eastfield Village
Box 145
East Nassau, NY 12062

1874 House
8070 SE 13th Ave.
Portland, OR 97202

18th Century Hardware Co.
131 East 3rd St.
Derry, PA 15627

Elcanco
60 Chelmsford St.
Chelmsford, MA 01824

Electric Glass Co., Inc.
1 E. Mellen St.
Hampton, VA 23663

The Elegant Cat
1440 B Street
Eureka, CA 95501

Elon, Inc.
198 Sawmill River Rd.
Elmsford, NY 10523

Empire Furnace & Stove
Repair Co.
793 Broadway
Albany, NY 12207

The Emporium
2515 Morse St.
Houston, TX 77019

Energy Marketing Corporation
Box 636
Bennington, VT 05201

Entol Industries Inc.
8180 NW 36th Ave.
Miami, FL 33147

Entwood Construction Frater-
nity, Inc.
R.R. 1
Wolcott, VT 05680

Espina Stone Co.
Box 185
Merrifield, VA 22116

The Essex Forge
12 Old Dennison Rd.
Essex, CT 06426

Evergreen Slate Co.
Box 248
Granville, NY 12832

Faneuil Furniture Hardware
94-100 Peterborough St.
Boston, MA 02215

The Farm Forge
6945 Fishburg Rd.
Dayton, OH 45424

Federal Street Lighthouse
38 Market Sq.
Newburyport, MA 01950

Felber Studios
110 Ardmore Ave.
Ardmore, PA 19003

Ferguson Cut Glass Works
4292 Pearl Rd.
Cleveland, OH 44109

Fine Woodworking Co.
4907 Quebec St.
College Park, MD 20740

David Flaharty, Sculptor
79 Magazine Rd., RD 1
Green Lane, PA 18054

Floorcloths, Inc.
Box 812
Severna Park, MD 21146

Floorcloths by Ingrid
8 Randall Rd.
Rochester, MA 02770

Florida Victoriani Architectural Antiques
901 First St. (Hwy 46)
Sanford, FL 32771

Flue Works, Inc.
86 Warren St.
Columbus, OH 43215

Focal Point, Inc.
2005 Marietta Rd., NW
Atlanta, GA 30318

Follansbee Steel Corp.
State St.
Follansbee, WV 26037

Fonthill
979 Third Ave.
New York, NY 10022

Form and Texture
12 S. Albion St.
Denver, CO 80222

French and Ball
Main Rd.
Gill, MA 01376

Frenzel Specialty Moulding Co.
4911 Ringer Rd.
St. Louis, MO 63129

Frog Tool Co., Ltd.
700 W. Jackson Blvd.
Chicago, IL 60606

Fuller-O'Brien
450 E. Grand Ave.
S. San Francisco, CA 94080

Furniture Revival Co.
Box 994
Corvallis, OR 97339

Fypon, Inc.
Box 365, 22 W. Penn Ave.
Stewartstown, PA 17363

Gargoyles, Ltd.
512 S. 3rd St.
Philadelphia, PA 19147

Gates Moore
River Rd., Silvermine
Norwalk, CT 06850

The Gazebo
660 Madison Ave.
New York, NY 10021

Gazebo & Porchworks
3901 N. Meridian
Puyallup, WA 98371

Douglas Gest Co.
RR 2
Randolph, VT 05060

Giannetti Studios
3806 38th St.
Brentwood, MD 20722

Gibbons Sash & Door
Rte. 1
Hurley, WI 54534

Gill Imports
Box 73
Ridgefield, CT 06877

Gladding, McBean & Co.
Box 97
Lincoln, CA 95648

Glen-Gery Corp.
Drawer S. Rte. 61
Shoemakersville, PA 19555

Glidden Coatings & Resins
3rd and Bern Sts., Box 1097
Reading, PA 19603

Goldblatt Tool Co.
511 Osage, Box 2334
Kansas City, KS 66110

Good Stenciling
Box 387
Dublin, NH 03444

Good Time Stove Co.
Rte. 112, Box 306
Goshen, MA 01032

The Gould-Mersereau Co., Inc.
21-16 44th Rd.
Long Island City, NY 11101

Graham's Lighting Fixtures
550 S. Cooper
Memphis, TN 38104

Grampa's Wood Stoves
Rte. 32, Box 492
Ware, MA 10182

Grand Silk House
357 Grand St.
New York, NY 10002

Great American Salvage
3 Main St.
Montpelier, VT 05602

Great Panes Glass Works, Inc.
1955 Market St.
Denver, CO 80202

Greeff Fabrics
155 E. 56th St.
New York, NY 10022

Greene's Lighting Fixtures, Inc.
1059 Third Ave.
New York, NY 10021

Greenhalgh & Sons
Farwell Rd.
Tyngsborough, MA 01879

Greensboro Art Foundry
1201 Park Terr.
Greensboro, NC 27403

Greg's Antique Lighting
12005 Wilshire Blvd.
W. Los Angeles, CA 90025

The Ground Floor
95½ Broad St.
Charleston, SC 29401

Gruber Building, Cleaning & Restoration, Inc.
110 Archer Lane
Williamsport, MD 21795

Guardian National House Inspection & Warranty Corp.
Box 115
Orleans, MA 02653

P. E. Guerin, Inc.
23 Jane St.
New York, NY 10014

Gurian's
276 Fifth Ave.
New York, NY 10001

Pat Guthman
342 Pequot Ave.
Southport, CT 06490

Haas Wood and Ivory Works
64 Clementina St.
San Francisco, CA 94105

Haines Construction Co.
11717 E. 42nd St.
Indianapolis, IN 46236

Half Moon Antiques
Box 141
Fair Haven, NJ 07701

Albert Hall & Associates
3926 High St.
Denver, CO 80205

Hallelujah Redwood Products
39500-J Comptche Rd.
Mendocino, CA 95460

Hammerworks Iron
75 Webster St.
Worcester, MA 01603

Hanks Architectural Antiques
311 Colorado
Austin, TX 78701

Hardwick Rafter Mfg.
Box 281
Hardwick, VT 05843

Harriss-Tarkett, Inc.
383 Maple St.
Johnson City, TN 37601

Harne Plastering Co.
Box 22
Libertytown, MD 21762

Hartco, Inc.
Oneida, TN 37841

W. R. Hasbrouck, Architect
Historic Resources
711 S. Dearborn St.
Chicago, IL 60605

Christopher Morris Hayes
Box 212 Main St. (Rte. 44)
Pine Meadow, CT 06061

Heads Up, Inc.
2980 E. Blue Star, Unit B
Anaheim, CA 92806

Hearth & Home Co.
Box 371
Brielle, NJ 08730

Hearth Realities
246 Daniel Ave. SE
Atlanta, GA 30317

Heartwood Owner-Builder School
Johnson Rd.
Washington, MA 01235

Heirloom Rugs
28 Harlem St.
Rumford, RI 02916

Ken Heitz
Box 161, Rte. 28
Indian Lake, NY 12842

Heritage Design
Box 103, 410 N. Maple St.
Monticello, IA 52310

Heritage Lanterns
70A Main St.
Yarmouth, ME 04096

S. M. Hexter Co.
2800 Superior Ave.
Cleveland OH 44114

Hi-Art Easst
6 N. Rhodes Center NW
Atlanta, GA 30309

David L. Hicks, Cabinetmaker
Rte. 1. Box 7
Labadie, MO 63055

Hilltop Slate Co.
Rte. 22A
Middle Granville, NY 12849

Historic Boulevard Services
1520 W. Jackson Blvd.
Chicago, IL 60607

Historic Charleston Reproductions
Box 622, 105 Broad St.
Charleston, SC 29402

Historical Replications, Inc.
Box 31198
Jackson, MS 39206

Hitchcock Chair Co.
Riverton, CT 06065

Murrel Dee Hobt, Architect
Box 322
Williamsburg, VA 23185

R. Hood & Co.
RFD, 3 College Rd.
Meredith, NH 03253

Hope Co., Inc.
Box 1348
Maryland Heights, MO 63043

Horton Brasses
Box 120, Nooks Hill Rd.
Cromwell, CT 06416

The House Carpenters
Box 217
Shutesbury, MA 01072

Housejoiner, Ltd.
RD 1, Box 860
Moretown, VT 05660

David Howard, Inc.
Box 295
Alstead, NH 03602

Howard Products, Inc.
411 W. Maple Ave.
Monrovia, CA 91016

Lyn Hovey Studio, Inc.
266 Concord Ave.
Cambridge, MA 02138

Hubbardton Forge Corporation
RD H
Fair Haven, VT 05743

S & C Huber, Accoutrements
82 Plants Dam Rd.
East Lyme, CT 06333

Hudson-Shatz Painting Company
429 W. 53rd St.
New York, NY 10019

Hudson Venetian Blind Service, Inc.
2000 Twilight Lane
Richmond, VA 23235

Roger Hulton
600 Oakwood Ave.
Toronto, Ontario, Canada
M6E 2X8

Humberstone Woodworking
9 Academy Rd.
Georgetown, Ontario,
Canada L7G 3N7

William Hunrath Co., Inc.
153 E. 57th St.
New York, NY 10022

Hunter Ceiling Fans
Box 14775
Memphis, TN 38114

Hurley Patentee Lighting
RD 7, Box 98A
Kingston, NY 12401

Hydrozo Coatings Co.
1001 "Y" Street, Box 80879
Lincoln, NE 68501

Iberia Millwork
500 Jane St.
New Iberia, LA 70560

Ice Nine
Glass Design
1507 S. 6th St.
Minneapolis, MN 55454

Illustrious Lighting
1925 Fillmore St.
San Francisco, CA 94115

Image, Inc.
528 Clarence Ave.
Oak Park, IL 60304

Import Specialists, Inc.
82 Wall St., 9th Fl.
New York, NY 10005

Irreplaceable Artifacts
526 E. 80th St.
New York, NY 10021

International Consultants, Inc.
227 S. Ninth St.
Philadelphia, PA 19107

International Terra Cotta, Inc.
690 N. Robertson Blvd.
Los Angeles, CA 90069

Iron Horse Antiques
RD 2
Poultney, VT 05764

Isabel Brass Furniture
120 E. 32nd St.
New York, NY 10016

Island City Wood Working Co.
1801 Mechanic St.
Galveston, TX 77550

William H. Jackson Co.
3 E. 47th St.
New York, NY 10017

Janovic/Plaza, Inc.
1150 Third Ave.
New York, NY 10021

J. J. Jaxon Co., Inc.
Box 618, 118 N. Orange Ave.
Eufaula, AL 36027

Lee Jofa
800 Central Blvd.
Carlstadt, NJ 07072

Jones & Erwin Inc.
979 Third Ave.
New York, NY 10022

Jerard Paul Jordan Gallery
Box 71, Slade Rd.
Ashford, CT 06278

Marvin Kagan, Inc.
991 Madison Ave.
New York, NY 10021

Katzenback & Warren, Inc.
950 Third Ave.
New York, NY 10022

Kayne & Son Custom Forged
Hardware
Rte. 4, Box 275A
Candler, NC 28715

Kenmore Carpet Corp.
979 Third Ave.
New York, NY 10022

Kenmore Industries
44 Kilby St.
Boston, MA 02109

Kensington Historical Co.
Box 87
East Kingston, NH 03827

Kentucky Wood Floors, Inc.
4200 Reservoir Ave.
Louisville, KY 40213

Jos. Kilbridge, Antiques of
Early America
Main St.
Groton, MA 01450

King's Natural Pest Control
224 Yost Ave.
Spring City, PA 19475

King's Chandelier Co.
Highway 14
Eden, NC 27288

Klise Manufacturing Co.
601 Maryland Ave.
Grand Rapids, MI 49505

Kohler Co.
Kohler, WI 53044

Mark Knudsen
1100 E. County Line Rd.
Des Moines, IA 50320

Kraatz/Russell Glass
Box 320c, Grist Mill Hill
Canaan, NH 03741

G. Krug & Son
415 W. Saratoga St.
Baltimore, MD 21201

Kyp-Go, Inc.
Box 147
Naperville, IL 60540

Lachin, Albert & Associates,
Inc.
618 Piety St.
New Orleans, LA 70117

J. & R. Lamb Studios
Box 291
Philmont, NY 12565

The Lamplighter Shop
Rte. 12-B
Deansboro, NY 13328

Langhorne Carpet Company
Box 175
Penndel, PA 19047

Chip LaPointe, Cabinetmaker
186 Emerson Pl.
Brooklyn, NY 11205

Tony Lauria
RD 2, Box 253B
Landenburg, PA 19350

John F. Lavoie
Box 15
Springfield, VT 05156

James Lea, Cabinetmaker
9 West St.
Rockport, ME 04856

Lebanon Oak Flooring Co.
Box 669
Lebanon, KY 40033

Lehman Hardware &
Appliances
Box 41
Kidron, OH 44636

Lemee's Fireplace Equipment
815 Bedford St.
Bridgewater, MA 02324

Brian F. Leo
7520 Stevens Ave. S.
Richfield, MN 55423

Gerald LePage
498 W. Main St., Rte. 66
Hebron, CT 06231

Al Levitan
Box 1012
Shepherdstown, WV 25443

Joe Ley Antiques
615 E. Market St.
Louisville, KY 40202

Howard Lieberman, P. E.
434 White Plains Rd.
Eastchester, NY 10709

Liberty & Co., Ltd.
2 Park Ave.
New York, NY 10016

C. Alan Lightcap
Box 173
Lambertville, NJ 08530

Litchfield House
Church St.
Roxbury, CT 06783

The Country Loft
South Shore Park
Hingham, MA 02043

The London Venturers
Company
2 Dock Sq.
Rockport, MA 01966

Lord & Burnham
CSB 3181
Melville, NY 11747

Louisville Art Glass Studio
Box 4665, 1110 Baxter Ave.
Louisville, KY 40204

Edward Ludlow
Box 646, Rte. 202-206
Pluckemin, NJ 07978

Ludowici-Celadon
Box 69
New Lexington, OH 43764

Luigi Crystal
7332 Frankford Ave.
Philadelphia, PA 19136

Lundberg Studios
131 Marineview Ave., Box C
Davenport, CA 95017

Lyemance International
Box 505
Jeffersonville, IN 47131

Kenneth Lynch & Sons, Inc.
78 Danbury Rd. Box 488
Wilton, CT 06897

Mad River Wood Works
Box 163, 4935 Boyd Rd.
Arcata, CA 95521

Magnolia Hall
726 Andover Dr.
Atlanta, GA 30327

Maine Architectural Millwork
Dennis Paul Robillard
Front St.
S. Berwick, ME 03908

Frank J. Mangione
21 John St.
Saugerties, NY 12477

Manor Art Glass Studio
20 Ridge Rd.
Douglaston, NY 11363

Mansion Industries, Inc.
14711 E. Clark
Industry, CA 91745

MarLe Company
170 Summer St.
Stamford, CT 06904

Manuscreens, Inc.
979 Third Ave.
New York, NY 10022

Marmion Plantation Co.
RD 2, Box 458
Fredericksburg, VA 22405

Marshalltown Trowel Co.
Box 738
Marshalltown, IA 50158

The Martin-Senour Co.
1370 Ontario Ave., NW
Cleveland, OH 44113

W. B. Maske, Sheetmetal Work
4419 Baltimore Ave.
Bladensburg, MD 20710

Mason's Masonry Supply, Ltd.
6291 Netherhart
Mississauga, Ontario,
Canada L5T 1A2

Master's Stained and Etched
Glass Studio
729 W. l6th St., No. B-1
Costa Mesa, CA 92627

Materials Unlimited
2 W. Michigan Ave.
Ypsilanti, MI 48197

Maurer & Shepherd, Joyners,
Inc.
122 Naubuc Ave.
Glastonbury, CT 06033

Mazza Frame & Furniture Co.,
Inc.
35-10 10th St.
Long Island City, NY 11106

McCloskey Varnish Co.
7600 State Rd.
Philadelphia, PA 19136

Meredith Stained Glass Studio
8472-C Tyco Rd.
Tysons Corner, VA 22180

Metropolitan Lighting Fixture
Co., Inc.
1010 Third Ave.
New York, NY 10021

The Metropolitan Museum of
Art
255 Gracie Station
New York, NY 10028

Michael's Fine Colonial
Products
Rte. 44, R.D. 1, Box 179A
Salt Point, NY 12578

Midwest Spiral Stair Co.
263 West Ave.
Elmhurst, IL 60126

W. Harley Miller
125 S. Church St., Box 945
Martinsburg, WV 25401

Newton Millham, Blacksmith
672 Drift Rd.
Westport, MA 02790

Carro!l Milligan
Box 62
Cave in Rock, IL 62919

Minnesota Trailbound School
of Log Building
3544½ Grand Ave.
Minneapolis, MN 55408

Mohawk Industries, Inc.
173 Howland Ave.
Adams, MA 01220

Tom Moore Steeple People
21 Janine St.
Chicopee, MA 01013

Duncan M. Morgan
21 Concord Ave.
Natchez, MS 39120

R. Jesse Morley, Jr.
88 Oak St.
Westwood, MA 02090

Thomas Moser, Cabinet
Makers
11 Cobbs Bridge Rd.
New Gloucester, ME 04260

Alice Moulton-Ely
144 E. Westminster Rd.
Lake Forest, IL 60045
Moultrie Manufacturing Co.
PO Drawer 1179
Moultrie, GA 31768
Mountain Lumber Co.
1327 Carlton Ave.
Charlottesville, VA 22901
M.R.S. Industries, Inc.
115 Fernwood Dr.
Rocky Hill, CT 06067
Mulberry Street Rugs
869 Via de la Paz
Pacific Palisades, CA 90272
Munsell Color
2441 N. Calvert St.
Baltimore, MD 21218

National Supaflu Systems,
Inc.
Rte. 30A, Box 289
Central Bridge, NY 12035
Native Wood Products, Inc.
Drawer Box 469
Brooklyn, CT 06234
Necessary Trading Co.
Main St., Box 305
New Castle, VA 24127
Nelson-Johnson Wood Pro-
ducts, Inc.
4326 Lyndale Ave. N.
Minneapolis, MN 55412
C. Neri Antiques & Interiors
313 South St.
Philadelphia, PA 19147
Newbury Carpets
22 Unicorn St., Box 609
Newburyport, MA 01950
Simon Newby, Cabinetmaker
Box C414
Westport, MA 02790
Newell Workshop
19 Blaine Ave.
Hinsdale, IL 60521
New Jersey Barn Company
Box 702
Princeton, NJ 08542
Newstamp Lantern Co.
227 Bay Rd.
North Easton, MA 02356
New York Marble Works, Inc.
1399 Park Ave.
New York, NY 10029
Nixalite of America
417 25th St.
Moline, IL 61265
E. A. Nord Company, Inc.
Box 1187
Everett, WA 98206
Norman Corporation
Box 323, 214-32 N. Cedar St.
Nevada, MO 64772
North Coast Chemical Co.
6300 17th Ave., S., Box 80366
Seattle, WA 98108
North Fields Restorations
8 Upham St.
Salem, MA 01970
North Woods Chair Shop
RFD #1, Old Tilton Rd.
Canterbury, NH 03224
Nostalgia, Inc.
307 Stiles Ave.
Savannah, GA 31401

Nowell's, Inc.
Box 164
Sausalito, CA 94965
Nutt, Craig, Fine Wood Works
2014 Fifth St.
Northport, AL 35476

Oak Leaves Woodcarving
Studio
RR#6, The Woods, No. 12
Iowa City, IA 52240
Ocean View Lighting &
Accessories
1810 Fourth St.
Berkeley, CA 94710
Oehrlein & Associates
1555 Connecticut Ave., NW
Washington, DC 20036
Old Carolina Brick Co.
Rte. 9, Box 77, Majolica Rd.
Salisbury, NC 28144
Old Colony Crafts
Box 155
Liberty, ME 04949
Old-Fashioned Milk Paint Co.
Box 222H
Groton, MA 01450
The Old Lamp Shop
Queen St., E.
Toronto, Ontario, Canada
M4L 1G1
Old Lamplighter Shop
Rte. 12-B
Deansboro, NY 13328
Old Mansions Co.
1305 Blue Hill Ave.
Mattapan, MA 02126
Old Stone Mill Corporation
Rte 8, Box 307
Adams, MA 01220
Old World Moulding
115 Allen Blvd.
Farmingdale, NY 11735
Old World Weavers
136 E. 55th St.
New York, NY 10022
Olde Theatre Architectural
Salvage Co.
1309 Westport Rd.
Kansas City, MO 64111
Orleans Carpenters
Box 107-C, Rock Harbor Rd.
Orleans, MA 02653
J. F. Orr & Sons
Village Green, Rte. 27
Sudbury, MA 01776
Owner-Builder Center
1824 Fourth St.
Berkeley, CA 94710

Donald M. Parrish, Inc.
3997 Holden Dr.
Ann Arbor, MI 48103
Megan Parry, Wall Stenciling
1727 Spruce St.
Boulder, CO 80302
Patterson, Flynn & Martin
950 Third Ave.
New York, NY 10022
Pelnick Wrecking Co.
1749 Erie Blvd., E.
Syracuse, NY 13210
Period Furniture Hardware
Co., Inc.
123 Charles St., Box 314
Charles St. Sta.
Boston, MA 02114

Period Lighting Fixtures
1 Main St.
Chester, CT 06412
Period Pine
Box 77052
Atlanta, GA 30357
Perma Ceram Enterprises, Inc.
65 Smithtown Blvd.
Smithtown, NY 11787
Edward K. Perry Company
322 Newbury St.
Boston, MA 02115
Pfanstiel Hardware Co., Inc.
Rte. 52
Jeffersonville, NY 12748
P & G New & Used Plumbing
Supply
155 Harrison Ave.
Brooklyn, NY 11206
Walter Phelps
Box 76
Williamsville, VT 05362
Michael Piazza, Ornamental
Plasterer
540 80th St.
Brooklyn, NY 11209
Pittsburgh Paints
1 Gateway Center
Pittsburgh, PA 15222
Pocahontas Hardware & Glass
Box 127
Pocahontas, IL 62275
Pompei Stained Glass
455 High St.
West Medford, MA 02155
Portland Stove Co.
Fickett Rd.
North Pownal, ME 04069
Portland Willamette Company
6800 NE 59th Pl., Box 13097
Portland, OR 97213
Portsmouth Paintworks
Partridge Replications
83 Grove St.
Peterborough, NH 03458
Pratt & Lambert
75 Tonawanda St.
Buffalo, NY 14207
Preservation Associates, Inc.
207 Potomac St.
Hagerstown, MD 21740
The Preservation Partnership
345 Union St.
New Bedford, MA 02740
Preservation Resource Group
(PRG)
5619 Southampton Dr.
Springfield, VA 22151
Preway, Inc.
1430 2nd St., N.
Wisconsin Rapids, WI 54494
Price Glover Inc., Antiques
817 Madison Ave.
New York, NY 10021
Putnam Rolling Ladder Co.,
Inc.
32 Howard St.
New York, NY 10013
E. W. Pyfer
218 N. Foley
Freeport, IL 61032

Quaker City Manufacturing
Co.
701 Chester Pike
Sharon Hill, PA 19079

Quality Woodworks, Inc.
Box 1117
Jasper, FL 32052

The Rambusch Co.
40 W. 13th St.
New York, NY 10011
Rastetter Woolen Mill
Star Rte., Box 42
Millersburg, OH 44654
Readybuilt Products, Co.
Box 4425, 1701 McHenry St.
Baltimore, MD 21223
Reggio Register Co.
Box 511
Ayer, MA 01432
Reisen Lumber & Millwork
1070 Morris Ave.
Union, NJ 07083
Rejuvenation House Parts Co.
901 N. Skidmore
Portland, OR 97217
Renaissance Decorative Hard-
ware Co.
Box 332
Leonia, NJ 07605
Renovation Concepts, Inc.
213 Washington Ave. N.
Minneapolis, MN 55401
Renovation Products
5302 Junius
Dallas, TX 75214
The Renovation Source, Inc.
3512-14 N. Southport Ave.
Chicago, IL 60657
Restoration Fraternity
Box 234
Lima, PA 19060
Restorations
382 11th St.
Brooklyn, NY 11215
Restorations Unlimited, Inc.
24 W. Main St.
Elizabethville, PA 17023
Restoration Treasures
Box 724
Cooperstown, NY 13326
Restore
19 W. 44th St., Suite 1701
New York, NY 10036
Restore-a-Tub and Brass, Inc.
1991 Brownsboro Rd.,
Brownsboro Plaza
Louisville, KY 40206
Rex Building Materials
405 Rogers Rd.
Toronto, Ontario, Canada
M6M 1A1
R. Wayne Reynolds
1330 Smith Ave.
Baltimore, MD 21209
S. Chris Rheinschild
2220 Carlton Way
Santa Barbara, CA 93109
Matthew Richardson,
Coppersmith
Box 69
Greenfield, MA 01302
Don G. Richmond
1036 Florida St.
San Francisco, CA 94110
D. A. Rinedollar
Box 14
Augusta, MO 63332
J. Ring Glass Studio, Inc.
618 N. Washington Ave.
Minneapolis, MN 55401

Rising & Nelson Slate Co., Inc.
West Pawlet, VT 05775

Ritter & Son Hardware
Box 578
Gualala, CA 95445

River Bend Timber Framing
Box 26
Blissfield, MI 49229

River City Restorations
200 South 7th St.
Hannibal, MO 63401

Robinson Iron Corporation
Box 785, Robinson Rd.
Alexander City, AL 35010

Rocker Shop of Marietta, GA
1421 White Circle NW, Box 12
Marietta, GA 30061

Rosecore Carpet Co., Inc.
979 Third Ave.
New York, NY 10022

Rowe & Giles
16740 Park Circle Dr., Box 210
Chagrin Falls, OH 44022

Erwin Rowland
181 E. 73rd St.
New York, NY 10021

Roy Electric Co., Inc.
1054 Coney Island Ave.
Brooklyn, NY 11230

Royal Windyne Ltd.
1022 Franklin St.
Richmond, VA 23220

Rue de France
77 Thames St.
Newport, RI 02840

Russell Restoration of Suffolk
Rte 1, Box 243A
Mattituck, NY 11952

Saint Louis Antique Lighting Co.
25 N. Sarah St.
St. Louis, MO 63108

The Saltbox
2229 Marietta Pike
Lancaster, PA 17603

Arthur Sanderson & Sons, Ltd.
979 Third Ave.
New York, NY 10022

Sandy Springs Galleries
233 Hilderbrand Dr., NE
Atlanta, GA 30328

San Francisco Victoriana
2245 Palou Ave.
San Francisco, CA 94124

Santa Cruz Foundry
Courthouse Sq.
Handford, CA 93230

San Valle Tile Kilns
1717 N. Highland Ave.
Los Angeles, CA 90028

Scalamandré, Inc.
950 Third Ave.
New York, NY 10022

Conrad Schmidt Studios
2405 S. 162nd St.
New Berlin, WI 53157

Schrader Wood Stoves & Fireplaces
724 Water St.
Santa Cruz, CA 95060

F. Schumacher & Co.
939 Third Ave.
New York, NY 10022

Schwartz's Forge & Metalworks
Box 205, Forge Hollow Rd.
Deansboro, NY 13328

I. Schwartz Glass & Mirror Co., Inc.
412-418 59th St.
New York NY 10022

Sculpture Associates Ltd., Inc.
40 E. 19th St.
New York, NY 10003

Sculpture Design Imports, Inc.
416 S. Robertson Blvd.
Los Angeles, CA 90048

John L. Seekamp,
472 Pennsylvania
San Francisco, CA 94107

The Seraph
Box 500
Sturbridge, MA 01566

The Shade Tree
6 Half-King Dr.
Burlington, CT 06013

Shaker Workshops, Inc.
Box 1028
Concord, MA 01742

Shakertown Corp.
Box 400
Winlock, WA 98596

Shanker Steel Corp
70-32 83rd St.
Glendale, NY 11385

Shaw Marble & Tile Co., Inc.
5012 S. 38th St.
St. Louis, MO 63116

Shenandoah Manufacturing Co.
Box 839
Harrisburg, VA 22801

Sherwin-Williams Co.
Box 6939
Cleveland, OH 44101

Calvin Shewmaker III
606 Cane Run
Harrodsburg, KY 40330

Ship 'n Out
8 Charles St.
Pawling, NY 12564

Silverton Victorian Mill Works
Box 877-35
Silverton, CO 81433

The Sink Factory
2140 San Pablo Ave.
Berkeley, CA 94702

Skyline Engineers, Inc.
58 East St.
Fitchburg, MA 01420

Smith-Cornell, Inc.
Box 686
Auburn, IN 46706

Smith Woodworks & Design
Box 42, RR 1
Califon, NJ 07803

Smithsonian Institution
Audiovisual Loan Program
Office of Museum Programs
2235 Arts and Industries Building
Washington, DC 20560

Society for the Preservation of New England Antiquities
Harrison Gray Otis House
141 Cambridge St.
Boston, MA 02114

Somerset Door & Column Co.
Box 328, S. Edgewood Ave.
Somerset, PA 15501

Southern Heritage
Metal Amenities Ltd.
Box 2782
Birmingham, AL 35202

Southington Specialty Wood & Lumber Co.
100 W. Main St.
Plantsville, CT 06479

Spanish Pueblo Doors
Box 2517
Santa Fe, NM 87501

Greg Spiess Building Materials
216 E. Washington St.
Joliet, IL 60433

Ronald Spivak's Custom Lighting, Pendulum Shop
424 South St.
Philadelphia, PA 19147

Spring City Electrical Mfg. Co.
Drawer A
Spring City, PA 19475

Squaw Alley, Inc.
401 S. Main St.
Naperville, IL 60540

Stair Specialist
2257 W. Columbia Ave.
Battle Creek, MI 49017

Stairways, Inc.
4323-A Pinemont
Houston, TX 77018

Standard Trimming Corp.
1114 First Ave.
New York, NY 10021

Stanley Galleries
2118 N. Clark St.
Chicago, IL 60614

Stark Carpet Corp.
979 Third Ave.
New York, NY 10022

Steptoe & Wife Antiques, Ltd.
3626 Victoria Park Ave.
Willowdale, Ontario, Canada M2H 3B2

Stewart Iron Works Co.
511 Enterprise Dr.
Covington, KY 41017

Stoneham Pewter
RFD 1, Box 656
Brookfield, NH 03872

Strafford Forge
Box 148
S. Strafford, VT 05070

Thomas Strahan Co.
10 New England Executive Park
Burlington, MA 01803

Daniel Strawser
126 Main St.
Stouchsburg, PA 19567

Studio I
6 Highland Cross, 2nd Fl.
Rutherford, NJ 07070

Stulb Paint & Chemical Co.
Box 297
Norristown, PA 19404

Strobel Millwork
Rte. 7, Box 84
Cornwall Bridge, CT 06754

Stroheim & Romann
155 E. 56th St.
New York, NY 10022

Structural Antiques, Inc.
1406 NW 30th St.
Oklahoma City, OK 73118

Structural Slate Co.
222 E. Main St.
Pen Argyl, PA 18072

Donald Stryker Restorations
154 Commercial Ave.
New Brunswick, NJ 08901

Sturbridge Yankee Workshop
Brimfield Turnpike
Sturbridge, MA 01566

Sunburst Stained Glass Co.
119 State St.
Newburgh, IN 47630

Sun Designs
Repstrom, Inc.
Box 206
Delafield, WI 53018

Sunflower Studio
2851 Road B½
Grand Junction, CO 81503

Sunrise Speciality & Salvage
2210 San Pablo Ave.
Berkeley, CA 94702

Sunshine Architectural Woodworks
Rte. 2, Box 434
Fayetteville, AR 72701

Sun System
Solar Greenhouses
60-D Vanderbilt Motor Pkwy.
Commack, NY 11725

Superior Clay Corporation
Box 352
Ulrichsville, OH 44683

Supradur Mfg. Corp.
Box 908
Rye, NY 10580

Swallow Woodworks
324 N. Schiller St.
Little Rock, AR 72205

Swiss Foundry, Inc.
518 S. Gilmore St.
Baltimore, MD 21223

Talas
213 W. 35th St.
New York, NY 10001

Taos Clay Products, Inc.
Box 15
Taos, NM 87571

Tennessee Fabricating Co.
2366 Prospect St.
Memphis, TN 38106

Terra Designs, Inc.
4 John St.
Morristown, NJ 07960

Richard E. Thibaut, Inc.
706 S. 21st St.
Irvington, NJ 07111

Thorn Lumber Co.
310 N. Raleigh St.
Martinsburg, WV 25401

Tiresias, Inc.
Box 1864
Orangeburg, SC 29116

The Toby House
517 E. Paces Ferry Rd., NE
Atlanta, GA 30305

Tremont Nail Co.
8 Elm St., Box 111
Wareham, MA 02571

Travis Tuck, Metal Sculptor & Blacksmith
RFD, Lamberts Cove Rd.
Martha's Vineyard, MA 02568

Turn of the Century Lighting
118 Sherbourne St.
Toronto, Ontario, Canada
M5A 2R2
Turncraft
Box 2429
White City, OR 97503
The Twigs, Inc.
5700 Third St.
San Francisco, CA 94124

United House Wrecking Corp.
328 Selleck St.
Stamford, CT 06902
Up Country Enterprise Corp.
Plantation Dr.
Jaffrey, NH 03452
Upland Woodstoves
2 Green St., Box 361
Greene, NY 13778
Urban Archaeology, Ltd.
137 Spring St.
New York, NY 10012

The Valley Craftsmen
Box 11
Stevenson, MD 21153
Valley Iron & Steel Co.
29579 Aubrey Lane
Eugene, OR 97402
Norman Vandal,
Cabinetmaker
Box 67
Roxbury, VT 05669
Albert Van Luit & Co.
4000 Chevy Chase Dr.
Los Angeles, CA 90039
Venturella Stained Glass
Studio
32 Union Sq. E.
New York, NY 10003
Vermont Castings, Inc.
Randolph, VT 05060
Vermont Iron Stove Works
424 Prince St.
Waterbury, VT 05676
Vermont Marble Co.
61 Main St.
Proctor, VT 05765
Vermont Soapstone Co., Inc.
Pond Rd., Box 77
Perkinsville, VT 05151
Vermont Structural Slate Co.,
Inc.
Box 98
Fair Haven, VT 05743
Victorian Collectibles, Ltd.
845 E. Glenbrook Rd.
Milwaukee, WI 53217
Victorian Interior Restoration
6374 Waterloo Rd.
Atwater, OH 44201
Victorian Lightcrafters, Ltd.
Box 332
Slate Hill, NY 10973
Victorian Lighting Works, Inc.
Gamble Mill
160 Dunlop St.
Bellefonte, PA 16823
Victorian Reproduction Enter-
prises, Inc.
1601 Park Ave., S.
Minneapolis, MN 55404

Victorian Reproduction
Lighting Co., Inc.
Box 654
Minneapolis, MN 55440
The Village Forge
Box 1148
Smithfield, NC 27577
Village Lantern
Box 8J, 598 Union St.
North Marshfield, MA 02059
Vintage Wood Works
Box 1157
Fredericksburg, TX 78624
W. D. Virtue
160 Broad St.
Summit, NJ 07901

Garrett Wade Co.
161 Ave. of the Americas
New York, NY 10013
Walbrook Mill & Lumber Co.,
Inc.
2636 W. North Ave.
Baltimore, MD 21216
Walker Industries
Box 129, 7384 Old Harding
Rd.
Bellevue, TN 37221
Wallin Forge
RR 1, Box 65
Sparta, KY 41086
Jack Wallis' Doors
Rte. 1, Box 22A
Murray, KY 42071
Walton Stained Glass
209 Railway
Campbell, CA 95008
William J. Warren & Son, Inc.
300 S. Holmes St.
Ft. Collins, CO 80521
E. G. Washburne & Co.
83 Andover St., Rte. 114
Danvers, MA 01923
Washington Copper Works
Washington, CT 06793
Washington Stove Works
Box 687, 3402 Smith
Everett, WA 98206
Watercolors, Inc.
Garrison-on-Hudson, NY
10524
Waterman-West
741 Ponce de Leon Court,
Suite 4
Atlanta, GA 30308
Waverly Fabrics
58 W. 40th St.
New York, NY 10018
J. P. Weaver Co.
2301 W. Victory Blvd.
Burbank, CA 91506
W. T. Weaver & Sons, Inc.
1208 Wisconsin Ave., NW
Washington, DC 20007
Lawrie Weiser
The Wallpaper Works
749 Queen St., W.
Toronto, Ontario, Canada
M6J 1G1
Weird Wood
Box 190
Chester, VT 05143
H. S. Welles Fireplace Co.
287 E. Houston St.
New York, NY 10002

Welsbach Lighting, Inc.
240 Sargent Dr.
New Haven, CT 06511
Holly Wesley
Hungry Point Farm
6 Old Deerfield Rd.
Welsh, MN 55089
West Barnstable Stove Shop
Box 472, Rte. 149
W. Barnstable, MA 02668
Westlake Architectural
Antiques
3315 Westlake Dr.
Austin, TX 78746
Martha Wetherbee
Star Rte, Box 35
Sanbornton, NH 03269
The Robert Whitley Studio
Laurel Rd., Box 69
Solebury, PA 18963
Jonathan Dexter Whitney
223 W. 19th St.
New York, NY 10011
John A. Wigen
RD 1, Box 281
Cobleskill, NY 12043
D. B. Wiggins
Hale Rd.
Tilton, NH 03276
Lt. Moses Willard & Co.
7805 Railroad Ave.
Cincinnati, OH 45243
Williams Art Glass Studios/
Sunset Antiques
22 N. Washington
Oxford, MI 48051
Helen Williams, Rare Tiles
12643 Hortense St.
N. Hollywood, CA 91604
Williams & Hussey Machine
Corp.
Elm St.
Milford, NH 03055
Williamsburg Blacksmiths
Buttonshop Rd.
Williamsburg, MA 01096
Willis Lumber Co.
Box 84
Washington Court House,
OH 43160
Winterthur Museum &
Gardens
Winterthur, DE 19735
M. Wolchonok & Son Inc.
155 E. 52nd St.
New York, NY 10022
S. Wolf's Sons
771 Ninth Ave.
New York, NY 10019
Woodbury Blacksmith & Forge
Co.
Box 268, 161 Main St.
Woodbury, CT 06798
Wood Classics, Inc.
106 Columbus Dr.
Tenafly, NJ 07670
Woodcraft Supply Corp.
41 Atlantic Ave., Box 4000
Woburn, MA 01888
Wood Moulding & Millwork
Producers
Box 25278, 1730 SW Skyline
Portland, OR 97225
Woodstock Soapstone Co.
Box 223/371, Rte. 4
Woodstock, VT 05091

The Woodstone Co.
Box 223, Patch Rd.
Westminster, VT 05158
The Woodworkers' Store
21801 Industrial Blvd.
Rogers, MN 55374
The Woodworkers' Store
retail outlets:
424 W. Lake St.
Minneapolis, MN 55408
3823 Stone Way N.
Seattle, WA 98103
2154 Massachussetts Ave.
Cambridge, MA 02104
340 S. Broadway
Denver, CO 80209
The Wrecking Bar
292 Moreland Ave., NE
Atlanta, GA 30307
Wrightsville Hardware
N. Front St.
Wrightsville, PA 17368

Yankee Craftsman
357 Commonwealth Rd.
Wayland, MA 01778
Ye Olde Mantel Shoppe
3800 NE 2nd Ave.
Miami, FL 33137
Yestermorrow
Warren, VT 05674
E. Stanford Young
1107 Cypress Point, Box 368
Placentia, CA 92670

Zina Studios, Inc.
85 Purdy Ave.
Port Chester, NY 10573
Emily Zum Brunnen Imports
5914 Fairfield Ave.
Shreveport, LA 71106